WALES

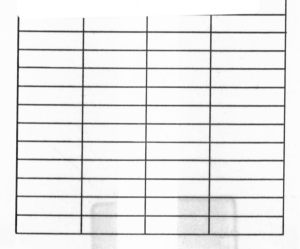

D1219418

First impression: 2016

The publisher acknowledges the support of the
Welsh Books Council

Cover: design: Olwen Fowler; photographs: Marian Delyth

Design: Marian Delyth and Richard Ceri Jones
Copyright of photographs: Marian Delyth

ISBN: 978 1 78461 347 1

Published and printed in Wales by
Y Lolfa Cyf., Talybont, Ceredigion SY24 5HE
e-mail ylolfa@ylolfa.com
website www.ylolfa.com
tel (01970) 832 304
facs 832 782

WALES

IN 100 PLACES

John Davies and Marian Delyth

Wales in 100 Places

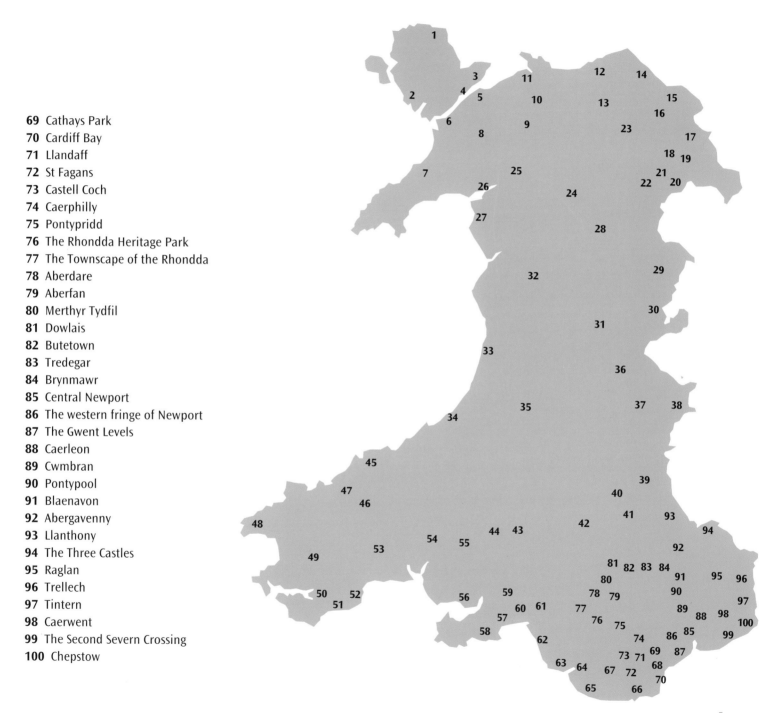

Introduction

I Mared a Iestyn

Choosing the hundred places in Wales that one really must see was a particular pleasure. I have been wandering around Wales since my mid teens, and I had seen almost all the places included here before reaching my mid-twenties. While preparing this volume, I was more systematic, although I have to confess that I had sent the original typescript to Y Lolfa before spending a night at the Lion Hotel in Trellech.

The order in which the locations are listed is intended to assist the traveller, rather than to suggest any order of merit. Number one hundred is as enthralling as number one. In the Welsh-language volume, place-name spellings followed those provided by *A Gazetteer of Welsh Place-names;* in this volume, the spellings are those of the Ordnance Survey maps.

During my travels, I came to realize how fortunate we are in Wales. Our country contains an astonishing range of examples of the fruits of human efforts – and I wish to stress that this book is wholly concerned with the fruits of human efforts. (The hundred places that should be visited because of their natural beauty could well be the subject of another volume.) This astonishing range is contained within a relatively small compass. Citizens of the larger nations of Europe cannot hope in the span of a single lifetime to visit all the highlights of their country's heritage. But Welsh residents and visitors to Wales can, by the time they reach three score years and ten, visit, appreciate and love all its glories.

I incurred many debts while preparing both the Welsh-language and the English-language versions of this book. My reliance upon the seven volumes in *The Buildings of Wales* series and upon the guidebooks published by Cadw will be obvious to anyone familiar with those admirable publications. I wish to thank Marian Delyth for her admirable photographs, particularly those which cast a new light on places that can be overfamiliar. I much admire her ability to capture, not so much the place itself, but the spirit of the place. At Y Lolfa, Lefi Gruffudd, Eirian Jones and Dyfed Elis-Gruffydd have been particularly helpful. As always, my greatest debt is to my wife, Janet Mackenzie Davies, my companion on many of my travels. It is a special delight to dedicate the book to the most recent of our grandchildren.

John Davies

Why 100 places? That was the question haunting me as I navigated a particularly narrow winding lane to reach one of them in my trusted camper. However, turning back was not an option – I had accepted the commission to photograph all of them. It was not merely the enormity of the task that appeared daunting at times, but some of the experiences I had during my travels proved to be quite challenging. On one occasion I found myself competing in a hundred-metre sprint with a bull but, mercifully, I succeeded in hurdling over a farm gate just in time – my camera still safely hanging from my neck. It seemed appropriate that I was photographing the Halleluja Monument (near Mold) at the time! In a spirit of protest I decided to omit that particular photograph.

The work itself was in reality a marathon, not a sprint, and thankfully I returned safely from my journey. Crossing the finishing-line and ticking off that one-hundredth place was a bitter-sweet moment. I felt like the lonely long-distance runner who had pounded many thousands of miles of tarmac before finally experiencing the joy of breaking the tape that marked the end of the challenge. But whereas the marathon runner will only have glimpses of cinematic images flowing in his memory, I have a store of digital files to treasure and to share for years to come. I also have a wealth of wonderful memories from the experience of roaming the length and breadth of this small country which I feel privileged to call my home.

The images that were selected to accompany the text of the book represent a small percentage of the photographs taken. It would be a considerable task to photograph one hundred places of one's own choice. To photograph one hundred places selected by others poses an additional challenge because we are not all excited by the same locations. I gained a new insight into Wales from the selections of my co-author and I thank him for sending me to a few secret places and some locations that I had not previously visited. However, I was a visitor and the images are those of the inquisitive visitor who is only scratching the surface of the subject-matter. I wished to stay a while longer in some places but the journey called me to move on. I hope to return again to dig a little deeper into those locations in the future. The constantly changing light on the varied landscape of such a small country, and the wealth of histories and characters within our wonderful communities, never cease to excite me. I hope that the photographs in some small way reflect those particular qualities.

I am grateful to those who assisted me in the creation of these images; for the hospitality and companionship that I experienced during my travels; Y Lolfa for their sterling production work, with a special thank-you to Richard Ceri Jones for his genial company, his craft and patience during the design process. Thanks are due also to the Welsh Books Council for the support of their commissioning programme.

Marian Delyth

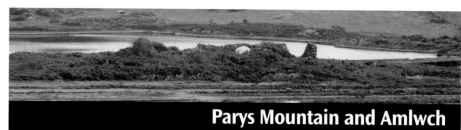

There are holes in the ground that are colourful, and holes lacking in colour. Gazing into the Penrhyn Quarry's void is a memorable experience, but the gazer only sees different shades of grey. When the vast open-cast workings on Dowlais Top were visible, brown and black were the only colours on offer. But Wales does have a magnificently chromatic chasm – the old copper workings on Parys Mountain, Wales's most striking industrial landscape. The colours are caused by the metals deposited there by volcanic action millions of years ago. The mineral rich soil sustains a number of unusual plants, lichens in particular.

As south-east Wales was industrialized far more intensely than any other part of the country, it may appear anomalous that industry has left its most dramatic remains on the northern edge of Anglesey. But it should be remembered that Anglesey's copper industry developed remarkably quickly in the last decades of the eighteenth century. According to the census of 1801, the parish of Amlwch (which included Parys Mountain), with its 4,977 inhabitants, was the fifth most populated place in Wales, after Swansea, Merthyr Tydfil, Carmarthen and Wrexham. (In 1801, Cardiff had only 1,870 inhabitants.)

The mountain was named after the Parys family, constables of Caernarfon Castle in the fifteenth century. It came to prominence in the 1760s, when the bottoms of the wooden ships of the British navy came to be covered with a sheet of copper (the origin of the phrase copper-bottomed), a development which led to a growing demand for the metal. Wales proved a prolific source, with the Nantlle Valley, Llanberis, and the southern part of the Llŷn Peninsula all having their mines. Then, on 2 March 1768, a rich vein was discovered on Parys Mountain. The second day of March became a day of annual celebration, and the vein's discoverer, Roland Puw, was rewarded with a bottle of whisky and a rent-free cottage for life.

Between 1768 and 1805, some 3.5 million tons of ore were extracted from the mountain, enough to produce 130,000 tons of copper. The mountain yielded profits of about £7 million, much of it finding its way into the coffers of Thomas Williams of Plas Llanidan (d. 1802), an entrepreneur who came close to controlling the entire world production of copper. Some of it went to the owners of the mountain – to Nicholas Bayly (d. 1782) and his descendants, the Paget family, marquesses of Anglesey, and to Edward Hughes (d. 1815) and his descendants, Barons Dinorben. It was the profits of Parys Mountain which financed much of the building of two of Wales's most distinguished country houses – Plasnewydd and Kinmel Park.

Initially, the ore was mined in levels and shallow shafts, but, by the 1790s, up to 15,000 tons of gunpowder a year were being used to wrest rock from the mountain. It was those explosions which created the huge chasm, in the base of which pools were dug in which copper was precipitated from the ore. Because of the depth of the pools and the steepness of the sides of the abyss, Parys Mountain is one of the most perilous places in Wales. The leaflet available at the car park urges visitors not to stray from the recommended route.

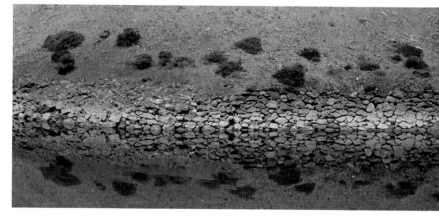

In the early nineteenth century, the rock beneath the bottom of the chasm came to be riddled with tunnels and shafts, some of them as much as 350 metres deep. These are the area of study of the Parys Underground Group, the members of which lead up to

nine-thousand people a year through the tunnels – perhaps the most exciting journey in Wales. The group's research has proved that Bronze Age people had mined ore on Parys Mountain and that the Romans had made objects cast from Anglesey's copper.

The prosperity of the mountain was not destined to endure. By 1844, it was noted that the workings had virtually come to an end, although speculators remained ever optimistic. In 1901, Amlwch had less than half the number of inhabitants it had had a century earlier. However, in the early twenty-first century, the price of copper rose markedly and companies from Australia, Canada and the United States expressed interest in restarting mining in Anglesey. Thus, the drama of the mountain may not yet have come to an end.

The work on Parys Mountain was more exhausting and dangerous than that in any other of the heavy industries of Wales. Visitors wrote horrific descriptions of miners swinging in their cages hundreds of metres above the bottom of the chasm. The rock had to be crushed into gravel. That was women's work and Thomas Williams (Twm Chwarae Teg [Tom Fair Play]) was praised for employing women who might otherwise be a burden on the Poor Law. They were the Copper Ladies, who are still part of the folklore of the area. Although Amlwch developed some of the graces of an urban community, little hard cash circulated there. Thomas Williams minted copper coins – Anglesey Pennies – to maintain the economy. They bore the image of a druid, and it was believed that about twelve million were produced. They remained in circulation until 1821, and are now avidly sought by collectors.

The pulverized ore was transported to Amlwch, where a harbour was built in 1793. Amlwch itself became a centre of some of the initial phases of coppermaking, but most of the ore was shipped to furnaces at Swansea, Holywell and Liverpool. Amlwch also came to produce chemicals, fertilizers, hats, candles and tobacco. Shipbuilding was undertaken in the harbour; the last ship – *Eilian* – was launched there in 1908. Now, the place is only a shadow of what it once was, but it still has one splendid showpiece. That is the original of the cultivar bred by the Amlwch solicitor, W. R. Jones, in his garden at Bryntirion. The cultivar is *Hoheria* Glory of Amlwch, a plant that has taken the name of Amlwch to all corners of the world.

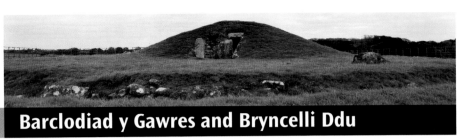

A visitor to Anglesey can see the remains of at least thirty chambered tombs, more than in any other Welsh county. Among the most interesting is Barclodiad y Gawres (the Giantess's Apronful) which is gloriously situated on a cliff above Porth Trecastell on the island's west coast. To those who believe that a chambered tomb should look something like the one at Pentre Ifan in Pembrokeshire – a huge capstone which seems to float above upright tapering boulders – Barclodiad y Gawres can, at first glance, be disappointing. The visitor's initial impression is of a grassy hillock which looks as if it was constructed quite recently. And it is quite recent, for it was raised in 1953. Neolithic people buried the stone framework of their chambers under a covering of soil; it is the erosion of the ages that has caused the stonework of Pentre Ifan and many another *cromlech* to be visible, and the purpose of raising the hillock was to ensure that Barclodiad y Gawres should have something of the appearance it had had when first constructed.

Barclodiad y Gawres is a passage grave in the tradition of Newgrange in Ireland, a splendid chambered tomb erected in the Boyne Valley sometime between 3000 and 2500 BC. The passage at Barclodiad y Gawres extends for seven metres and leads to a cross-shaped chamber. It is believed that the remains of cremated bodies were placed in the arms of the cross and that rituals were conducted in the centre of the chamber; there, remains of parts of frogs, toads, snakes, mice and eels have been found, an indication that there were those who were concocting witches' brew some four thousand years before the age of Macbeth. (The concocting is admirably interpreted at Oriel Ynys Môn in Llangefni.) The most remarkable aspect of the monument are the four stones bearing carvings – spirals, lozenges, angles and zigzags – ritual symbols which denote the beginnings of art in Wales.

Carvings were also found on a stone in another of Anglesey's chambered tombs – Bryncelli Ddu, located about ten kilometres

east of Barclodiad y Gawres. (The stone is now in the National Museum of Wales; a replica has been placed in the chamber.) Like Barclodiad y Gawres, Bryncelli Ddu is a passage grave in the Newgrange tradition, and, like Newgrange, its chamber has astrological significance. On 21 December 1967, the archaeologist, M. J. O'Kelly, was the first in modern times to see light snaking through the Newgrange passage at sunrise on the winter solstice. (By now, fifty people come every year to Newgrange on the morning of 21 December to witness the snaking light; they are chosen by lottery and in 2007 there were 28,106 applicants.) On 21 June 2005, Steve Burrow from the National Museum was the first in the modern era to see light snaking through the Bryncelli Ddu passage at sunrise on the summer solstice. (A display at the National Museum provides some idea of the experience.)

Although the carvings in Anglesey's chambered tombs are intriguing, the most fascinating carved stone on the island is in St Cadwaladr's Church, some twelve kilometres west of Bryncelli Ddu. The death of Cadwaladr in the year 682 is the first entry in *Brut y Tywysogyon* (The Chronicle of the Princes). With the death of Cadwaladr, states the *Brut*, 'the Britons lost the crown of

Porth Castell Beach near Barclodiad y Gawres

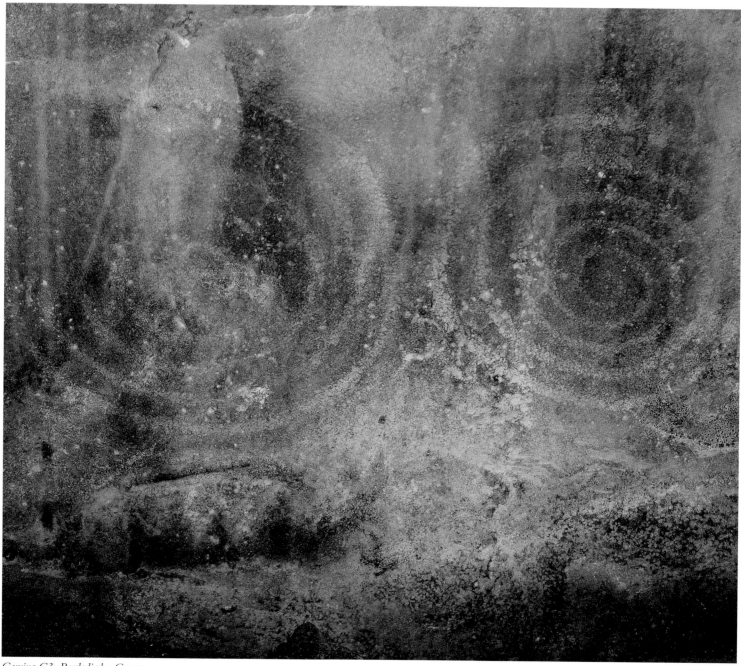

Carving C3, Barclodiad y Gawres

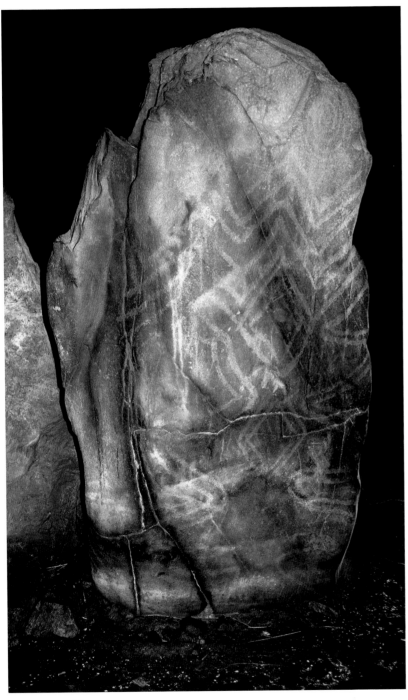

kingship and the Saxons acquired it', a statement consistent with the tradition that Cadwaladr was the last ruler of the Britons (the Welsh) whose authority was recognized in the greater part of the old Roman province of Britannia. (In later centuries, the appearance of a new Cadwaladr was the great hope of the prophetic poets.) However, the inscription at St Cadwaladr's Church commemorates, not Cadwaladr, but his grandfather Cadfan. On the north wall, a stone bears the curly letters favoured by the centres of learning of mainland Europe in the seventh century. The words are CATAMANUS REX SAPIENTISSIMUS OPINATISSIMUS OMNIUM REGUM (Cadfan, the wisest and most illustrious of all kings). As very little is known of Cadfan, his eulogistic memorial is somewhat puzzling. It may have been commissioned by his son, Cadwallon (d. 633), virtually the last Welsh ruler with the power effectively to intervene in what would become the kingdom of England.

Llangadwaladr is only two kilometres from Aberffraw, the 'special seat' of the kings of Gwynedd. Apart from some fine Romanesque work in St Beuno's Church, nothing, apart from a modern memorial to the princes of Gwynedd, is visible which might indicate the significance of the site, and it is likely that Aberffraw was the symbol of Gwynedd's sovereignty rather than in any sense the capital of the kingdom. Although Gwynedd had the resources to maintain a royal court and to sustain the institutions of an embryonic state, transport was so underdeveloped that it was not a matter of bringing resources to the headquarters of the ruler, but rather of the ruler journeying ceaselessly to take advantage of local resources. In every *cwmwd*, there was a *llys* – the dwelling of the ruler during his visits – where villeins on the demesne supplied the needs of the peripatetic ruler. Only one of the *llysoedd* of Gwynedd has been carefully examined – Rhosyr near Newborough, much of which was excavated between 1992 and 1996. For those seeking to understand the governance of Gwynedd under Llywelyn I and Llywelyn II, Rhosyr is the place to go.

Carving C16, Barclodiad y Gawres

The contrast between the two towns commissioned by Edward I on either side of the Menai Strait is intriguing. Caernarfon, which was to be the headquarters of English power, is remarkably Welsh in spirit and language. Beaumaris, which was planned at the last moment, hardly shares those merits. But, whatever else may be said about Beaumaris, the symmetry of its castle is superb.

By the early 1290s, castle building had been afoot in Wales for well over two hundred years. Perhaps the earliest to be built was the motte-and-bailey commissioned about 1055 at Womaston, on the edge of the later Radnorshire, by Ralph, a Norman and a nephew of Edward the Confessor. The essence of motte-and-bailey castles, and of the more ambitious castles which succeeded them, was a keep surrounded by defences. The finest Welsh castle in that tradition is Pembroke, where the massive round keep erected about 1204 is surrounded by the curtain walls of the inner

ward; to the south-east lies the outer ward, also surrounded by curtain walls.

The weakness of such structures was the possibility that besiegers might seize the wards, thus enclosing the defenders in the confined space of the keep. The answer to the weaknesses of the keep-castle was the concentric castle – two wards, the inner wholly enclosed within the outer. A concentric castle did not have a separate keep. The inner ward was the keep, and even if the outer ward were overrun, the defenders would have under their control the extensive space of the inner ward. As the walls of the inner ward were higher than those of the outer ward, the defenders could strike back from a position of strength.

It would appear that it was the Crusaders in Outremer (the Holy Land and its neighbours) who were the first to build concentric castles; Krak des Chevaliers, which is now in Syria and which was completed about *c*.1250, is considered to be the prototype. In western Europe, some already existing castles – Dover, for example – were surrounded by additional defences, but soon castles were built which were concentric from their beginnings. Between 1268 and 1272, a concentric castle was built at Caerphilly, with a greater emphasis on water defences than would be found in the fullest development of the style. Of the first wave of castles (1277–80) commissioned in Wales by Edward I, Flint was a tentative version of the Pembroke tradition, but those at Aberystwyth and Rhuddlan were essentially concentric constructions.

Beaumaris belongs to the end of the second wave. The original intention of Edward I, after he had destroyed Llywelyn ap Gruffudd's principality, was to commission powerful castles at Caernarfon, Conwy and Harlech – strongholds which would ensure that he would have tight control over Snowdonia – and to strengthen some of the castles of the Welsh rulers, Cricieth and Dolwyddelan among them. However, after the Welsh Revolt

of 1294–5, it was felt that a further stronghold was necessary, especially to ensure English control over the shipping in the Menai Strait. On the mainland, Caernarfon Castle dominated the south-western entrance to the Strait, and a castle at Beaumaris was built to command its north-eastern approaches.

The three castles commissioned by Edward I immediately after his victory in 1282–3 were all built on rock, locations where the landform imposed restrictions on what could be built. That was not true of Beaumaris Castle, which was built on a fine marsh (*beau marais*), a crucial factor in determining its shape. As the landform of the *beau marais* imposed no restrictions upon the shape of the castle, it was possible to aim for perfect symmetry.

In his castle-building ventures, Edward I's chief adviser was James of St George, whose knowledge of military architecture was unrivalled. By 1282, he had already played a part in the construction of seven castles for the king, and he was determined that his creations should be as beautiful as they were impregnable. The progress of the work at Beaumaris was aided by the fact that the expenditure on the king's other castles was coming to an end. Between the summer of 1295 and the autumn of 1298, Edward spent £11,289 on Beaumaris (at least £15 million in today's money). He was in financial difficulties by the end of the 1290s, and the work came to a standstill. It was resumed in 1306, but not with the same urgency as before. After *c.*1330, no further building

work was undertaken. Thus, Beaumaris is an unfinished castle; in particular, the walls were not raised to their intended height and the towers were not crowned with turrets.

But, even in its uncompleted state, and after centuries of weathering and stone robbery, the castle is magnificent. Caernarfon Castle is more of a presence, Conwy Castle is more ingenious and Harlech Castle is more threatening, but none of them can compete with Beaumaris's symmetry – the three towers on the west side perfectly matching the three towers on the east side, the bulk of the southern gatehouse in splendid accord with the bulk of the northern gatehouse, the peerless regularity of the towers of the outer curtain wall, and the solidarity of the building delectably reflected in the waters of the moat.

Those visitors who are not sated even by Beaumaris Castle should go to the banks of the Menai Strait to gaze at the wonderful panorama of Snowdonia, to the parish church to appreciate the skilled carving on the lid of the coffin of Joan, wife of Llywelyn the Great, and to the old gaol, where the exhibition invests imprisonment with a certain charm. While wandering around Beaumaris, it is easy to believe that it could be the most attractive town in Wales if it could shake off some of its colonialist traditions.

The lid of the coffin of Princess Joan

When the Menai Bridge was opened on 30 January 1826, it was immediately acknowledged that Thomas Telford had designed a masterpiece. Its praises were sung by Pushkin in Moscow, the chief architect of Berlin, Karl Freidrich Schinkel, came to Wales specifically to admire it, and it was portrayed on thousands of pieces of porcelain. The elegance of the bridge and the splendour of its location were part of its appeal, but it was its length which dazzled contemporaries. The section – 176 metres in length – which is suspended from the chains which stretch between the two towers, won it recognition as the longest suspension bridge in the world. It retained that status until 1834, when a suspension bridge 271 metres long was erected across the River Sarine near Fribourg in Switzerland. By now, Kashi-Tackyo Bridge in Japan, with a length of 1,991 metres and opened in 1998, heads the list of suspension bridges.

Suspension bridges have a long history. Hurling ropes across a river and attaching some sort of bridge to them is a craft which dates back at least to the Bronze Age. Constructing a suspension bridge of iron is a much more recent activity. The oldest still in use is a bridge linking Scotland with England across the Tweed. It is known as the Union Bridge, a name which may well change in the coming years. The suspended part of the bridge is 137 metres long. When opened in 1820, it was the longest such bridge in the world; in a mere six years, it was demoted to second place.

Its length is one of a large number of fascinating facts relating to the Menai Bridge. The deck is suspended from 16 chains. Each of them originally consisted of 935 iron bars giving a total of 14,960 bars, all of which were pickled in linseed oil (not in wine, as Lewis Carroll maintained) in order to delay the onset of rust. The chains were made at Upton Magna near Shrewsbury; they were transported by canal to Chester and then by sea to the Menai Strait. Ropes pulled by 150 men dragged the chains – each weighing over 20 tons – to the tops of the towers, and their achievement was celebrated by a brass band and the cheers of a host of onlookers. Unlike the Forth Bridge, the Menai Bridge does not need to be painted time and time again. Over the last century, its metalwork was only thoroughly painted in 1940 and in 2005. The 1940 painting was part of the work of replacing the original iron with steel links. The bridge was intended for carriages drawn by horses, and it was the coming of motorized traffic that led to the replacement. Until 1940, bus drivers drove empty buses across the bridge after insisting that passengers should walk across it.

All this is explained in exemplary detail in the Bridges Museum in the town of Menai Bridge (Porthaethwy). There, visitors are reminded that the bridge was only a small part of Telford's ambitious scheme to build a highway which would cut the time needed to link London with Dublin, a link which

increased in importance following the British parliament's absorption of the Irish parliament in 1801. Telford constructed the highway through the heart of Snowdonia; it is remarkable that, in crossing that mountainous terrain, no part of it has a gradient of more than 5 per cent, proof that the bridge is a masterpiece within a masterpiece.

To the poet, Dewi Wyn o Eifion, the outstanding feature of the bridge was its height. The bridge's great height was necessary because, in the 1820s, sailing ships rising thirty metres out of the water regularly sailed through the strait. Thus, it was necessary to ensure that the bridge was a hundred foot (30.77 metres) above water level. It is relevant to cite another of Telford's masterpieces, the suspension bridge across the Conwy; as tall ships did not sail up the Conwy, that bridge could squat humbly.

When Robert Stephenson was designing the railway bridge across the strait in the 1840s, he too had to take into account the height of the ships of the era. As the weight of a train is much greater than the weight of a horse-drawn carriage, the railway bridge had to have a central pillar. Indeed, it was the rock in the middle of the strait on which the pillar stands – Craig y Fyrdan (loosely translated as Britannia Rock) – which gave the bridge its name. The Britannia Bridge was build as a tube – the earliest such bridge in the world – and the story of raising the 1,500-ton tubes from the water to their position on the towers is one of the most dramatic in the history of construction in Wales. As Prince Albert was deeply interested in technology, he and the queen came to see the bridge in 1852, two years after it was opened – one of the three visits which Victoria made to Wales during her 64-year reign.

The Britannia Bridge did not arouse as much enthusiasm as did the Menai Bridge, but its history was more dramatic. The greatest excitement was in 1970 when the bridge was almost totally destroyed by fire. When it was reopened in 1972, it had been transformed; the tube had disappeared, steel arches had been inserted, a road bridge had been built above the railway, and the lions which had stirred the imagination of y *Bardd Cocos* (the cockle-selling poet, John Evans) had become almost invisible.

Of all the characteristics of the bridges, the most interesting is their designers' pride in their work. The Menai Bridge bears the prominent inscription THOMAS TELFORD ENGINEER; the Britannia Bridge bears the equally prominent inscription GEORGE STEPHENSON ENGINEER. It is not only their masterpieces that are cheek by jowl; as both are buried in Westminster Abbey, they are also cheek by jowl.

The summit of Bangor Mountain is the best place to look at Bangor. The viewer can appreciate the bulk of the chief building of the University College (there are those who cannot bring themselves to refer to Bangor University), which dominates the city with almost the same panache as its cathedral dominates Lincoln. Also visible is Bangor's High Street – the longest street in Wales, it is claimed, and one better seen from a distance than from close by.

At the centre of Bangor's lacklustre streets stands the cathedral. The name, Bangor, has its origins in the wicker fence which surrounded the original Christian sanctuary. (There are four places called Bangor in Wales, two in Ireland, one in Brittany, and at least twenty in the countries to which the Welsh and Irish emigrated.) The sanctuary was founded by Saint Deiniol (d. *c*.572); remnants of his *clas* were discovered in the 1890s. There are no indubitable references to Bangor as the seat of the bishop of the north-west until the end of the eleventh century, but it is likely that Deiniol was an abbot-bishop and that Elfoddw,

described by a chronicler in 768 as *archiepiscopus Guenodatae regione*, was bishop of Bangor.

The essence of the present cathedral is what was built between 1480 and 1530, along with the results of the extensive renovation carried out between 1868 and 1884, the work of George Gilbert Scott, who was also responsible for renovation at St Davids and St Asaph cathedrals. Had the renovation not been undertaken, Bangor Cathedral would look similar to St Beuno's Church, Clynnog Fawr, built at the turn of the sixteenth century, probably by the same builders as were employed at Bangor. The cathedral's interesting features include the tomb of Owain Gwynedd; it is located beneath the high altar, despite the efforts of the archbishop of Canterbury to ensure that a man who had challenged canon law should not have so distinguished a resting-place. The building's chief treasure is the Mostyn Christ, a wood carving of the late fifteenth century; as the carving has no stigmata, it is a rare image of Christ before rather than after the crucifixion.

From the cathedral, the visitor should climb the steep hill up to the building which used to house Bangor Normal College,

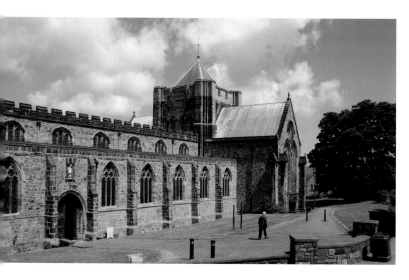

an institution absorbed by the University College in 1996. (Normal, in this context, is a loan from French educational practice; the first institution in France to have the title *école normale* was intended as the model for all other similar institutions.) According to Gwyn Alfred Williams, the Normal College was the only truly Welsh national institution ever to be located at Bangor. It came into existence in 1858, as the result of a campaign led by Hugh Owen to establish an institution for the training of Welshmen intending to become elementary schoolmasters. Wales already had training colleges –Trinity, Carmarthen (1848), for men and St Mary's, Caernarfon (1856; later at Bangor), for women. They, however, were Anglican colleges which trained teachers for the denominational schools of the National Society. Hugh Owen sought to provide non-denominational training, and Bangor Normal was the only such institution in Wales for men until the establishment of Caerleon Training College in 1914. The Normal College attracted students from all over Wales, a contrast with the University College, which was very much a college for students from the north. Proof of the nation-wide catchment area of the Normal College and the provincial catchment area of the University College, argued Gwyn, was the fact that the latter did not defeat the former at rugby until 1913.

The Arts and Crafts building of the Normal College is highly appealing, and the uncluttered profile of the University College –

the masterpiece of the Wolverhampton architect, Henry H. Hare – has a splendid dignity. Hare's building has its eccentricities – the professors' corridor, for example, and the less than successful attempt to provide Bangor with an Oxbridge court. (The court at Lampeter is much more convincing.) But it is delightful to wander around the court and to imagine that one is in communion with 'dewiniaid Bangor' (the sages of Bangor), 'llusernwyr canrifoedd coll' (the lamplighters of the lost centuries) of the language, literature and history of Wales.

There is more to Bangor than religion and education. Evidence of the city's ambition to be a major holiday resort can be seen in its 407 metre pier (1896). Particularly dignified is the gateway built as a memorial to the northerners who died in the First World War, an attempt to claim that Bangor is the north's chief urban centre – an audacious claim in view of the fact that there are in the north at least eight towns with larger populations.

Visitors to Bangor should end their tour by walking along the estuary of the Cegin in order to visit Porth Penrhyn. Established in 1790 as the place from which to export the slates of the Penrhyn Quarry, it was in 1800 linked to the quarry by tramroad. The North Wales Path which connects Bangor with Prestatyn begins by following the track of the tramroad and passes an intriguing building which looks like a round dovecote. Within it are seats where 12 people can companionably defecate together.

The privy adjoins the boundary of the park of Penrhyn Castle, a building which everyone should visit if only to be angered by the way in which the Douglas-Pennant family spent the wealth produced by the Penrhyn Quarry. The place can be enjoyable too, for Thomas Hooper's attempt to interpret the Romanesque can be very inventive, and sometimes rather comical.

It is said that the brewer Arthur Guinness, irritated by the toll charged on the porter he exported from Ireland to Britain, sailed to Holyhead to find a building where he could brew his black ale free of toll. He was informed of a vast building located across the Menai Strait; he saw the building, considered it suitably large and made a bid for it. Unfortunately, the Crown refused to sell Caernarfon Castle, and, consequently, it is Irish taverns, not Welsh taverns, that have sprung up in almost every city in the world.

In being impressed by the size of the castle, Arthur Guinness was sharing the experience of every visitor to Caernarfon. It is big, enormously big; it stretches for 152 metres, and some of its towers are among the largest ever built. A castle can be defined as a defensive building, a building from which to attack and an administrative centre. Caernarfon Castle was all of these, but in its

essence it was intended as an overwhelming statement – proof that the resources of the king of England were so limitless that any defiance of his power was doomed to failure.

Edward I's choice of Caernarfon as the location of the most prominent of his Welsh castles was wholly deliberate. It had been the site of a Roman fort. In Welsh tradition, the place was 'the old stronghold of the Emperor Constantine'. 'The king', noted Tony and Glenda Carr, 'was shrewd enough to realize the propaganda possibilities of a place watched over by the spirits of Magnus Maximus, Helena and Constantine.' (Edward's other chief castles were also located in places which had legendary or historical links with the traditions of the Welsh – Conwy replacing the monastery which was the spiritual heart of Gwynedd and the burial-place of Llywelyn the Great, Harlech built on the rock above the sea lauded at the beginning of the story of Branwen Ferch Llŷr, and Beaumaris displacing Llanfaes, Gwynedd's chief port and the burial-place of Joan, the wife of Llywelyn the Great.)

Every part of Caernarfon Castle is as defensible as every other part. It therefore does not belong to the earlier tradition of castle building best illustrated at Pembroke – a tradition which emphasizes the keep, the stronghold which would be defended when all other parts of the castle had been seized by its attackers.

By the late thirteenth century, the favoured design was that of the concentric castle, best illustrated at Beaumaris. However, Caernarfon is not a concentric castle; rather is it a series of towers and curtain walls. It was built remarkably rapidly, with the main expenditure occurring in 1283, 1284 and 1285. Edward I spent about £25,000 on it, more than twice as much as was spent at Beaumaris. He borrowed much of the money from the Riccardi Company, bankers at Lucca, Tuscany. The origins of the loan were characteristic of the far-flung associations of the building; Edward I's chief advisor in his castle-building ventures was James

A glimpse of the Gwynedd Council Offices at Caernarfon

of the castle. Dewi–Prys Thomas sought to symbolize the most remarkable feature of Caernarfon – that a town established to consolidate victory over Welshness has become the chief stronghold of Welshness. I remember talking to Éamon de Valera. On his visits to Wales, it was Caernarfon which had impressed him most. 'Welsh was spoken everywhere in the streets', he said. 'And it was a town; it was a town.'

It is a mere step from the council offices to *y maes*, a place where it was possible, when Caernarfon was Wales's ink capital, to meet the nation's chief reporters. It is the place to begin one of the walks through the town described in the pamphlets available at the tourist office. The visitor should walk to Llanbeblig and to the Roman fort at Segontium, and return via Hen Walia. From Lôn Parc, there is a splendid view across the Seiont to the castle. Blessed are the *Cofis* and the prospective *Cofis* (one of the dedicatees of this book among them) who live in houses offering such views.

of St George, a native of Savoy, who drew upon his knowledge of military architecture in Europe and beyond. It has been claimed that the eagles on the main tower represent a conscious attempt to construct an imperial palace in the Roman tradition and that the octagonal towers with their bands of different coloured stone were replicas of the walls of Constantinople – although James of St George could probably have found other precedents for the towers.

From the castle, the visitor should walk around the town walls. They extend for only 734 metres, compared with the 1,300 metres at Conwy, but the sight of them from the sea makes Caernarfon as much of a European icon as is Aigues-Mortes. The most interesting building within the walls is the offices of Gwynedd Council, particularly the extension designed by Dewi-Prys Thomas. Although the authors of *The Buildings of Wales: Gwynedd* (2009) are not enthusiastic about Thomas's work, it is a fascinating attempt to create an administrative centre inspired by principles very different from those which inspired the designers

Almost two-thousand years ago, the Romans – the invaders – were responsible for some remarkable building projects in Wales – establishing the legionary fort at Caerleon, for example, laying the foundation of the hundreds of kilometres of roads, and constructing the walls of the city of Caerwent. But it was the Britons – the natives – who were responsible for the marvel of the era – Tre'r Ceiri, the most astonishing of the six hundred and more hillforts built in Wales during the Iron Age. With a surface area of 2.5 hectares, it is not among the largest of Wales's hillforts; Garn Goch near Llangadog has a surface area of 11 hectares, but delectable although Garn Goch is, Tre'r Ceiri is superlative. In later centuries, the people of Llŷn were convinced that it had been built by giants. (*Ceiri* is a version of *cewri*, the Welsh word for giants; there is no basis to the belief that *ceiri* comes from *caerau*, the Welsh word for forts.)

Part of the appeal of Tre'r Ceiri is its location on the second highest of the three peaks of Yr Eifl. It is 485 metres above sea level, and the bulk of the highest peak, Y Garn Ganol (564 metres), deprives the fort of a view northwards. But the views in every other direction are magnificent. Almost the whole of Snowdonia and the Llŷn Peninsula are visible, and, on a clear day, it is possible to see on the far horizon across Cardigan Bay the graceful outline of the Preseli Hills.

The entrance to the path leading to the fort is situated on the B4417 about a kilometre south-west of the village of Llanaelhaearn. Virtually no publicity is given to the fort, but a few hardy souls find their way there. As the path rises 276 metres in a walk of about 740 metres, the path to the summit of the fort is very steep. As one climbs, the curtain walls come into view. To visitors who are acquainted with forts surrounded by earthen ramparts – Pendinas near Aberystwyth, for example – the first surprise at Tre'r Ceiri is the abundance of stone. The fort is a village of dry-stone houses surrounded by dry-stone walls, and it

is astonishing that the cementless constructions have survived for two-thousand years.

There were five entrances, and the path leads to the most important of them. There, it is evident that parts of the fort have been helped to survive. The site was thoroughly examined in 1956, and, since then, some strengthening and restoration has been undertaken. For example, the bastions on each side of the main entrance have been renewed, and attempts have been made to distinguish between untouched and restored work. The curtain wall is at its best on the north side, where the steps which led to the rampart walk are discernible. The path leading to the northern entrance crosses the fort, but it is difficult to traverse because of the many clusters of stone. These were the walls of the dwellings of the inhabitants of Tre'r Ceiri. At least 150 houses were built, most of them round in shape and about 2.5 metres in diameter.

Yr Eifl from Aberdesach

It is believed that a pole in the middle of each dwelling held up a roof made of reeds, gorse or turf. With thick walls, a fire in the middle of the floor, and neighbours in close proximity, life in one of Tre'r Ceiri's houses was no doubt sociable and snug.

The artefacts found in the fort date from AD 100 to 400, although it is believed that the origins of the fort are considerably earlier. If it is credible that, at the fort's apogee, every dwelling at Tre'r Ceiri housed a family, the village would have had a population of some six hundred. Why so many people should have settled in such a windswept place on land that produced little but gorse, heather and whinberries has been a matter of much speculation. The Roman historian, Tacitus, noted that General Agricola defeated the Ordovices about AD 80, a victory accompanied by great slaughter. Perhaps the tribal remnant established an almost inaccessible stronghold on Yr Eifl, just as the Incas are believed to have done at Machu Picchu following their defeat at Cajamarca. That may be overimaginative, and a more prosaic interpretation may be that it was a shelter used occasionally, perhaps by shepherds in summer, and that their permanent dwellings in the lowlands have been obliterated by centuries of agricultural activity.

After visiting one village that was abandoned, it may be fitting to visit another – Porth Nant, a village which in 1910 adopted, on very shaky historical grounds, the name Nant Gwrtheyrn (Vortigern's brook). It was established in the 1850s as a barracks for those – Irish people in the main, initially – who worked at the granite quarries of Yr Eifl. Although there is a road to the place by now, the village was built on the assumption that ships would transport the products of the quarries and would supply the needs of the inhabitants. The barracks were destroyed by a landslide in 1925, but long before then a chapel and a neat row of houses had been built, home to a community whose members had totally abandoned the place by the 1950s. A trust led by Dr Carl Clowes bought the village for £25,000 in 1978 with the intention of adapting it as a Welsh-language learning centre. Although the venture has faced difficult times, it now prospers and the village can offer accommodation to 58 people. For those prepared to drive down the steep hill to the village, or are fit enough to make the journey on foot, going to Nant Gwrtheyrn is a requisite part of a visit to northern Llŷn. And for the tired walker, there is no better place to rest that in Tafarn y Fic in Llithfaen, which is owned by the most remarkable co-operative venture in Wales.

Llanberis is as near as it gets to the top of the list of Wales's 'must see' places. Indeed, it is difficult to think of any other place of its size (2,018 inhabitants) which offers so many attractions. Some of the most interesting – the Dinorwic Slate Quarry, the National Slate Museum and the Dinorwic Power Station – are aspects of the area's industrial history. (Incidentally, although the three are associated with Llanberis, they are all located within the community of Llanddeiniolen.)

Strategic considerations gave rise to the earliest of the attractions – Dolbadarn Castle, which was built in 1225 on the orders of Llywelyn ap Iorwerth, who was convinced that control over Llanberis Pass was essential to the security of his realm. It is a bulky round tower which stands above Llyn Peris. It was probably its picturesque location which inspired J. M. W. Turner to make

two paintings of it, although the artist, Ogwyn Davies, argued that Turner's interest in the building sprang from his sympathy for Owain ap Gruffudd, who was, it is believed, imprisoned in the castle. If the right of the first-born is accepted, Owain was the true heir to Gwynedd, and some of the poets lamented the action of his younger brother, Llywelyn ap Gruffudd, who insisted that he should languish in prison for decades.

In the spring of 1283, the forces of Edward I captured Dolbadarn Castle, the last Welsh stronghold to fall in the war of 1282–3. After the record of the capture, there were no further references to the area for hundreds of years. The factor which re-aroused interest in Llanberis was its role as the starting point for the ascent of Snowdon. In 1831, it was noted that there was 'no place more public than the higher ground of Eryri during the summer', a development which Llanberis's hoteliers, guides and shopkeepers were eager to exploit.

Tourism, however, was a minor importance compared with the development of slate-quarrying. Small-scale slate-working had been occurring for centuries and a major step was taken in 1788 when a partnership began working the rock above Llyn Peris. In 1809, the venture became the property of the local landowner, Thomas Assheton Smith of Vaynol, and it would be he and his descendants who would profit from the wealth of the Dinorwic Quarry. The quarry was linked by tramway with Y Felinheli (Port Dinorwic – now a redundant place-name) in 1825, a year in which the quarry made a profit of £16,807. Its prosperity reached its peak in the 1880s, when the parishes of Llanberis and Llanddeiniolen had 9,919 inhabitants, compared with 1,503 in 1801.

The activity of this increasing population resulted in one of the most striking industrial landscapes in Europe. From the surface of Llyn Peris, Elidir Fawr rises eight hundred metres to its summit; more than half this vast hillside has been carved into terraces.

Alongside the terraces is the waste rock which flows down the mountain as if there were an intention to fill Llyn Peris with rubble. There are even more dramatic industrial wounds in Wales – the chasm at Parys Mountain, for example, and the great void of Penrhyn Quarry – but those do not adjoin a major road. As the terraces of the Dinorwic Quarry can be clearly seen from the A4086, they represent the most visible industrial remains in Wales. It is a memorable experience to stand on the shore of Llyn Peris, and to realize that it was workers hanging from ropes and equipped with pickaxes and explosives who were responsible for this astonishing sight.

The Dinorwic Quarry was closed in 1969, and a museum was established in the old workshops. The institution became the North Wales Slate Museum and then the National Slate Museum, one of the branches of the National Museum of Wales. Apart from St Fagans, it is the most appealing of the seven branches of that estimable institution. As its website states, visitors get the impression that they have strayed into a place 'where quarrymen

and engineers have just put down their tools and left the courtyard for home'. There are dwellings there too – four terraced houses from Fron Haul, Tanygrisiau; three of them have been furnished in the styles of 1869, 1901 and 1969.

The most interesting experience for a visitor to the museum is to watch one-time slate workers splitting the rock. The most impressive object in the museum is a waterwheel 15.4 metres in diameter, which was, until 1925, a central feature of the work of the quarry.

Of all the wonders of the Llanberis area, the most remarkable is the Dinorwic Power Station which was opened in 1984. The station pumps water from Llyn Peris (100 metres above sea level) to Llyn Marchlyn Mawr (580 metres above sea level); the water then falls 480 metres to power the generators located in a vast chamber sited behind the old quarry – the largest man-made underground chamber in the world. The station uses more energy than it produces; nevertheless, as it produces electricity when demand is at its height, and uses electricity to pump water up to Llyn Marchlyn Mawr in the middle of the night, when demand for electricity is at its lowest, it is claimed that the station is responsible for a reduction of 140,000 tons a year in the amount of carbon dioxide released into the atmosphere.

The most popular attraction at Llanberis is the Snowdon Mountain Railway. Trains run on the 7.524-kilometre-long narrow gauge line which allows visitors to reach the summit of Snowdon, 1,085 metres above sea level, in an hour, more or less the amount of time the most rapid competitors in the Snowdon Race take to run from Llanberis to the summit and back. The railway was opened in 1896, and relied wholly on steam until 1986 when a few diesel engines were introduced. As coal was scarce after the Second World War, there was a time when the railway was powered by burning soldiers' old boots.

The years between the Act of 'Union' and the great changes of the late eighteenth century are considered to be 'the age of the gentry'. Of the gentry of the period, the most memorable is Sir John Wynn (1553–1627). That is partly because he wrote *The History of the Gwydir Family*, a volume full of droll and boastful comments, and partly because he is mentioned in a wide variety of sources ranging from material relating to the life of Bishop William Morgan, to plans to drain Traeth Mawr, Porthmadog, and campaigns to hold *eisteddfodau*, all of them offering evidence of his rapacious and irascible personality.

Sir John was the great-grandson of Maredudd ap Ieuan (d. 1468), a refugee from the anarchy of Eifionydd who gained possession of Gwydir Castle *c*.1500. For centuries, there had been a square keep at Gwydir, which was incorporated into the new building erected in the 1550s for Maredudd's son, John Wynn ap Maredudd. The new building was a sumptuous mansion rather than a castle, although it did have some defensive features. It incorporated elements from Maenan Abbey, dissolved in 1536,

a spiral staircase in particular. Sir John Wynn enlarged the mansion, as did his son, Richard (1588–1649), who commissioned the finely-carved panelling lining the walls of the dining-room. The result was an irregular, picturesque, pile put together over several centuries – a marked contrast with Plas Mawr, the superbly coherent mansion erected in Conwy for Sir John's kinsman, Robert Wynn.

Following the death of Sir John's grandson in 1674, Gwydir passed to his daughter Mary and her husband, Robert Bertie, Baron Willoughby d'Eresby. The descendants of Mary and Robert had a variety of surnames, and it was for them that Gwydir House in Whitehall, the London home of the Welsh Office, was built in 1772. By the 1870s, Clementina Elizabeth Drummond-Willoughby owned 65,820 hectares of land, 12,300 in Caernarfonshire, 31,000 in Perthshire and 22,520 in Lincolnshire and Rutland, making her one of the richest landowners in the kingdom. Although members of the family endowed a school in Betws-y-Coed and paid for some renovation at Dolwyddelan Castle, they spent little time at Gwydir. Grimsthorpe Castle in Lincolnshire and Drummond Castle in Perthshire are still owned by the family, but the bulk of the Gwydir estate was sold to Lord Carrington in 1895. In an auction in 1925, most of the estate's farms were sold to their tenants. The solicitors for the sales were Lloyd George and George; it is intriguing that Lloyd George received commission from the extinction of the patrimony of Sir John Wynn.

Following a fire in 1912, Gwydir was despoiled; in 1921, the panels of the dining-room were sold to William Randolph Hearst, who intended to install them in his castle, San Simeon, in California. There were further fires in the 1920s, and the place was empty until 1944 when an attempt was made to renovate it. The attempt was abandoned after 20 years, and the castle was unprotected until Peter and Judith Welford bought it in 1994. The amount of work they have done is astonishing. The most exciting chapter in the story is the discovery of the dining-room panels in a storeroom near New York, where they were still in the boxes in which they had been placed on the orders of William Randolph Hearst in 1921. The panels were reinstalled in 1998, and now the dining-room looks exactly as it did in the time of

Richard Wynn. The castle is regularly open to the public, but the best way of appreciating it is to spend a night in one of the two rooms let to visitors. Guests can wander through the gardens in the moonlight, enjoying the cedars, yews and oaks, and avoiding the peacock dung copiously produced by the birds (fifty at the last count) which have long been a feature of Gwydir.

From the castle, a path leads uphill to Gwydir Uchaf. There, in 1604, Sir John Wynn commissioned the building of a house – a Trianon, so to speak, to go with the Versailles at the bottom of the hill. A year before the death of Richard Wynn in 1674, a chapel was completed near the house. It was a private family chapel, and, consequently, it did not suffer from the rebuilding, the 'restoration' or the medievalization which befell virtually every parish church in Wales in the nineteenth century. In 1952, Grimsthorpe Estates Limited, the family company of the Willoughbys, gave the chapel to the Ministry of Public Buildings and Works; in 1984, it came under the care of Cadw. The importance of the chapel is that it offers a rare illustration of the pattern of worship favoured by High Churchmen in the second half of the seventeenth century. Although it contains rows of pews facing the central aisle, most of the congregation would have sat on chairs immediately before the Communion-table in the shadow of a coat of arms which emphasized the loyalty of the

A carving on the tomb of Hywel Coetmor (d. c.1440) in Gwydir Chapel, Llanrwst

worshippers to the royal family. The chapel's chief glory is its painted ceiling, which abounds with particularly angelic-looking angels.

Gwydir Uchaf is not the only Gwydir Chapel in the area. To see the other, the visitor should cross the bridge across the Conwy to Llanrwst. The bridge – attributed, perhaps not wholly falsely, to Inigo Jones – is one of the most elegant in Wales. It was built in 1636, and, mercifully, it has not been adapted to serve modern traffic. Gwydir Chapel, Llanrwst, an appendage to St Grwst's Church, was built for Richard Wynn in 1634. It contains a number of memorials to the Wynn family, but the most interesting object within it is the coffin which is claimed to have contained the body of Llywelyn the Great (d. 1240). As Harri Webb put it:

Next morning I went to pay my respects
To the empty sarcophagus.
There were also present
Two lawnmowers and a milking stool.

Unlike their nearest neighbours, the Welsh are not noted for doting on their gardens. Therefore, it was a surprise to find that *The Oxford Companion to the Garden* has individual entries on eighteen gardens in Wales – Aberglasney, Bodnant, Bodysgallen Hall, Chirk Castle, Dyffryn, Erddig, Gnoll, Hafod, Margam, the National Botanic Garden of Wales (Middleton), Piercefield, Plas Brondanw, Plasnewydd, Portmeirion, Powis Castle, Raglan Castle, Tredegar House and Tretower Court. Because of its age, Powis Castle garden, where the yews took centuries to reach their present astonishing size, has a claim to be considered Wales's finest garden, but few would contest Bodnant's right to that title; indeed, in a recent poll, Bodnant was voted the most popular garden in Britain. There are gardens in Britain which are at least as rich in plants as is Bodnant – Kew in London, for example, or Wisley in Surrey – but they are gardens on flat land and thus lack the drama of Bodnant.

The story of Bodnant begins in 1874 when Henry Davis Pochin (1824–95) bought a house and 25 farms north of the village of Eglwys-bach on the east side of the Conwy. As he had made a fortune inventing more economical ways of manufacturing soap and paper and investing in Cornwall's china-clay deposits, money was not a problem for him. He built a new house, which was described by Edward Hubbard (*The Buildings of Wales: Clwyd*) as resembling 'a hotel in some staid Victorian spa'. But the house is not the attraction. Pochin had already tried his hand at gardening at Haulfre in Llandudno, but Bodnant, with its more spacious opportunities and its magnificent views of Snowdonia, was much more of a challenge. He employed Edward Milner, a disciple of Joseph Paxton at Chatsworth, to design the garden, and by Pochin's death Bodnant's best known feature – the 55-metre tunnel of Golden Chain (*Laburnum x wateri Vossii*) – had already been planted. Milner also oversaw the planting of the earliest conifers in the Nant Hiraethlyn ravine, among them the *Sequoiadendron giganteum* planted in 1886, which is now forty-five metres tall.

Bodnant was inherited by Pochin's daughter, Laura, and her husband Charles McLaren (1850–1934), a nephew of the radical politician, John Bright. McLaren received the title Baron Aberconway in 1911. It was Henry McLaren (1879–1953), the son of Laura and Charles, who commissioned Bodnant's greatest glory – the series of terraces and the rich planting in the ravine. He combined his gardening with a political career (he was parliamentary secretary to Lloyd George when the latter was President of the Board of Trade) and with a career as an industrialist (he was chairman of English China Clay, of the shipbuilding company, John Brown, and of the Tredegar Iron and Coal Company, the company which sank the Pochin and McLaren pits in the Rhymney and Sirhowy Valleys).
With so close an association with Blaenau Gwent, it is hardly

Bodnant's Pin Mill and Canal Terrace

surprising that it was from a neighbouring district – Llanelly, Breconshire – that he attracted F. C. Puddle in 1920 to become head gardener at Bodnant. F. C. Puddle was followed in the post by his son, Charles, and then his grandson Martin, a succession which tragically came to an end in 2005 when Martin drowned in the Bodnant lily pool.

Henry McLaren was elected president of the Royal Horticultural Society, a position which became almost hereditary in the family. He invested in the ventures of plant hunters such as George Forest, Frank Kingdon Ward and E. H. Wilson, who combed remote areas for their botanical treasures. As often as not, their discoveries were first seen in the West at Bodnant – *Rhododendron aberconwayi* among them. Plant breeding was undertaken in the garden, and the cross between *Viburnum farreri* and *Viburnum grandiflorum* gave rise to the cultivar *Viburnum x bodnantense* and its sub-forms.

Henry McLaren inherited the barony in 1934, and in 1949, four years before his death, he gave Bodnant to the National Trust, although he retained possession of the house and the mausoleum, the burial-place of the family. His son, Charles McLaren (1913–2003), the third baron, continued to make use of the house and, from 1961 to 1983, he was president of the Royal Horticultural Society. But, unlike his Liberal ancestors, Charles was a high Tory. In 1939, he went to Germany at the request of Lord Halifax with the intention of yielding more than Hitler had gained at Munich.

Bodnant offers a range of attractions – dramas, operas, exhibitions, displays of birds of prey – but it is the plants that are the true attraction. The spring is the best time to visit, although it is worth going there at any time when the gardens are open. (They are closed from the end of November until the beginning of March.) In April, the rhododendrons are at their best and the *Magnolia campbelli* magnificent. At the end of May, one's face can be caressed by the laburnum chains; in the summer, the roses are splendid, and in September the visitor can appreciate the world's largest collection of *eucryphia*, plants collected in Chile and south-eastern Australia. The end of the day in late October is the most romantic time to go to Bodnant, when the red and the gold of the leaves frame the sun setting over Snowdonia.

It would have been delightful to be around before any bridges had been built across the Conwy estuary. Then, the castle must have reared up like a magical vision across the water. But, as Telford's and Stephenson's bridges are also masterpieces, it could be argued that they enrich rather than impoverish the view. That cannot be claimed for the ill-judged bridge erected in the 1950s, but tribute should be paid to the ingenuity of the designers of the tube laid on the river bed in 1991 to carry the A55, the first attempt in Britain to build a road in an underwater tube rather than in a tunnel.

The Conwy crossing is a place of obvious strategic importance, and thus the need for a stronghold there had been realized six-hundred years before Edward I commissioned the castle. The fort on Deganwy Mountain, east of the estuary, had been the chief court of Maelgwn Gwynedd (d. *c.*547), a place where there was delight in the luxuries imported from the coasts of the Mediterranean Sea. In about 1080, Robert of Rhuddlan commissioned a castle on the site of the fort, a castle that was rebuilt by the Welsh *c.*1213. As Dafydd ap Llywelyn did not wish that stronghold to come into the possession of Henry III, he insisted that it should be demolished. (One of the most harrowing documents to survive from the wars of the thirteenth

Conwy Harbour; the hill in the distance is crowned by the ruins of Deganwy Castle

century is a letter by an English soldier who was shivering defenceless in the castle's ruins.) The castle was rebuilt for Henry III, but was demolished in 1263 on the orders of Llywelyn ap Gruffudd.

Edward I camped in the remains of Deganwy Castle in 1283, but, rather than rebuilding it and founding anew the borough which had been established adjoining it, he chose to fortify the Conwy estuary by establishing a castle and borough on the western side of the river. Among the motives for the change of location was the fact that the rock upon which Conwy Castle was built jutted out into the estuary and was therefore accessible to shipping, a facility not offered by the prominence crowned by Deganwy fort. A further consideration was that the presence of an English castle on the west side of the estuary meant that the place lost its status as the spiritual heart of Gwynedd, a status it had had since the establishment of Aberconwy Abbey in 1186. The abbey was relocated at Maenan, 12 kilometres to the south, where the coffin of Llywelyn the Great was transported from its original place of internment at Aberconwy.

Edward moved rapidly. Work on Conwy Castle began in March 1283, and there were hundreds of workers there within a few months. Originally, it would appear that Conwy was intended as the headquarters of the territories of the king of

England in north-west Wales. It was there that Edward and his wife Eleanor spent much of their sojourn in Wales in 1283–4, and the castle's royal apartments are among the most opulent built in thirteenth-century Europe. The secretariat which administered the king's policy in Wales was located at the castle, and it was undoubtedly to the needs of the clerks that the most intriguing feature of Conwy can be attributed – the row of twelve stone privies built into the town walls. More was spent on Conwy than on any other of Edward I's Welsh ventures, partly because of the cost of the walls, which stretch for 1,300 metres compared with the 734 metres at Caernarfon.

Conwy's premier role was not destined to endure, for Caernarfon became the chief town of the northern principality. Yet, despite the impressiveness of Caernarfon, it lacks the splendour of Conwy. As Goronwy Edwards put it: 'Conway [*sic*] is incomparably the most magnificent of Edward I's Welsh castles.' It does not have the perfect symmetry of Beaumaris's concentric castle. Conwy is a linear castle, as is Caernarfon, but it is a more ingenious building. That can be seen from an examination of the western bastion. In Caernarfon, the great gatehouse is pierced by a straight entry – much fortified admittedly; in Conwy, an attacker would first have to break through the fortifications of the western bastion, and then turn ninety degrees to the left in order to attack the defences of the main entrance. Furthermore, despite the drama of the profile of Caernarfon Castle, that of Conwy Castle is more memorable.

With its eight round towers, four of them capped with turrets, and with the entire structure mirrored in the water of the river, it is one of the great sights of Europe.

The delights of the castle and its walls should be enough to satisfy any visitor to Conwy. But there is more to see. It is worth visiting St Mary's Church, if only to gaze at what remains of the original burial site of Llywelyn the Great and at the memorial to John Gibson (1790–1866), a native of Conwy who was in his day considered to be the world's most skilful carver of marble. Even more interesting is Aberconwy House, the oldest town

house in Wales. Built c.1420, it enchanted a wealthy American, who would have taken it apart and shipped it off across the Atlantic had not the National Trust intervened. Still more splendid is Plas Mawr, built for Robert Wynn c.1585. With its stepped gables and its wealth of plasterwork, it is the finest town house erected in Britain in the sixteenth century.

A visit to Conwy should end in a walk along the estuary to enjoy the view across Conwy Sands to the Great Orme. It was on the sands, around 1850, that the first game of golf was played in Wales. Sadly, it is an activity that has spread.

Gruffudd ap Llywelyn (d. 1063) was the first and the last Welsh king to bring the whole of Wales under his authority. His headquarters was Rhuddlan, and thus it would not be too much to claim that Rhuddlan was the first capital of Wales. Indeed, as Rhuddlan was, at the height of Gruffudd's power, the centre of a sovereign Welsh polity – whatever that meant in the mid-eleventh century – it could be asserted that Rhuddlan is the only real capital that Wales has ever had. It is hardly surprising therefore that the motto of the old district council was 'Rhuddlan, Crud Cymru' (Rhuddlan, the cradle of Wales).

Gruffudd's choice of Rhuddlan was far-sighted. As it was in the middle of a sea marsh, it was defensible; it was possible to flee from it along the estuary of the Clwyd; the resources of the fertile land of the Vale of Clwyd were on hand; it was conveniently located for the fulfilment of Gruffudd's major ambition – to restore to Welsh rule the land which the Mercians had seized between the Dee and the Clwyd.

Gruffudd's career and hopes came to an end in 1063, but the merits of Rhuddlan were realized by Robert, the cousin of the first of the earls of Chester, Hugh of Avranches. With his energy, pride, avarice and cruelty, Robert was the epitome of a Norman knight. In 1073, he commissioned a castle at Rhuddlan, the base for his efforts to gain authority over the territories west of the Clwyd. The motte of his castle – Twt-hill – rises about 18 metres above the waters of the Clwyd, and to its east it is possible to trace the banks and the moat of his borough, which, as the home of eighteen burgesses, was the largest built by the Normans in the first wave of their attacks upon Wales.

Robert's power proved short-lived. Following his death at the hands of the Welsh in 1088, control of Rhuddlan became the measuring rod of the success or otherwise of the rulers of Gwynedd. On the occasions when their power waned, Rhuddlan was a stronghold of the kings of England. At the height of the career of Owain Gwynedd (d. 1170), Rhuddlan was part of Gwynedd, as it was during the apogee of the influence of his grandson, Llywelyn ap Iorwerth (d. 1240) and his great-great-grandson, Llywelyn ap Gruffudd (d. 1282). In 1258, Llywelyn ap Gruffudd founded a Dominican friary at Rhuddlan; remains of the building may be seen in the outbuildings of Abbey Farm.

Matters changed dramatically in 1277, when Llywelyn ap Gruffudd was obliged to yield to Edward I all his territories east of the Conwy. Even before the agreement was sealed, Edward had commissioned the building of a stone castle at Rhuddlan, the first Welsh castle in which that genius of an architect, James of St George, was involved. Apart from Caerphilly, which was built for Gilbert de Clare, the most powerful of the lords of the March, Rhuddlan was the first concentric castle to be built in Wales. It does not have the superb symmetry of Beaumaris, but its two gatehouses exude dignity and strength, and ingenuity was employed in linking the castle with the Clwyd. Rhuddlan Castle was built four kilometres from the sea and the original channel of the Clwyd was tortuous. Straightening it became a priority and,

The memorial at St Asaph to the translators of the Bible into Welsh

Parliament Street, Rhuddlan

between 1277 and 1290, there were 100 *fossatores* creating what may be considered to be the earliest canal in Wales.

The castle survived fairly well until the middle of the seventeenth century, but, after suffering siege in 1646, much of it was demolished in order to ensure that it would be impossible to defend. From then until 1947, when a renovation programme was launched, the castle was a quarry for the local inhabitants, and its most obvious feature today is that the dressed stone which formed the outer layer of the lower parts of the walls has disappeared.

The chief significance of Rhuddlan in the era of conquest was the fact that it was there, on 19 March 1284, that the Statute of Wales was promulgated, the document which laid out the way in which the territories seized by Edward I would be administered. On the 'Parliament House' in the High Street, there is a plaque which claims that it was at a parliament held in that building that the statute was authorized. There is no substance to the claim; the building contains stonework carved in the thirteenth century, but that was probably material pilfered from the castle.

Part of Edward I's intention in spending substantial sums on the defences and the accessibility of Rhuddlan was to ensure that it would be the seat of the bishop of the north-east. The king asked the Pope to recognize it as the centre of a bishopric, at the expense of St Asaph. The cathedral there had been destroyed by fire in 1282, and there was substance to the argument that a new start should be made at a more defensible location. The Pope did not reply, and what can now be seen at St Asaph is the shell of the building erected between 1284 and 1391, together with the renovation work undertaken by George Gilbert Scott between 1867 and 1875. The chief splendours of the cathedral are the two rows of stalls in the choir, rows carved following the indignities it suffered during the Glyn Dŵr Revolt. From 1601 until his death in 1604, the bishop of St Asaph was William Morgan, and, in the cathedral cemetery, there is a striking memorial to him and his fellow-translators of the Bible into Welsh.

South of the cathedral stands the H. M. Stanley Hospital, originally the workhouse in which Stanley (then John Rowlands, 1841–1904) spent his early years. He claimed he suffered cruelty at the workhouse; cruelty certainly became ingrained in him, as is evident from his willingness to aid Leopold of the Belgians in the king's campaign to reduce the inhabitants of the Congo to servitude.

Following the Acts of 'Union' of 1536 and 1543, Denbigh became the administrative and legal centre for the counties of Denbigh and Montgomery, and was thus, along with Caernarfon, Carmarthen and Brecon, the capital of one of the 'quarters' of Wales (Flintshire came under the supervision of Chester.)

The place to begin is St Marcella or Whitchurch. It was the religious centre of this part of the Vale of Clwyd long before a castle was built on the rocky ridge a kilometre to the west. St Marcella is one of the finest of the two-aisled churches so characteristic of this part of Wales. (Abergele is perhaps the finest.) Among the most memorable of its monuments is the tomb of John and Joan Salusbury of Lleweni, his effigy carved ten years after his death in 1578, and hers carved when she was still alive; the tomb features the couple's nine sons and five daughters. Joan was a member of the Myddelton family, and the church contains a brass plate to Richard Myddelton (d. 1575), his wife and their nine sons and seven daughters. But the most interesting of the church's monuments is that to Humphrey Llwyd, whose map of Wales was published at Antwerp two years after his death in 1568; fittingly, the monument is crowned by a globe.

The chief marvel of the area is located on a hill south of the present town – the great gatehouse of the castle. It is often claimed that the gatehouse at Harlech is the most formidable of the military structures of medieval Wales. That is probably true, but of all the strongholds built in Wales in the thirteenth century, the most ingenious is Denbigh's great gatehouse. It is a cluster of three octagonal towers enclosing an octagonal hall. Even at Conwy, there is nothing as inventive, and, although it was built for Henry de Lacy, earl of Lincoln, there can be little doubt that James of St George, Edward I's chief adviser on military architecture, had a hand in it.

The former Town Hall, Denbigh

45

The same inventiveness is not apparent in the design of the medieval walled town of Denbigh. The walls extend for 1,100 metres (compare the 1,300 metres at Conwy), but as the site was steep and lacked adequate water, Denbigh's inhabitants had, by the sixteenth century, abandoned the land within the walls. In the empty space, the earl of Leicester – who had gained possession of the lordship of Denbigh in 1563 – commissioned the construction of perhaps the oddest building to be erected in sixteenth-century Wales. Work on it ceased in 1584, but had Leicester's project been completed, Denbigh would have had the only cathedral to be built in the territories of Elizabeth I during her reign – the intention was to replace the cathedral at St Asaph – and the only Protestant church to be built in Wales in the sixteenth century. The church was designed as a place to hear sermons, and it may be considered to be the precursor of the host of chapels built in Wales in subsequent centuries.

Extramural Denbigh began developing shortly after the lordship came into the possession of de Lacy. Little of it survives apart from the ruins of the friary, the only Carmelite house established in medieval Wales. Located behind a garage and with bricks supporting the tracery of the east window, it looks very desolate.

Wandering the streets of Denbigh is a pleasant experience, although the town does not sparkle as does Ruthin. The one-time offices of Gwasg Gee, Wales's most famous nineteenth-century publishing house, is located in Swan Lane; hopes of turning it into the museum of printing in Wales have not yet been fulfilled. Also in Swan Lane is a Congregational chapel, a building described in *The Buildings of Wales: Clwyd* under the name *Trefn y Moddion* (The order of service). The Calvinistic Methodist chapel, also in Swan Lane, is historically more significant. It was in that chapel – although not in the present building – that Thomas Jones, a layman, administered in 1810 the sacrament of baptism, an act which was among the factors leading to the establishment of the Calvinistic Methodist denomination in 1811. Thomas Jones was one of the first Calvinistic Methodist preachers to be ordained, and it was probably in Swan Lane that the earliest sermon by an ordained minister of the denomination was delivered.

Of the other buildings in the town, among the most interesting is the former Bluecoat School, now the home of Canolfan Iaith Clwyd (the Clwyd Language Centre), which houses the Wireless in Wales exhibition, a fascinating collection of radio sets brought together by that distinguished resident of Denbigh, David E. Jones. By far the largest building in the town is what was until 1995 the North Wales Mental Hospital. The location of the hospital gave the name of Denbigh a somewhat sinister meaning among many of the inhabitants of the north, but the massive pile, with its symmetry and the ingenuity of its gables, is a building of distinction.

The immediate environs of Denbigh are rich in places of interest, among them Plas Clough (1567), the earliest building in Wales with stepped gables in the Dutch tradition, and Gwenynog, the garden of which features in one of Beatrix Potter's books. Near the ruins of Lleweni stands the largest industrial building (*c.*1785) surviving from eighteenth-century Wales; it produced bleach for the linen industry. One of the most intriguing of Denbigh's structures – a cockpit from the seventeenth century – was re-erected at St Fagans in 1970. The museum is eager to ensure that the buildings there are used as they were used originally – weaving in the woollen mill, for example, and baking in the bakery – but it is unlikely that there will ever be cock-fights in the cockpit.

The tomb of John and Joan Salusbury and their sons at St Marcella's Church, Denbigh

St Marcella's Church (left)

The memorial to Humphrey Llwyd (centre)

Two of the daughters of John and Joan Salusbury carved on the tomb of their parents (right)

There were several occasions when English monarchs were unfortunate in their dealings with Wales. Edward II was seized in Wales in 1326, and was dethroned and murdered. Richard II suffered the same fate in 1399. Edward V left the borders of Wales in 1483; he was captured, dethroned and then

Winefride's Well

disappeared in the Tower of London. Two years later, Richard III was killed by an army which emerged from Wales. The Tudors were more fortunate, perhaps because – unlike all the other royal dynasties of England – not one Tudor monarch set a foot on the land of Wales.

Of the Stuarts, Charles I was executed because of his readiness to take advantage of the second Civil War, a war which began in Wales. The role of Wales – and of Holywell in particular – in the fate of his son James II is more diverting. James's great hope was to have a son, a son he was determined to raise as a devout Roman Catholic. By 1687, he and his wife, Mary, had been married for fourteen years, and none of the children born to them had survived infancy. It was believed that if Mary were to give birth to a healthy son, a miracle would be needed. The best place to pray for a miracle was Winefride's shrine at Holywell. James went there; he prayed, and James Edward was born on 20 June 1688. It was the fear that the Holywell miracle would ensure a succession of Catholic monarchs which led to the dethronement of James and to the 'Glorious Revolution' of 1688.

According to tradition, the Holywell shrine stands where a spring gushed forth at the place where Winefride's head fell following her beheading for defending her virginity. (As she was the niece of St Beuno, rejoining her head and body was a small matter.) A well-chamber surmounted by a chapel was built *c.*1500, buildings commissioned, it is believed, by Baron Stanley, husband of Margaret Beaufort, mother of Henry VII. They are among Wales's finest examples of Perpendicular Gothic architecture. The vaults of the chamber are particularly impressive, as is the basin with its steps down to the water. Adjoining the chamber's entrance is an open-air pool where pilgrims seeking to bathe are still welcomed.

The strength of the flow from St Winefride's Well was harnessed by eighteenth-century industrialists. The results of their work can be seen in the Greenfield Heritage Park, which lies between the well and the Dee estuary. Greenfield is one of the places (Bersham is another) which underlines the folly of interpreting the industrial history of Wales solely in terms of the south. Admittedly, there were only about 45,000 people employed in heavy industries in the northern coalfield in 1901, when there were 320,000 people employed in such industries in that of the south. But in the south, the great majority were involved in the same activity – the mining of coal – while in the north they were involved in a remarkable variety of activities.

The variety was at its most marked at Greenfield, where there were copper works, lead mines, collieries, factories making paper and vitriol and centres for the spinning of cotton, silk and wool. Copper manufacturing was the chief industry and, in 1774, Dr Johnson counted nineteen works within two miles of St Winefride's Well. By then, work had begun on the rich vein of copper ore on Parys Mountain, and, in the 1780s, there were forty ships ceaselessly transporting copper ore from Amlwch to Holywell. There was an iniquitous aspect to the trade, for among the products of Holywell were the copper ornaments which were exchanged for slaves on the coast of west Africa.

Wandering through Greenfield, following the directions provided by industrial archaeologists and seeking to understand the skilful use of water-power, is a fascinating experience. The path crosses Wat's Dyke, the precursor of Offa's Dyke, and ends in something quite unexpected – the ruins of a twelfth-century Cistercian monastery. Basingwerk Monastery was founded in 1131, probably by Ranulph, earl of Chester. Although it did not belong to the mainstream of the monasticism of *Pura Wallia*, it would seem that the monks contributed to the compilation of the Chronicle of the Princes. If it is true that the splendid roof of the nave of Cilcain church was transported there from Basingwerk, the dismembering of the monastery must have begun shortly after its dissolution in 1535. Little of the abbey church has survived, but the outline of the monastic buildings can be traced and the western wall of the refectory is still fairly complete.

While Basingwerk is a ruin, there is in the vicinity of Holywell a religious house which is complete and functioning. It is at Pantasaph, about three kilometres west of St Winefride's

Well. Its founding was a matter of much controversy. In 1849, Rudolph Feilding and his wife Louisa, heiress of the Pennant family of Plas Downing, commissioned a new Anglican church at Pantasaph. A year later, Rudolph and Louisa were received into the Roman Catholic Church and decided that St David's, Pantasaph, should be a Roman Catholic Church. They were challenged in court by the bishop of St Asaph and throughout the kingdom a storm of protest arose against Catholic 'rapacity' – a widespread fear in the 1850s. The bishop was unsuccessful and a fund was established to raise money to build an Anglican church to replace that which had been 'lost'. Enough money was raised to build two churches, one at Brynford and one at Gorsedd.

St David's Church, Pantasaph is a memorable building. Adjoining it, Rudolph Feilding established a friary for the Capuchin friars, one of that order's five houses in Britain. (It is the

cowl of the Capuchins – the *capuccio* – which gave rise to the word *cappuccino*.) The friars maintain a retreat centre where the most unbelieving of visitors receive balm for the soul.

Industrial remains in the Greenfield Heritage Park

As Ewloe is only three kilometres from Queensferry, it is the most easterly of the castles of the Welsh princes. The castle is the most striking evidence of the boldness of the princes of Gwynedd as they increasingly pushed the boundaries of their territory towards Chester. Possession of the mineral riches and the fertile land located between the Clwyd and the estuary of the Dee was central to the ambitions of Owain Gwynedd (d. 1170), his grandson, Llywelyn ap Iorwerth (d. 1240), and Llywelyn's grandson, Llywelyn ap Gruffudd (d. 1282). In 1167, Owain succeeded in capturing all the invaders' castles in that region and thus he probably felt that there was no reason for him to commission the building of another castle there. The claim that Ewloe Castle was originally built in the 1160s is therefore unlikely to be true. His achievement was repeated by Llywelyn ap Iorwerth, and it has been suggested that it was he, *c*.1210, who commissioned the D-shaped keep – a shape characteristic of several of the castles of the Welsh rulers – on a slope above the Nant Gwepra ravine.

Nevertheless, it is generally agreed that it was under Llywelyn ap Gruffudd that the castle was built. The earldom of Chester came into the possession of the future Edward I in 1254, and it may have been that development which caused Llywelyn to commission the building of Ewloe Castle. In 1277, Llywelyn lost all his territories in the north-east, but, unlike other castles of the Welsh rulers, Ewloe did not become a link in Edward I's chain of Welsh strongholds. It slowly decayed until the 1960s, when the Ministry of Public Buildings and Works began clearing the brambles and repointing the walls.

The result of the work of the ministry, and its successor, Cadw, is one of the most attractive monuments in Wales. The main appeal of Ewloe Castle is that the wanderer comes across it almost by accident. Most of the castles of Wales can be viewed from afar, but Ewloe lurks in the trees, almost immediately above the ravine in which Owain Gwynedd sought to ambush Henry II in 1157. There is something exceptionally neat and trim about the ruins – the curtain walls which enclose the two wards, the round tower which is part of the walls of the outer ward and the free-standing D-shaped tower in the middle of the inner ward.

Ewloe Castle's chief significance is that it is an indicator of the extent of Gwynedd at its medieval apogee, but it must be confessed that it is almost unknown to history; the sole reference to it dating from the Middle Ages is a passing mention in 1311. But a wealth of history is attached to the castle – or rather the castles – located four kilometres to its south-east. Hawarden's Old Castle was begun in the 1070s as part of the attempt of Hugh of

Avranches, earl of Chester, to gain possession of the north-east. It was built within an Iron Age fort, but little is known of it for it was wholly destroyed by Llywelyn ap Gruffudd in 1265. It had been the home of the Montalt family, stewards of the earldom of Chester, and under the provisions of the Treaty of Montgomery (1267), the site was returned to Roger de Montalt on condition that it would not be refortified. But it was, for there was certainly a castle at Hawarden on the eve of Palm Sunday (21 March) 1282, when it was attacked by Llywelyn's brother, Dafydd – the assault which presaged the destruction of the polity which Llywelyn and his ancestors had sought to create.

GLADSTONE

Hawarden Castle was rapidly captured by Chester-based English forces, who set about strengthening and enlarging it. What survives today is a round keep, a rather old-fashioned structure to be erected in the late thirteenth century, but one which crowns its high motte with dignity. The castle had no further role in the Wars of Independence nor did it feature in the Glyn Dŵr Revolt. It was twice besieged in the Civil Wars of the seventeenth century, and, following those wars, was rendered ineffective as a military stronghold. It was bought in 1653 by John Glynne, whose descendants in the 1870s would own 2,800 hectares of land in Flintshire. The medieval enthusiast, Stephen Glynne (1807–74), delighted in the ownership of an ancient monument, which he made more picturesque by adding to its irregularity.

In the eighteenth century, the Glynne family gained possession of Broadlane Hall, which was renamed Hawarden Castle. The building, which is rarely open to the public, was enlarged and castellated in 1810. It became the home of William Ewart Gladstone following his marriage in 1839 to Catherine, the sister of Stephen Glynne. Gladstone's study contains an impressive collection of axes, presented to him by leading statesmen who were intrigued by his delight in felling trees. It was while felling in Hawarden Park that he heard in December 1868 that he was to be prime minister, an office he held for almost fifteen years.

Hawarden is rich in memorials to Gladstone. His collection of books – over thirty thousand of them – are in St Deiniol's Library. In front of the library stands the Gladstone statue intended for, but rejected by, the city of Dublin, which was, by the time of the statue's completion (1923), the capital of the Irish Free State. St Deiniol's Church contains the cenotaph of Gladstone and his wife (their bodies are in Westminster Abbey), and a stained-glass window donated by Armenian patriots. The finest memorial to Gladstone – the gift of his family – is the west window of the church. The last work of Edward Burne-Jones, it portrays Mary and the baby Jesus with angels, shepherds and magi. It is the finest stained-glass window in Wales.

Mold has yielded the most magnificent artefact to have been found in Wales – the gold cloak discovered in 1833 in Bryn-yr-ellyllon cairn. (The cairn has been destroyed, but a plaque noting the place of its discovery can be seen on Chester Road.) The cloak was hammered out of a single ingot of gold, probably in *c*.1750 BC. It was torn while being pulled from the cairn, and some parts of it have disappeared; the largest part was bought by the British Museum in 1836, and, as other pieces came to light, the cloak, which weighs over half a kilogram, was reassembled. It was exhibited at Wrexham in 2005, and there are hopes in Mold that a home for the cloak, and other Bronze Age artefacts from the north-east, will be established there. If that happens, the town will win international renown.

Mold is a remarkably attractive place. Indeed, along with Ruthin and Aberaeron, it is among Wales's most appealing county towns. The roots of the place may be found in its north-eastern corner. There one can find the key to the name Mold/Yr Wyddgrug – the *mont hault* (high hill)/the *grug* (hill) *gŵydd* (prominent). Before the end of the eleventh century, the *mont* or *grug* had been surmounted with a wooden castle which became the responsibility of the Montalt family, the stewards of the earldom of Chester. As the family had another castle eight kilometres away at Hawarden, Mold Castle was not rebuilt in stone. Consequently, the centre of the town developed around the parish church rather than the castle.

The nave of St Mary's Church, Mold, is one of Wales's best examples of the Perpendicular Gothic style. The work was financed by one of the north-east's major landowners – Baron Stanley, husband of Margaret Beaufort, mother of Henry VII. As the nave's walls are replete with stone carvings, the visitor gets an impression of greater opulence than is usual in Perpendicular Gothic buildings. Among the carved motifs are the three legs of the Isle of Man, an island of which Baron Stanley was lord. The west tower was completed in 1773, and it is an interesting example of an eighteenth-century architect's attempt to interpret the architecture of the late fifteenth century. The graveyard contains the grave of Richard Wilson, the most famous painter to be born in Wales. He died at Colomendy near Mold in 1782, and in 1851 two rather feeble *englynion* (Welsh alliterative stanzas) were carved on the tomb, the product of a competition organized by the Mold branch of Cymdeithas y Cymreigyddion (The Welsh Literary Society).

The Church in Wales is not the only denomination which has a distinguished place of worship in Mold. A Calvinistic Methodist chapel was built there in 1819. The town's population doubled in the following forty years, creating the need for a much larger building. The result was Bethesda (1863), the chapel with the finest neo-classical façade in Wales. (It is very similar to the Lammas Street Baptist chapel in Carmarthen, but it is better located and is more elegant.)

It was the industrial development of the district – coalmining and lead-ore mining in particular – which caused Mold's

The Tower near Mold

population growth. One of the chief collieries was Leeswood Green, some four kilometres south-east of Mold. In 1869, the miners, enraged by wage cuts and by the prohibition of the use of Welsh underground, attacked the colliery manager. In the court case that followed, there were riots in Mold, riots which can be considered to be the northern version of the Merthyr Rising (1831). Four protesters were shot dead and at least ten were seriously wounded. Although he denied the assertion, the riots are one of the themes of *Rhys Lewis*, the best of the novels of Daniel Owen (1836–95). Daniel Owen portrays Mold as a border town where Welsh and English coexisted; he is commemorated there by a statue, a cultural centre and a shopping precinct.

Although Flint was intended as the county town of Flintshire, Mold came to assume a growing role as an administrative centre. It was acknowledged as the county town in 1833, and its importance increased following the establishment of the Flintshire County Council in 1889. As heavy industry declined in the area, Mold came to depend largely upon administration, the main cause of the increase in its population from 4,263 in 1901 to 9,568 in 2001. In 1966, work began on a civic centre north-east of the town. Until 1974, the 187,000 inhabitants of Flintshire were administered from Mold; with the establishment of the county of Clwyd in that year, the number administered rose to 365,000. The civic centre was therefore enlarged, work which weakened the integrity of the original design. As the Flintshire established in

1996 has only 148,000 inhabitants, one wonders whether the administrative buildings are now too extensive? The most interesting building on the site is Theatr Clwyd (1973–6), which in 1998 became the home of Clwyd Theatr Cymru, Wales's premier theatre company. The building has five auditoriums, which can, together, accommodate 1,360 spectators.

Mold is located at the centre of an area rich in historic attractions. South of the town stands The Tower, built in the mid fifteenth century for Rheinallt Gruffydd ap Bleddyn, one of the patrons of the poet, Lewys Glyn Cothi; it is one of Wales's twelve fortified tower houses. To the north stands Rhual, a well-proportioned house built in 1634, which contains a particularly elegant staircase. In 1736, Rhual's owner commissioned the Hallelujah Monument which purports to mark the place at which an army of Welshmen – who were, of course, Christian – defeated a force of pagan Englishmen. The Welsh were led by St Germanus, and the war cry 'Hallelujah' was enough to ensure victory. That, at least, is what tradition maintains.

St Mary's Church, Mold

It is hardly ever possible to state that a particular building is unquestionably the best of its kind in Wales. But there can be no doubt that All Saints, Gresford, is Wales's finest parish church. It contains some features which have survived from the thirteenth and fourteenth centuries, but the essence of what is visible there now is a completely coherent realization of what a church of *c.*1500 should be. It has similarities with churches built at that time in the Cheshire Plain, although it surpasses all of them;

indeed, several architectural historians have commented upon the anomalous fact that the finest of the Cheshire churches is in Wales.

It has been claimed that it was the wealth of Thomas Stanley, husband of Margaret Beaufort, the mother of Henry VII, which financed the building of the church. Nevertheless, unlike St Mary's Church, Mold, symbols such as the three legs of the Isle of Man are absent there, and it is therefore likely that the income produced by its chief treasure – a miraculous image of the Virgin Mary – financed its construction.

The first thing that strikes the visitor is the large number of yew trees in the churchyard. Yet, it is not Gresford's yews that are praised in the verse, 'The Seven Wonders of Wales'. (The yews praised are those of Overton.) It is Gresford's bells that are praised – eight originally, but twelve after a further four were added in 2006. The tower sustaining them is not as lively as that at St Giles, Wrexham, but it has a highly attractive, subtle dignity. Inside, the splendour of the wooden roof, the purity of the pillars and arches of the nave, the soft light that comes through the windows of the clerestory and the glory of the east window are breathtaking. The stained-glass is of the highest quality, although its colour was almost destroyed in 1966 when the glass was washed with a chemical cleaning fluid.

The church is further enriched by a wealth of monuments. The earliest (1313) is an effigy in armour of Madog ap Llywelyn ap Gruffudd, a descendant of the royal house of Powys Fadog. There are numerous monuments to the Trevors of Trevalyn, a prominent family in the public life of Denbighshire in the century following the 'Union'. The monument to John Trevor (d. 1589) is in Welsh; although a Roman Catholic, he insisted on being buried in a Protestant church in order to spend eternity among his ancestors. His effigy only shows his head and legs; the same is true of the effigy of Efan Llwyd (d. 1639) at Llanarmon-yn-Ial, which

seems to suggest that there were sculptors in Denbighshire who did not want to portray abdomens.

The crypt holds the most moving object in the church. It is a lump of coal mined at the Gresford Colliery on 22 September 1934, a few hours before the explosion which killed 266 colliers. There have been only five disasters in Britain more lethal than that at Gresford – Senghenydd (1913) 439 dead, Barnsley (1886) 388 dead, West Haughton (1910) 344 dead, Cilfynydd (1894) 281 dead, and Abercarn (1878) 268 dead. As Gresford has always been

Items from the Gresford Colliery exhibited at The Bersham Heritage Centre

an essentially rural village, only twelve of the dead lived there; the colliery's workforce was drawn from a wide area, and thus the disaster was a tragedy for the whole of the industrial north-east. Consciousness of that is still evident today, as can be seen from the many contributions to the disaster website.

An unknown poet wrote a ballad about the disaster, verses redolent with bitterness. The bitterness is understandable, bearing in mind that the employers argued that, as the colliers had only worked half a shift on 22 September 1934, only half a shift's wages should be paid to their dependants. The enquiry dragged

on until 1937; in the court case which followed the publication of its report, William Bonsall, the colliery manager, was fined £140.

Following many a colliery disaster, the dead are fittingly commemorated in funeral services. That, for example, is what happened following the Maerdy explosion of 1885, when the eighty-one who died – the grandfather of the author of these comments among them – were buried in Ferndale cemetery. However, only twelve bodies were raised from Gresford Colliery. The site of the disaster was sealed, and 254 of the dead colliers still lie where they were killed. In 1982, a monument to the dead was unveiled. It was made of the winding gear of the pit; the wheel is portrayed on the leaflet bearing the words of the hymn 'Gresford', the anthem of the colliers.

Until 1964, much of the village of Gresford was in Flintshire. The Flintshire established following the Conquest had three non-contiguous parts. The *cantref* of Tegeingl in the north-east was separated from the *cwmwd* of Maelor Saesneg in the south-east by the lordships of Mold, Hawarden and Hope, which would become part of Flintshire in 1536, and the lordship of Bromfield and Yale which would become part of Denbighshire in that year. In the centre of the lordship of Bromfield and Yale lay the *taeogdrefi* (bond villages) of Marford and Hoseley. They did not extend over more than 300 hectares, but, for some unknown reason, they became part of Flintshire. It is worth going to Marford, if only to see the village built between 1803 and 1815 by the owners of the Trevalyn estate, a village which is a remarkable exercise in the picturesque. The great days of Marford and Hoseley were the years 1961–8, when taverns were closed on Sunday in Denbighshire and open in Flintshire, an era when there was much jollification in the Red Lion and the Trevor Arms.

Cottages at Marford

One of the most interesting walks in Wales follows the Clywedog River from Coedpoeth to Wrexham. (The Clwyd, Dugoed, Dee, Severn, Ithon, Teifi and Wnion rivers all have tributaries called Clywedog; the Clywedog which joins the Dee is the one under discussion here.) The valley floor is owned by the National Trust, and it is difficult to believe, while walking through its leafy glades, that the path traverses one of the most significant industrial landscapes in Britain.

The chief attraction along the path is Bersham, the first place in Wales where iron ore was smelted using coke rather than charcoal. The venture was launched in 1721 by Charles Lloyd, the brother of the founder of Lloyds Bank, only twelve years after Abraham Darby had devised the method at Coalbrookdale in Shropshire. (The fact that both the Lloyd family and the Darby family were Quakers assisted the adoption of Coalbrookdale methods at Bersham.) Bersham may well have been the first place in the world, outside Shropshire, where iron ore was smelted with coke, a method not used in the south Wales coalfield until the 1760s. The switch from charcoal (half-roasted wood) to coke

(half-roasted coal) had revolutionary implications. It released the iron industry from reliance upon the limited supply of timber. Charcoal was produced by the pound and coke by the ton, a change fundamental to what came to be called the Industrial Revolution. In the early eighteenth century, iron production had been a minor activity in virtually every part of the country; with the use of coke, production came to be centralized in coalfields. Indeed, it could be claimed that it was the pioneering work carried out at Coalbrookdale and Bersham which created the distinction between rural and industrial areas.

In 1753, the Bersham works came under the management of Isaac Wilkinson, and, from 1763 onwards, of his son, John. In their era, Bersham concentrated not so much on making iron, as on manufacturing objects made of iron, a marked contrast with most of the ironworks of the south. Bersham was famous for its cannons, which were hollowed out by an invention on which John Wilkinson secured a patent in 1774. The same invention was used to hollow out the cylinders made for the engines of Boulton and Watt, work which demanded exact measurements. Indeed, it is claimed that John Wilkinson was the first to realize the importance, in making engines, of wholly correct measurements. As ironworks came to rely increasingly on energy produced by coal, the location of Bersham, a works originally founded in the late seventeenth century to make use of the water-power created by the flow of the Clywedog, became less advantageous. John Wilkinson bought the Brymbo estate; he established a colliery there and founded an ironworks, a venture which gave rise to the largest industrial business in Denbighshire.

John Wilkinson was a quarrelsome man. Disputes arose between him and his brother and partner, William, and both of them hired gangs of thugs to dismember the Bersham works, apparently in order to avoid the costs of dissolving the partnership through law suits. But law suits were held, during John's lifetime

The Minera Leadmines located near the start of the Clywedog Trail

Objects on the site of the former Bersham Colliery

and after his death in 1808. By the 1820s, the works were in ruins. Between 1987 and 1991, the site was excavated; eventually, that enlightened body, the Wrexham Council, renovated the ironworks and established the Bersham Heritage Centre near the A483.

The Clywedog Trail continues to the King's Mills; there, the river powered the mills to which the medieval residents of Wrexham Regis were obliged to bring their grain for grinding. It is worth leaving the trail in order to see Croes-foel Farm, where a plaque commemorates Robert Davies (1675–1748), his father and his two brothers. The Davies family were responsible for the finest artwork to stem from Wales's heavy industry. The speciality of Robert and his relations was iron gates, and splendid examples of their work may be seen at Erddig, Leeswood, Ruthin, Chirk and Wrexham. Some of the iron they used came from Bersham, and it was in their forge at Croes-foel that they created their masterpieces.

After passing Rhostyllen, the walker should turn away from the Clywedog Trail in order to visit one of the wonders of Wales

– Erddig. In 1973, Erddig came into the possession of the National Trust, which immediately set about saving the mansion from collapse. The shafts and tunnels of the Bersham Colliery had caused Erddig to sink a metre and a half. Over a million pounds were spent on re-creating its foundations, and the mansion was opened to the public in 1977.

The central part of Erddig was built in 1683 at a cost of £677 10s. 9d. for Joshua Edisbury, who was impoverished by the venture. In 1718, the house came into the possession of John Mellar, who, c.1724, commissioned the two wings. The result was a long brick building in an unadorned Palladian style. (Tredegar House, which was built more or less in the same period, is a more attractive version of the same mode.) Mellar had a negro servant whose portrait he commissioned, the beginning of a tradition which lasted for generations. Consequently, the portraits of the servants, and the doggerel which sometimes goes with them, are Erddig's most interesting feature.

Following the death of Mellar in 1733, the mansion passed to his nephew, Simon Yorke (1696–1767), the first of seven generations of Yorkes to live at Erddig. Neither Simon, nor his son Philip (1743–1804), followed the fashion of the time of erasing the formal garden surrounding the house, and, as a result, Erddig has one of the finest pre-Romantic gardens in Wales. Its greatest glory are the screens and gates attributed to Robert Davies.

The most interesting of the Yorkes of Erddig was the last, Philip (1905–78). Wrexham has a tavern called Squire Yorke; its sign shows Philip riding a penny-farthing bicycle, his favourite means of transport.

For centuries – probably for more than half a millennium – Wrexham has been the largest town in the north. Indeed, for a period in the seventeenth century, it was the largest town in Wales. The statistics tend to mask Wrexham's importance. The census of 1801, for example, records that Wrexham had 2,575 inhabitants. The figure, however, refers only to the parish of Wrexham Regis, which constituted only a small part of the built-up area of the town. Unlike other urban areas of the north – Caernarfon, for example, or Denbigh – Wrexham lacked borough roots. Until it attained borough status in 1857, it was merely a collection of twelve townships.

As discoveries at Brymbo, Borras and Llay have shown, the region had inhabitants from the Neolithic to the Iron Age. However, it would appear that the Romans made little impression upon the district. By the eighth century AD, the area was part of the kingdom of Mercia – Offa's Dyke lies west of Wrexham – but, by the thirteenth century, it was under the rule of the lords of Powys Fadog. Following the Conquest, Wrexham was one of the small villages of the lordship of Bromfield and Yale, which had its caput at Holt Castle.

Since the fertile land west of the bend in the Dee – an area where there were places with fascinating names such as Cacca Dutton and Dutton-y-brain – lacked a trading centre, Wrexham grew to fill the vacuum. The most obvious evidence of the prosperity of late medieval Wrexham is the scale of the church of St Giles. The nave was built in the fourteenth century and was remodelled in the Perpendicular Gothic style in the late fifteenth century. The church's chief glory is its splendid tower, a more exuberant version of that of St Peter's Monastery, Gloucester (Gloucester Cathedral since 1541). The arms of the Isle of Man are visible in the church, an indication that it received the patronage of Baron Stanley, lord of Man, and his wife Margaret Beaufort, mother of Henry VII, although the tower was completed some time after his death in 1504 and hers in 1509. The tower is the sole building in Wales a replica of which has been built across the Atlantic, the result of the fact that Elihu Yale (1649–1721) lies buried at the foot of the tower. He was the chief benefactor of the university in Connecticut which bears his name. (A photograph of the tower at Yale may be seen on page 624 of *The Encyclopaedia of Wales*.)

The water which seeps through Wrexham's rocks is hard and rich in minerals, and the land around the town is suitable for barley growing, two factors which ensured that it was, by the seventeenth century, Wales's chief centre of beer brewing.

Originally, Wrexham developed as a trading centre and the home of industries based upon the agricultural produce of the district, but, with the growth of industry, its prospects were transformed. By 1901, the town and the industrial areas surrounding it had 70,154 inhabitants; Colwyn Bay and its vicinity, home to about 14,000 people, was its closest northern competitor. Proof of the growth of Wrexham was the number of dignified buildings erected there, among them the Wynnstay Arms (now the Crest Hotel), where, in the eighteenth century, the district's Jacobites drank toasts to the 'king over the water'.

Growth was not without its drawbacks. Ancient streets were demolished when the railway from Ellesmere was driven through the town in the 1880s. Brynffynnon (c.1635), the largest house in the old Wrexham, was demolished c.1914; the Town Hall (1715), the town's most impressive public building, was demolished in 1939. The greatest loss was St Mark's Church (1862), demolished in 1959. The church, with its 60-metre spire (14 metres taller than the tower of St Giles), was an astonishing structure.

As so much of the old distinction has gone, there is a tendency to belittle Wrexham. But its inhabitants have rejoiced in their town. Indeed, it has been the subject of the enthusiasm of more historians than any other town in Wales (D. Leslie Davies,

A. H. Dodd, A. N. Palmer, Stanley Williamson), and, through the efforts of A. Alister Williams, Wrexham is the only Welsh town with its own encyclopaedia (2001). The most appealing of the attempts to record the delights of the area is the work of a local doctor, Harry Drinkwater, who, between 1903 and 1915, made memorable paintings of hundreds of the plants which flourish in Wrexham and its vicinity. Many of the paintings can be seen in Wrexham Museum, one of the best museums in Wales.

North of the museum stands St Mary's Cathedral (1857), the seat of bishops who, from 1898 until 1987, had responsibility for all the Roman Catholics in Wales apart from those living in Monmouthshire and east Glamorgan. The area of their responsibility was the bishopric of Menevia (Mynyw, an ancient name for St Davids), a name restricted in 1987 to the diocese based at Swansea. The cathedral displays one of the bones of Richard Gwyn, who was martyred in 1583 and canonized in 1980. Like Wales's two other Roman Catholic cathedrals, it was designed by E. W. Pugin, son of the artist who decorated the Palace of Westminster.

From the cathedral, it is a mere step to what remains of the brewery of the Wrexham Lager Company, where brewing began in 1883. The brewery closed in 2000, and its remains are a sad memorial to the time when Wrexham had nineteen breweries. (According to George Borrow, who visited Wrexham in 1854, the only Welsh words current in the town were 'cwrw da' [good beer].)

For many, the most interesting place in Wrexham is the ballroom of the Wynnstay Arms. It was there, in 1876, that the Welsh Football Association was founded. For decades, the national team was a venture of the north-east – of Wrexham, in particular. The team played in sixty-six international matches before it included any footballers from the south.

The first stronghold to be established in the vicinity of Chirk was the extensive fort built by the Romans *c.* AD 49 across the Ceiriog at Weston Rhyn – evidence of the resistance they expected from the inhabitants of the north-east, and of their determination to ensure control over the territory where the Deva (Chester) legionary fort would be built in AD 75. Then, for a thousand years, evidence of what was happening in the area is non-existent. It is believed that the earl of Chester, during his incursions into the north-east, commissioned the building of a motte, some small remains of which can be seen near Chirk's St Mary's Church; the remains of another motte are located west of Chirk Bridge. The real story starts after the Conquest, when Edward I granted Chirk and Chirkland to Roger Mortimer (d. 1326).

Of the castles built following the Conquest, Chirk is the only one which is habitable. That does not mean that the castle has survived intact from its earliest days. When the original work was completed *c.*1310, what stood above the Ceiriog Valley was a square castle with round towers at each corner and a half-tower in

the middle of all four walls. It thus had similarities with the inner ward of Beaumaris Castle, but without the great gatehouses. The castle was modified repeatedly over the centuries, and it is only the northern side which now conveys an impression of what was built in the early fourteenth century. Members of the Fitzalan family, lords of Chirkland from 1334 until the last decades of the fifteenth century, were responsible for some additions.

In 1595, Thomas Myddelton (1550–1631) bought the castle which by then was merely the shell of a medieval stronghold. Myddelton, a native of Denbigh, had made a fortune in London, part of which he spent financing the publication in 1630 of *y Beibl Bach* (the 'Little Bible'). His son, also Thomas (1586–1667), was the leader of the Parliamentary forces in the north during the Civil War, and it was probably during that upheaval that the castle's towers lost their upper floors. Consequently, the impression the castle gives today is that of a squat building crouching on its hill. Thomas Myddelton the first ensured that the interior became a luxurious mansion, but much renovation was needed following the destruction of the Civil War. The rooms of the north wing were revamped in the neo-Classical style in the later eighteenth century, and, in the 1840s, the main rooms were decorated under the guidance of A. W. N. Pugin. Indeed, apart from his work at the Palace of Westminster, Pugin's genius is best appreciated at Chirk. Further work was undertaken in the years immediately before the First World War at the request of Baron Howard de Walden, the promoter of drama in Wales and tenant of the castle from 1911 to 1946. The result is a building which contains elements from every era from the thirteenth century to the twentieth – a hotch-potch, perhaps, but a very attractive one.

In the era of Roger Mortimer, the castle was surrounded by a hunting park; it long survived and it was reported in 1675 that it contained five-hundred deer. Early in the eighteenth century, one of the finest formal gardens in Britain was laid out at Chirk.

The vista stretching north of the castle had its climax in the gates which Robert Davies began constructing in 1712, gates which represent the craft of the smith at its most superlative. By the 1760s, however, garden designers sought to emulate 'Nature' rather than to create a contrast with it. As the Myddeltons of Chirk were wealthy enough to keep up with fashion, the castle's splendid formal gardens were short-lived. It was William Eames, among the most renowned of the landscape architects of the Romantic Age, who turned the undeviating walkways into winding paths, and the straight lines of trees into clusters of shrubs enclosing secluded glades. Through his work, the castle was surrounded by one of the finest parks designed in accordance with the ideas of artists such as Claude Lorraine and Poussin of what constituted 'real Nature'. In the 1870s, the yew trees which are the basis of Chirk's wealth of topiary were planted; there was further planting in the twentieth century, with the emphasis on the introduction of plants from all corners of the world. An advantage of the move from formality to informality was the

decision to move Robert Davies's gates from their location north of the castle to a site near a public road, a place where even those reluctant to pay to visit the castle can admire them.

From the gates, it is a short walk to other glories of Chirk. They include the aqueduct and railway across the Ceiriog. The aqueduct (1801) was designed by Thomas Telford; it stands 21.5 metres about the river. The viaduct (1848) was designed by Henry Robinson; it stands 30 metres above the river. The B5070 road offers a splendid vista of the two structures. The vista is of the ten arches carrying the canal standing a little in front of, and slightly lower than, the fifteen arches carrying the railway. The two bridges are cheek by jowl, and present, as Edward Hubbard (*The Buildings of Wales: Clwyd*) put it, 'a spectacle of Roman grandeur'.

The visitor should not leave Chirk without wandering around the village. The parish church should be visited if only to work out the genealogy of the Myddeltons by reading the inscriptions on their numerous tombs. North of the church, there is a reminder that Chirk was once a mining village – Halton High Barracks, a street of back-to-back houses with the upper row offering access to the lower row. They are unique among the working-class houses of Wales, but, as their condition indicates, no organization is taking care of them.

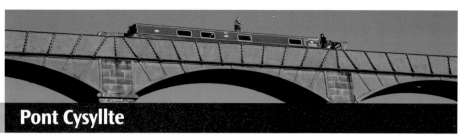
In the main, 2009 was not a year for cheerful news, but one announcement was the cause of much rejoicing. On 27 June, it was announced in Seville that UNESCO was adding the Pont Cysyllte Aqueduct to its list of World Heritage Sites. Consequently, Wales appears thrice on the list – Pont Cysyllte, Edward I's castles in the north-west (1986) and the industrial landscape of Blaenavon (2000). (There is a case for claiming more; the accolade has been given to six sites in Slovakia.) The aqueduct certainly fulfils the chief criterion for the listing of a structure – that it represents 'a masterpiece of mankind's creative genius'.

The best place from which to have the first sighting of the aqueduct is the path that branches off the B5434 at the bottom of the Dee Valley. There, the enormous scale of the structure can be immediately appreciated – the thirty-five pillars elegantly tapering from eight metres in width at the base to five metres at the top, and the nineteen arches of wrought iron each sealed to its neighbour through a combination of cloth, sugar and molten lead. This is truly 'the stream in the sky'. Splendid though the view from the valley bottom is, the great adventure is the journey across the aqueduct by barge. The original intention was to lay down a path and construct railings on both sides of the waterway, but this was done only on the eastern side. Nervous travellers should face that side, where there is at least some barrier between them and the brink.

The story of the aqueduct is part of the complex history of canals in this part of the world. In the era of the 'rage for hydraulics' which stemmed from the duke of Bridgewater's plan launched in 1759 to link Manchester and Liverpool by canal,

the chief development in the northern borderland was the opening of the Chester-Ellesmere Canal in 1779. Plans were then prepared to link the Mersey with the Severn by a canal which would go through the centre of the Denbighshire coalfield. Thousands of pounds were spent on its construction – such a canal was considered essential to the prosperity of Wrexham – but, as the land of the area was largely limestone and sand, water poured into the canal rapidly disappeared. The intention of constructing a waterway across the northern coalfield was abandoned. The hope of connecting the Mersey with the Severn by canal was not fulfilled, but the branch which would have linked that canal with the Ellesmere Canal was constructed.

The 12-kilometre link was completed between 1795 and 1805, and it was as part of the link that Pont Cysyllte was built.

The chief industrial advisor of the Ellesmere Canal Company was William Jessop (1745–1814), but, as he was responsible for a host of ventures, the task of designing the aqueduct increasingly became the responsibility of a younger canal engineer –Thomas Telford (1757–1834). There can be no doubt that its chief glory – its great height – is wholly attributable to Telford. Jessop had intended to place three locks on each side of the aqueduct, an arrangement which would have caused it to be eight metres lower than it is, and one which would have been profligate with water as well as causing long delays on the one side and the other.

In 1794, Telford had ensured that the Shropshire Union Canal crossed the River Tren in an iron trough; he argued that such a design – which could maintain the level and the flow of the canal – would also be suitable for the Dee crossing. He won the argument, and, on 26 November 1805, eight-thousand people came to celebrate the opening of the wonder he had designed. (In November 2005, a similar number came to celebrate the aqueduct's two-hundredth anniversary.)

Work on the aqueduct was proceeding satisfactorily when it was announced that the plan for a canal across the northern coalfield was to be abandoned. Had that decision been made before the construction of the aqueduct had started, it is likely that it would never have been built. It cost £45,000 (at least £5 million in current money), and represented a large investment in a venture which did not lead anywhere. The terminus of the canal was the wharf on the north side of the Dee, a useful place to load

the products of the industrialization that was afoot at Cefnmawr. Tramroads were built to link the wharf with the coalfield, but the venture fell far short of the hopes of the Wrexham industrialists. Yet, perhaps the industrial uses of the canal were greater than is generally assumed; in 1854, for example, George Borrow was informed that the slates of the Berwyn Quarry were shipped from the wharf.

In 1808, the canal was extended from the wharf to Llangollen and on to the Dee near Llantysilio. There, Telford designed a weir – Horseshoe Falls – which permitted water from the river to flow into the canal feeder. Thereafter, the chief function of the Llangollen Canal and Pont Cysyllte was to supply water to the network of canals in the western Midlands of England. By 1939, when commercial use of the canal came to an end, it was considered that it, like most of the canals of the kingdom, was redundant. What saved Pont Cysyllte from demolition was the fact that it was, by then, carrying a large body of water to the cities of northern England – to Liverpool in particular. It is widely believed that, in the second half of the twentieth century, Liverpool's desire to have water from Wales was a defining happening in the nation's political history. Perhaps there should also be awareness that it was Liverpool's desire to have water from Wales that saved the nation's greatest glory.

The year 1763 saw the passage of one of the earliest Acts of Parliament relating to turnpike roads in Wales. It was concerned with connecting Llangollen to the kingdom's network of highroads. Its implementation meant that Llangollen was the first picturesque place in the north to have a convenient link with major centres of population. In 1788, Thomas Pennant warmly recommended the place to visitors, as did almost all the eighty and more authors who wrote travel books on Wales between 1789 and 1815. In 1808, Llangollen was also connected with the canal network, and it became even more accessible when the post road to Holyhead was completed in 1830. By the deaths of Eleanor Butler (1829) and Sarah Ponsonby (1831) – 'The Ladies of Llangollen' – up to thirty stagecoaches a day trundled through the town.

Valle Crucis Abbey

In July 1854, George Borrow arrived at Llangollen – on foot. The first night he was there, he was charmed by a harpist, perhaps one of the harpists (or harpers) who hurt the ears of Felix Mendelssohn on his visit in 1829, when he condemned the 'dreadful out-of-tune rubbish' which was heard in every one of Llangollen's hotels. Borrow spent fifteen weeks in Wales in 1854, ten of them at Llangollen, and the popularity of *Wild Wales* (1862) further underlined the importance of the town to tourism in Wales.

The rulers of Powys had appreciated the merits of the district centuries earlier. In the ninth century, Cyngen (d. 854), king of Powys, caused a cross to be raised in memory of his great-grandfather, Eliseg, 'the king who freed Powys from the grasp of the English through fire and sword', to quote the inscription

which the memorial once bore. The cross has disappeared, and had Edward Lhuyd not copied the inscription on its pillar in 1696, it would now be impossible to have any idea of its content. Following the death of Cyngen, Powys came under the rule of his nephew, Rhodri, king of Gwynedd, but the sovereignty of Powys was restored by Bleddyn ap Cynfyn in the 1070s.

Powys split in the twelfth century, with the Llangollen region becoming the centre of northern Powys, or Powys Fadog. The spiritual heart of Powys Fadog was the monastery of Valle Crucis, the last of the Cistercian monasteries of *Pura Wallia* to come into existence (1201). The Cistercian monastery of Strata Marcella, founded near Welshpool in 1170, was located in southern Powys or Powys Wenwynwyn. As there were Cistercian monasteries in all the other leading Welsh-ruled territories, the lords of Powys Fadog presumably believed that to have a monastery of that order was essential to their status. Valle Crucis was founded by Madog ap Gruffudd (d. 1236), grandson of Madog ap Maredudd (d. 1160), the last of the rulers of united Powys. Its ruins stand near the Eliseg Pillar or Cross – the cross which gave rise to the name Valle Crucis.

Of the eight Cistercian monasteries of *Pura Wallia* (Whitland, Strata Florida, Strata Marcella, Cwm-hir, Llantarnam, Aberconwy, Cymer and Valle Crucis), it is Valle Crucis which has

the most extensive remains. The western façade of the abbey church still stands, as does much of the sanctuary and the south transept, work in an austere form of the Decorated Gothic style. The chapter house is particularly impressive; above it, in what was the monks' *dorter*, sixteen gravestones are exhibited. The memorial to Madog ap Gruffudd (d. 1306), the great-grandson of the founder and the great-grandfather of Owain Glyn Dŵr, is among the best to survive from fourteenth-century Wales. In the fifteenth century, the *dorter* was revamped to include a handsome hall in which the abbot entertained his guests. That, no doubt, was the hall in which the poets Gutun Owain and Guto'r Glyn feasted, licking their lips over the food and wine provided for them by Abbot Siôn and Abbot Dafydd.

The chief stronghold of Powys Fadog was Castell Dinas Bran which stands on a hilltop 230 metres above Llangollen. It is worth walking from Valle Crucis to the summit, if only to gaze at Creigiau Eglwyseg, which are so architectural in form that they look as if they were carved by giants. It is believed that the castle was built for Gruffudd ap Madog (d. 1270), son of the founder of Valle Crucis. It has a keep within its own moat, together with curtain walls enclosing a rectangular ward which has a two-towered gatehouse. The lords of Powys Fadog lost their territories as a result of the Conquest, and the area, which included

The case of a visitor to the Llangollen International Eisteddfod

contains the neo-Gothic grave of 'The Ladies of Llangollen'. The home of the 'Ladies' – Plas Newydd – bears little resemblance to what it was in their day, and little of their innovative garden survives.

Llangollen's present renown is the result of the success of its International Eisteddfod, which has grown so large that it now has its own fringe festival. The only permanent building associated with the eisteddfod is the Royal Pavilion; grafting the word royal on to the pavilion has bemused all who believe in the ideals which inspired those who established the eisteddfod in 1947.

Llangollen, became part of the lordship of Bromfield and Yale. Its lord, John de Warenne, commissioned a new castle at Holt, a more accessible location than Dinas Bran, which fell into ruin. However, enough survives to provide an eye-catching view for those strolling along the banks of the Dee at Llangollen.

The path down the slope from Castell Dinas Bran leads to the bridge over the canal, a starting point for Wales's finest water trip – the crossing of Pont Cysyllte aqueduct. Nearby, is the starting point of one of Wales's finest train journeys – that on the reopened track between Llangollen and Corwen. The bridge across the river – one of the 'seven wonders of Wales' – takes the walker to St Collen's Church, where the wooden roof rivals in splendour those at St Davids and Ruthin. The churchyard

Ruthin is unique. Peter Smith noted that there was a time when the towns of Wales sparkled with black-and-white houses. 'Now', he wrote, 'only Ruthin remains. It should be scrupulously preserved as a national monument, as our last reminder of a departed urban gaiety before it was effaced by the dull reign of stone and stucco.' Among the black-and-white buildings is the Old Court (now the National Westminster Bank). One of the major sources of Welsh medieval history came to light in the building – the court rolls of the lordship of Dyffryn Clwyd. They extend almost unbroken from the 1290s until the 1530s; consequently, more is known of that lordship in the later Middle Ages than is known about virtually any other part of Wales.

The place to begin exploring Ruthin is the *hin* (edge) *rhudd* (red) – the ridge of sandstone which stands above the Clwyd

Valley. It was there, in the 1270s, that a castle was built for Dafydd, brother of Llywelyn ap Gruffudd. The castle was probably the place where Dafydd in 1282 planned his attack upon Hawarden Castle, the attack which sealed the fate of the royal house of Gwynedd. The castle came into the possession of the de Grey family, and was rebuilt, possibly in accordance with plans prepared by Edward I's adviser on military architecture, James of St George. It was attacked during the Glyn Dŵr Revolt, suffered during the Civil War and was partially demolished in 1826 when a mansion was built on the site. Consequently, it is now difficult to discern the shape of the de Grey stronghold, although it is likely that it was a substantial structure with two wards and a large gatehouse.

The 1826 mansion was built for Frederick West, and his wife Maria, who had inherited 2,200 hectares in Denbighshire from her Myddelton ancestors. William Cornwallis-West was the only Liberal Unionist to be elected in Wales in the general election of 1886. In 1900, his son, George, married the widow of Randolph Churchill, thus becoming the stepfather of Winston Churchill, who was a mere fortnight the younger. Ruthin Castle was sold in 1920; it became a private clinic and then a hotel. (Ruthin is the only place in Wales, apart from Manorbier, where a visitor can book a bed within the walls of a medieval castle.)

In the late thirteenth century, Ruthin acquired a church as well as a castle. Originally, St Peter's was a chapel of ease of St Meugan's parish church, Llanrhudd, but it attained the status of a collegiate church served by Augustinian canons. It is essentially a fourteenth-century building, the tower of which was, in the nineteenth century, surmounted by a handsome spire. Its greatest glory is the splendid roof of the north aisle. The church abounds in memorials, including that to Gabriel Goodman (1528–1601), who assisted William Morgan in publishing his translation of the Bible in 1588. Goodman was responsible for the most delightful

feature of Ruthin – the parochial close. He bought the buildings of the dissolved college and adapted them as Christ's Hospital, an almshouse accommodating twelve beadsmen and a clergyman. Adjoining the hospital, he established a grammar school. Little of the original work remains, but the revamping over the centuries

'The Eyes of Ruthin'

has succeeded in retaining much of the original atmosphere. The close is adorned with iron gates (1727), the work of Robert Davies, the most talented smith in the history of Wales.

The gates lead to St Peter's Square, the heart of Ruthin. In it stand the dignified buildings of the Castle Hotel and the more endearing ones of the Myddelton Hotel, with its three rows of dormer windows forming 'the Eyes of Ruthin'. Apart, perhaps,

for Montgomery, Ruthin is the most delightful of all the towns of Wales. The wanderer should stroll along Castle Street, Record Street and Clwyd Street. The former is the location of Ruthin's finest black-and-white building – Nantclwyd House, with its fine timber-framed porch. Reopened to the public in 2007, it contains rooms furnished in the style of seven periods between 1475 and 1942. Record Street commemorates the building erected between 1785 and 1790 to house the documents of the Court of Great Session. In 1889, the record office became the headquarters of Denbighshire County Council. Ruthin had long replaced Denbigh as the county town, partly because it was nearer the most densely populated part of the county – the area around Wrexham. (The offices opened in 2005 as the headquarters of the restored county are less appealing.)

The chief attraction in Clwyd Street is the old gaol, opened in 1775 to serve the counties of the north-east. After it ceased to be a prison (1916), it became a library and then an archive repository. In 2002, the central part of the building became a museum of incarceration. Visiting it is a fascinating, if rather chilling, experience; indeed, in 2006, those taking part in a night–

the Art Fund's £100,000 prize. The centre was opened in a small building in the late 1970s. The splendid structure, designed by Jonathan Sergison and Stephen Bates, was opened in 2008. Its undulating roofs reflect the profile of the Clwydian Range and within the building are three galleries and six artists' studios. The multifariousness of the exhibitions held in so small a place as Ruthin (5,218 inhabitants) is truly astonishing.

The Ruthin Craft Centre

time visit claimed to have had a number of paranormal experiences. Everything is there – the six cells for women (more than twelve times that number for men), the quilted cell, the treadmill, the chapel and the place where the murderer, William Hughes, was hanged in 1903. Visitors can follow the stories of individual prisoners, stories that are often painfully poignant.

In the future, perhaps the chief attraction of Ruthin will be its Craft Centre, which, in 2009, was on a short-list for the award of

Penllyn is puzzling. The *cantref* has never had more than 6,000 or 7,000 inhabitants, hardly more than 0.3 per cent of the population of Wales. Yet, of the first six wardens of the Guild of Graduates of the University of Wales, three had been brought up in Penllyn. Wales has about thirty-five full-scale open-air statues of Welsh heroes (two in Caernarfon, one in Tregaron, one in Llangeitho, and so on; incidentally, do we have any such statues of heroines?). Five of them are in Penllyn – Thomas Charles,

The statue of Thomas Charles at Bala

Lewis Edwards, Thomas Edward Ellis, O. M. Edwards and Ifan ab Owen Edwards. Why is a district that is home to only 0.3 per cent of the inhabitants of Wales the location of almost 15 per cent of the statues of its heroes?

When seeking the opinions of the inhabitants of Penllyn, the usual answer is that the *cantref* is the heart of Wales, and the cradle of all that is best and most vigorous in Welsh cultural tradition – the area where Bibles were first distributed, where Welsh Calvinistic Methodism was at its most intellectually challenging, the birthplace of the father of Welsh nationalism (Michael D. Jones), the home of those prepared to suffer for their Liberal beliefs, and so on. All that may well be true, but perhaps there is a simpler explanation for the remarkable contribution of the inhabitants of Penllyn. In 1713, a native of Edeirnion, Edmund Meyrick, died, leaving in his will sufficient funds to found the Tŷ Tan Domen grammar school in Bala. The place offered a vigorous education – 'from 9.30 to 12.30 Latin, and from 1.30 to 3.30 Mathematics. Afterwards, from 7.30 to 9.30, Prep', wrote R. T. Jenkins, the school's most brilliant ex-pupil. Ysgol Tŷ Tan Domen, it could be argued, was the key to Penllyn's disproportionate contribution to the history of Wales.

The *tomen* (the motte), which gave the school its name, was a nine-metre high hillock, the highest motte in Wales apart from that at Cardiff Castle. It may have been constructed by the Normans, but it became the chief stronghold of the lord of Penllyn. In 1202, it was seized by the forces of Llywelyn ap Iorwerth, thus causing Penllyn, which had traditionally been linked with Powys, to draw closer to Gwynedd. In about 1310, Roger Mortimer (d. 1326), the chief justice of the Principality of Wales, founded the borough of Bala, the last borough to be established in medieval Wales. The view from the summit of the motte provides a clear impression of the layout of the borough. The school building at the foot of the motte (*tan domen*) became

the offices of Gwasg y Sir and the newspaper, *Y Cyfnod*; now, Neuadd y Cyfnod is a restaurant.

Bala is a pleasant town in which to stroll, although it contains no outstanding buildings. Perhaps the most interesting is the White Lion Hotel (1759 and later) where George Borrow had a memorable breakfast in 1854: 'pot of hare; ditto of trout; pot of prepared shrimps; dish of plain shrimps; tin of sardines; beautiful beef-steak; eggs, muffin; large loaf, and butter, not forgetting capital tea'. (In the 1990s, the George Borrow Society held a weekend course in the hotel to celebrate the breakfast.)

In the mid-eighteenth century, Bala was mainly known as the home of stocking-knitters, an industry which produced a profit of £200 a week. George III, who considered that Bala stockings were the only ones that relieved the pains of his rheumatism, was a regular customer. It was also a cultural centre, and the eisteddfod held there in 1789 is considered a crucial turning-point in the history of the festival. But, by then, a Carmarthenshire man, Thomas Charles, had settled in Bala, and the town rapidly became a stronghold of Calvinism; with its lakeside location, it was talked of, somewhat fancifully, as the Geneva of Wales. On becoming a Methodist stronghold, it ceased to be a centre for *eisteddfodau*; no National Eisteddfod would be held there until 1967.

Websites relating to Penllyn show that the main attraction of the *cantref* is Tryweryn – not Tryweryn the drowned valley (Llyn Celyn), nor Tryweryn of the imprisoned Irish rebels (the Sinn Féin University), nor even Tryweryn of the distillery (the Welsh whisky of F. J. Lloyd Price of Rhiwlas), but Tryweryn of white-water rafting. For many, the best known place in Penllyn is the National White Water Centre, located about half a kilometre south of the Llyn Celyn dam. Opened in 1986, its main feature is the rush of water released from the lake into the Tryweryn, a flow which allows thrilling water rafting to be experienced there when other rivers have little water in them.

But to Welsh patriots, Llyn Celyn itself is the most significant place in Penllyn. Liverpool's ability to obtain an Act of Parliament in 1957 authorizing the corporation to take possession of the valley and to insist that its inhabitants abandon their dwellings – although not a single Welsh MP had voted for the act – was considered to be proof that the Welsh national community, under the arrangements then pertaining, was totally powerless. The fact that increasing numbers of the inhabitants of Wales came to realize the implications of those arrangements created a new context for Welsh politics. The Liverpool Corporation, which has apologized for the drowning, ensured that a memorial chapel was built on the lakeside and that graves from the flooded cemetery were placed alongside it. Visiting the chapel is a moving experience, but the dignified memorial designed by John Meirion Morris has yet to be built. A small version of it is on display at the United Nations in New York; it portrays a mythical bird rising out of the water – perhaps singing protest songs.

According to *The Encyclopaedia of Wales*, 'the people of Blaenau Ffestiniog constitute the most remarkable society in Wales', consisting as it does of 'individuals, all of whom are bonkers, but none of whom are boring'. Blaenau Ffestiniog was the largest place to come into existence as a result of the growth of the slate industry. In 1901, the urban district of Ffestiniog had 11,435 inhabitants, compared with 5,848 in Llanddeiniolen, 5,223 in Llanllyfni and 5,218 in Bethesda, the three other slate-producing centres with populations of more than 5,000. A century later, when Ffestiniog had declined to 4,830, Llanddeiniolen to 4,885, and Llanllyfni to 3,919, Bethesda topped the list with 4,515 inhabitants. Despite the contraction of all four places, they are still essentially industrial centres. That, at least, is the belief of the Snowdonia National Park authorities judging by the care taken to ensure that none of them are within the park's boundaries; in 2010, however, the Ffestiniog community council asked for the town to be part of the park.

The best way to go to Blaenau Ffestiniog is by train, either from Porthmadog via the Ffestiniog Railway or from the Conwy Valley via the old LNWR line. The Ffestiniog Railway opened in 1836, closed in 1946, and partially reopened in 1955; it was completed in its present form in 1983, and the journey on one of its steam trains is the most romantic way of reaching Blaenau Ffestiniog. There are merits also to the journey from the Conwy Valley, particularly the view the train offers of Dolwyddelan Castle, the most splendidly sited of all the castles of the north. It is a pity that Blaenau Ffestiniog can no longer be reached by the old GWR line from Bala; the central part of that line disappeared under the waters of Llyn Celyn before Richard Beeching had a chance to recommend its closure.

Located under the shadow of mountains, rich in chapels (as many as twenty-six at one time) and in terraced houses, and blessed with abundant rain (3,000 mm a year compared with 640 mm at Rhyl), Blaenau Ffestiniog seems like a piece of the southern coalfield transplanted in the hills of Merioneth. But, as most of the coal tips of the south have been cleared, more industrial scars are visible in Blaenau than in any other town in Wales. The place offers the best opportunity in Wales to visit

abandoned workings. The slates of the old county of Caernarfon were quarried on the surface, either in galleries or in vast open-air chasms. Those of Merioneth were mined in enormous underground chambers, some of them large enough to contain St Paul's Cathedral. A visit to Llechwedd with its sixteen caverns and its forty kilometres of tunnels is even more memorable than a visit to Big Pit at Blaenavon. It is claimed that the weddings held at Llechwedd are the deepest in the world.

In 1884, at the height of its prosperity, Llechwedd produced 24,000 tons of slates, less than half the amount produced by the slate mines of the Oakeley Company. That company, founded in 1882, came into existence as the result of the marriage of William Oakeley with Margaret, the daughter and heiress of Robert Griffith of Tanybwlch (d. 1750). Unlike the other entrepreneurs involved in slate production at Blaenau, the Oakeley family were local landowners with Welsh roots; in the time of William Edward Oakeley (d. 1912), Tanybwlch was the centre of an estate of three thousand hectares. The most productive part of the Oakeley empire was Gloddfa Ganol, which, with its twenty-six levels of caverns and its 80 kilometres of tunnels, was the largest underground quarry in the world. At its apogee in the 1890s, the Oakeley Company produced sixty 60,000 tons of slates a year. Gloddfa Ganol was closed in 1971; it reopened, partly as a tourist attraction, in 1978. It came into the ownership of the McAlpine Company in 1997, when the tourist element was abandoned; by now, it is owned by Welsh Slate, part of the Irish company, Rigcycle, but production ceased in 2010. The property of the Oakeley Company included the Cwm Orthin Quarry, located at a remote site about two kilometres north-east of Moelwyn Mawr. Visiting the remains of Cwm Orthin is a particularly poignant experience.

Of all the slate mines of Blaenau Ffestiniog, it is Manod that has the most interesting story. Located east of the town, Manod was the most accessible of the mines of the region. On 12 August 1941, a lorry-load of paintings arrived there, paintings from the National Gallery in London that had previously been stored at Penrhyn Castle or at Neuadd Prichard-Jones in Bangor. It was the fear that those buildings might be bombed from the air that led to the decision to place the paintings in underground chambers.

The chief problem facing the removers was the fact that the road to the mine ran beneath a bridge carrying the Bala to Ffestiniog railway, a bridge that offered clearance of only 3.38 metres. It was therefore impossible to transport to Manod the Gallery's large paintings, in particular the largest of them all – Van Dyck's portrait of Charles I. The level of the road had to be lowered by 75cm; evidence of the digging is still apparent. The Van Dyck portrait passed under the bridge with a centimetre to spare. Inside the mine, rooms with a constant temperature were constructed, and it was claimed that the paintings stored in them suffered less cracking and blistering than they would have suffered had they remained in the gallery. Eventually, virtually all the National Gallery's paintings came to Manod, and the last did not leave the mine until the end of 1945. Until the late 1980s, Manod was maintained as a place to store treasures in time of war. However, as she believed that only politicians should be saved in a time of nuclear attack, Mrs Thatcher insisted that the maintenance should cease.

The main road from Maentwrog to Harlech (the A496) goes through the village of Ynys. It is worth leaving the highway and following the lane to Llechollwyn, where there is a splendid view of the estuary of the River Dwyryd. The combination of the golden sands of Traeth Bach and the azure waters of the estuary is delightful, but the most intriguing feature is the trickle of white on the slope immediately across the river. The trickle is Portmeirion, Wales's most remarkable village.

Portmeirion was built on a promontory that was part of the estate created by David Williams (1800–69), Merioneth's first Liberal MP (1868–9), whose candidature in the general election of 1859 gave Conservative landlords the opportunity to evict their disobedient tenants. David Williams commissioned the construction of Castell Deudraeth, a bulky building erected in the 1840s on the site of a castle mentioned by Giraldus Cambrensis. His son, Osmond Williams, was also MP for Merioneth (from 1900 to 1910). Osmond's wife's sister's son was Clough Williams-Ellis (1883–1978), heir to the Brondanw estate near Llanfrothen.

In 1931, Clough bought Castell Deudraeth from his uncle, adding it to the land he had bought in 1925 at Aber Iâ on the estuary. Clough's description of his upbringing at Llanfrothen is fascinating – he himself monoglot English, and all the other children in the village monoglot Welsh. (The wheel turns; Clough's grandson, Robin Llywelyn, is the most imaginative of present-day Welsh-language novelists.)

By 1925, Clough had already displayed his architectural and horticultural skills at Plas Brondanw, a place worth visiting if only to admire the topiary work which frames the view of Cnicht, a handsome pyramidal peak. However, Portmeirion, as Clough renamed Aber Iâ, offered great possibilities. He believed that sensitively designed architecture could add beauty to the most beautiful of places, although it is difficult to believe that any planning authority today would permit an architect to create a fantasy, including buildings no one else wanted, in a place as unspoilt as Aber Iâ.

Clough's intention was to foster environmentally-friendly

architecture, and he was responsible for one of the few examples in Wales of a tourist development which enhances rather than disfigures the landscape. And in essence, Portmeirion is a tourist development, which, by now, offers accommodation to over two-hundred people. Clough was not wealthy; to finance his vision, he needed the income from his hotel at Aber Iâ, in addition to his earnings as an architect. Financial issues, as well as the pause in building during the Second World War, explain why the work of completing Portmeirion (assuming that it has been completed) lasted from 1925 to 1975.

Clough wanted to introduce something of the panache of Italy to Merioneth. It is said that his inspiration was Portofino on the Riviera di Levante; if so, the imitation is better than the original, for, compared with Portmeirion, Portofino is disappointing. Portofino grew organically, and that is also the impression given by Portmeirion. Yet, as can be seen from the careful models Clough designed in the 1920s, the essential plan was in his mind from the beginning. He sought a petite and compact village, although he used several stratagems – paint, acclivity, arches and window size – to suggest that Portmeirion is bigger than it is.

Among its most delightful features are the Campanile, the Hercules Hall, the Gothick Pavilion, the Belvedere and the Colonnade. The latter was brought from Bristol in accordance with Clough's intention of making Portmeirion a refuge for homeless buildings. Among the structures brought from elsewhere in Wales are the porch from Nercwys Hall and the panelled room from Emral Hall (both in Flintshire). The last building constructed in the village was the Toll House, completed when Clough had reached his ninety-second year. Among Portmeirion's attractions are quirky little things – memorials to particularly warm summers, for example, and the extensive use of piscatorial motifs.

The year 2008 was the fortieth anniversary of the event which did more than anything to bring Portmeirion to public notice – the broadcast of the television series *The Prisoner*, which was filmed in the village. Its cult followers hold conferences at Portmeirion, and perhaps it is possible to find some of the Kafkaesque features of the series in the works of Robin Llywelyn, who was, in his childhood, a witness to the filming.

For those who have exhausted the charms of Portmeirion –

The Dogs' Cemetery at Portmeirion

if they can be exhausted – the beach and the paths of the Gwyllt are at hand. The Gwyllt is a ten-hectare woodland which stretches north of the village, an area rich in shrubs which thrive in the mild microclimate of Portmeirion. The miserly can reach the Gwyllt via a path from the A487, thus avoiding paying the entrance fee. The honest pay. On returning to the main road, it is worth glancing at the building which once housed the Minffordd post office, the office used by Bertrand Russell – who was then living at Plas Penrhyn on the fringes of Portmeirion – when sending telegrams during the Cuban Crisis in 1963 to Khrushchev and Kennedy begging them not to destroy the world.

Of the chief castles of the north-west, Conwy seems to float, Caernarfon is a statement of power, Beaumaris squats comfortably and Harlech glowers menacingly. Harlech glowers partly because of its location on a promontory sixty metres above the sea, and partly because of the vast size of the gatehouse, which defends the only side of the castle accessible over level ground. It is worth walking down the steep hill to the vicinity of Ysgol Ardudwy in order to see the castle frowning down upon the salt-marsh. The view from the south is even more dramatic because, from there, the castle rears up with all the splendour of Snowdonia as its background.

The four chief castles of the north-west were all located on sites that had special significance for the Welsh, a fact of which Edward I, with his deep-seated belief in historical propaganda, was undoubtedly aware. In the *Mabinogion*, the story 'Branwen Ferch Llŷr' begins with Bendigeidfran fab Llŷr sitting on the rock of Harlech – probably the exact location of the castle – and when wooden buildings were erected in the inner ward, the *llys* at Ystumgwern, the administrative centre of Ardudwy, was dismantled to provide the timber.

Like Beaumaris, Harlech is a concentric castle. That is, the inner ward is located wholly within the outer ward. However, the curtain walls of the outer ward are a mere shadow of what they once were, and are almost wholly towerless; thus, unlike Beaumaris, where the outer curtain walls with their sixteen towers are still largely complete, Harlech does not give the impression of concentric perfection. Although the defences of the outer ward are now minimal, those of the inner ward are hugely impressive. The chief fascination of Harlech is the multiplicity of the defences obstructing attackers seeking entrance through the gatehouse – three portcullises and three massive doors, and, above the passage, holes through which projectiles could be hurled.

Most of what is now visible was built between 1283 and 1289;

the work was at its most intense in 1286, when over nine-hundred workers were employed on the site. A wall was built to protect the path to the Water Gate, an essential element in ensuring the security of the castle. As the sea has retreated almost a kilometre from the foot of the rock on which the castle stands, it is now difficult fully to appreciate the ingenuity of the seaward defences.

As Harlech Castle is so remote, it may seem odd that its history was more eventful than that of any of the other chief castles of the north-west. It was besieged during the revolt of

Madog ap Llywelyn (1294–5), when grain ships from Ireland proved the usefulness of the Water Gate. It was besieged again during the Glyn Dŵr Rising, when the ability of a garrison of five English soldiers to resist the besiegers for months provided proof of the effectiveness of its defences. Owain Glyn Dŵr captured the castle in the spring of 1404, and from then until it was recaptured by the forces of the English king early in 1409, it was the headquarters of Owain's principality. Indeed, the castle is the only extant structure in Wales which was home to a ruler who claimed the allegiance of the entire population of Wales.

In the course of the following quarter of a millennium, Harlech was the last stronghold of a lost cause, not on one but on two occasions. During the Wars of the Roses, the Yorkists seized power in the territories of the English crown in 1461, but, under Dafydd ab Ifan ab Einion, the castle held out for the Lancastrians until 1468. (It is claimed that it was his defiance which inspired the words of 'Men of Harlech'.) In the first of the Civil Wars of the seventeenth century, Parliamentary forces were victorious by May 1646, but Harlech remained a Royalist stronghold until March 1647.

As was the case with the rest of Edward I's Welsh castles, Harlech Castle was adjoined by a borough. It became the county town of Merioneth, but as Ardudwy lacked the resources to maintain a successful town, the borough dwindled. In 1536, when borough constituencies were established in all the other Welsh counties, Merioneth received no such representation.

Harlech languished until 1867, when it was linked to the railway network. The glories of Ardudwy were discovered, and the area was opened up to tourism. St David's Golf Club was established in 1894, and in 1910 Harlech acquired one of Wales's finest houses built in the Arts and Crafts style – Wern-fawr, built for George Davidson, an interesting combination of a millionaire and an anarchist. In 1927, the house became the core of Coleg Harlech – traditionally known as 'the college of the second chance', although it is doubtful whether the 350 students who attended the college between 1927 and 1939 had ever had a first chance. It was the existence of Coleg Harlech which led to the establishment of Theatr Ardudwy (1972), a development which means that the inhabitants of Harlech (there are 1,406 of them)

have more opportunities for theatrical experiences than are available to far more populous communities.

Visitors should not leave Harlech without seeing the outcome of a venture undertaken in the 1990s – the renovation of Lasynys-fawr, the modest mansion built c.1660 which was home to Ellis Wynne (1671–1734), author of *Gweledigaetheu y Bardd Cwsc* (The Visions of the Sleeping Bard). The book is one of the classics of Welsh prose and is proof that among the Welsh gentry – at least among those of the county of Merioneth – there were writers who had a superb command of the Welsh language at least a century and a half after the passage of the Act of 'Union'. The splendid renovation work is an excellent example of a local group successfully giving substance to their pride in their community.

Lasynys-fawr

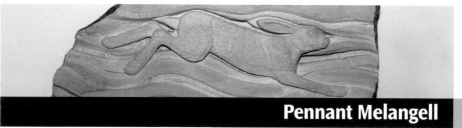

It is necessary to go to one of Wales's remotest places in order to see the country's finest example of Romanesque art. The road that leads to it (the B4391) branches off from the A490 shortly after that road has passed through Llanfyllin and Llangynog – two places that should be visited on the return journey. From Llangynog, a narrow road winds up Cwm Pennant, and it is in that valley, at the point where the road ends at the foot of the Berwyn mountains, that a church comes into view – a substantial church bearing in mind the scantiness of the local population.

The church commemorates one of the most delightful of the stories associated with the early saints. Melangell was a refugee from Ireland who found refuge in Cwm Pennant. There, where she and the animals of the district lived in fearless concord, Eden seemed to have been recreated around her. When Brochwel, prince of Powys, came to hunt in the valley, a hare found shelter beneath her skirts, and the hunting dogs refused to go near the holy virgin. Brochwel, impressed by Melangell's sanctity, gave her land on which to found a nunnery. The story was fully recorded

in the seventeenth century, but it was known centuries earlier, as can be seen from the fourteenth-century statue of Melangell and the hare in the nave of the church, and from the carvings on the fifteenth-century screen.

The history of the church is complex, as is the history of its chief treasure – St Melangell's shrine. The shrine was built *c*.1160, but it was demolished during the Protestant Reformation and its stones were scattered. The stones were brought together again in the nineteenth century, and following further work in 1958 and between 1988 and 1992, the shrine now presents a credible impression of what was constructed in the late twelfth century. It stands on four columns and two half columns, the capitals of which are carved in a refined form of Celtic/Romanesque. Seeing it in so remote a place is a thrilling experience. Nothing similar to it has been found anywhere else in Europe. Only 2 per cent of Wales's listed structures are on the Grade One list; they include the chief castles of the north-west, the Pont Cysyllte Viaduct, Newport's Transporter Bridge and St Melangell's Shrine.

The church is open daily, but no longer has a regular congregation. Indeed, it probably never had one of any size, and, in the Middle Ages, it was more a place of pilgrimage than a parish church. That is certainly what it is today, with members of the Orthodox Church showing particular fondness for it. It finds favour among supporters of the Green Movement also, for Melangell, patron saint of hares, can be seen as a symbol of the need to protect the world of nature. Near the church stands a cottage in which mental, emotional and spiritual support is available. The centre is open on Tuesday, Wednesday and Thursday of each week, and the fellowship provided there adds greatly to the experience of visiting Pennant Melangell.

On returning to Llangynog, it is worth looking at one of the most extensive industrial landscapes in mid Wales. Lead ore was mined in the area in prehistoric and in Roman times, but it was in the first half of the eighteenth century that the industry reached its apogee. In the 1730s, Llangynog was one of the chief lead-mining centres in Europe, and the most important landlord in the area, William Herbert (d. 1747) of Powis Castle, reputedly received a profit of £121,000 from his mines. Lead-mining had declined markedly by the nineteenth century, when much of the evidence

for it was buried under the waste from slate quarrying, an industry which began in the area in the eighteenth century. It was the hope of sustaining the quarries and reviving lead-mining which inspired the promoters of the light railway which was opened in 1904 between Llangynog and the line linking Oswestry with Welshpool. The hopes of the promoters were not fulfilled, but the railway, which ran through the delectable Tanat valley, carried passengers until 1951.

From Llangynog, the B4391 takes the traveller over the Berwyn mountains to Bala. It is worth following that road for a few kilometres in order to stop and look back at that wonder, Craig Rhiwarth. In the Bronze Age, the rock was crowned with a cairn which, in the Iron Age, was surrounded by the walls of a hillfort. Discovered within the walls were the foundations of at least fifty houses, thus making Craig Rhiwallt one of the most interesting hillforts in Wales.

Indeed, there is hardly anywhere in the country more interesting than this area – a hillfort which rivals Tre'r Ceiri; a *llan* which rivals Llantwit Major; Romanesque art which surpasses anything in Chepstow or Ewenni; industrial remains which can be compared with those on Parys Mountain; a spiritual centre equal to that at The Pales, and an old railway line which, if re-opened, would offer journeys as enjoyable as those on any of Wales's restored tracks.

A further treat awaits – Llanfyllin, one of the most attractive of Wales's country towns. There, permission should be sought to view one of the rooms in the Council House in the High Street. The room contains thirteen large murals painted *c.*1812 by Captain Augerau, a French prisoner-of-war in Llanfyllin, who married the local vicar's daughter. As the murals are in the neo-classical tradition, they are an interesting contrast with that other example of Wales's prisoner-of-war art – the neo-baroque church created by Italians at Henllan in the Teifi Valley during the Second World War.

The shrine of Melangell at St Melangell Church, Pennant Melangell

It comes as a surprise to discover that, in 1801, Welshpool was the sixth largest town in Wales. In that year, it had 2,872 inhabitants, compared with 1,870 in Cardiff. (It had 6,269 inhabitants in 2001, when 305,353 people dwelt in Cardiff.) The surprise arises from the tendency to forget that, before the coming of the railways, transport on water was of central importance. Of British rivers, the one navigable for the greatest distance was the Severn, and the highest point water craft on that river could reach was Pool Quay, three kilometres from Welshpool. Thus, it was from Pool Quay that much of the produce of mid Wales was transported, and it was from Pool Quay that a large part of the needs of the inhabitants of mid Wales was supplied.

Trade on the river was declining by 1801, largely because the Montgomeryshire Canal reached Welshpool in 1796. The coming of the canal further encouraged the growth of the town, which, in 1821, was still larger than Cardiff. A decade later, Welshpool had yielded the status of being the largest town in Montgomery-shire to Newtown, which was linked to the canal in 1819.

Many of the buildings in central Welshpool date from the town's most flourishing period – the eighteenth and early nineteenth centuries. The extensive use of brick, an unusual building material in Wales in that period, can be ascribed to water transport. On a hill east of the town centre stands St Cynfelyn, a church which poses interesting questions about ecclesiastic building in sixteenth-century Wales. In the early decades of that century, many churches were rebuilt or enlarged, an activity which virtually came to an end following the Reformation. As it is believed that the nave and the chancel roof of St Cynfelyn were erected in the later sixteenth century, they perhaps represent the earliest example in Wales of work on a Protestant church.

South of the town stands Smithfield, the largest animal market in Wales and one of the largest sheep markets in Europe.

During the weekly Monday marts, the bleating of the sheep and the shouts of the auctioneers make for a remarkably lively scene. The walk to Smithfield skirts the most attractive feature of Welshpool – the canal basin. On a warm summer's day, the place is crowded with barges, for unlike the canals of the south, the Montgomeryshire Canal is linked to the kingdom's general canal network. When the five kilometres north of Llanymynech are reopened, the basin will be accessible from much of southern Britain. On its bank stands the Powysland Museum, Wales's oldest county museum; indeed, apart from Caerleon Museum (1859), it is the oldest museum in Wales. Founded in 1874, it was a venture of the Powysland Club (1867), which also founded the longest-lived of Wales's local history journals, *The Montgomeryshire Collections* (1869–). Among the museum's exhibits are some of the tiles which adorned the floor of Strata Marcella Abbey,

the Cistercian monastery which stood four kilometres north-east of Welshpool. The abbey church was an extensive building, with a length of 83 metres compared with the 72 metres at Tintern, but the tiles are virtually all that remain of that noble structure.

The most memorable site in the vicinity is Powis Castle, which came into existence as a square keep similar to that at Dolwyddelan. The keep was probably built for Gwenwynwyn ab Owain Cyfeiliog (d. 1216), but it was his grandson, Owain ap Gruffudd (d. 1309), who commissioned most of the medieval features that are visible today. During Owain ap Gruffudd's lifetime, what had been a dynasty of native Welsh rulers became a dynasty of Marcher Lords, a change symbolized by his adoption of the name Owen de la Pole. Owen's daughter, Hawis Gadarn (d. 1353), married John Charlton, and the castle was held by the Charlton family until 1421, when it passed by marriage to the Grey family. Edward Grey sold the castle to Edward Herbert in 1587; by the 1870s, the Herbert family, owners of 13,575 hectares of Montgomeryshire, were the largest landowners in the county.

It was Edward Herbert and his immediate descendants who were responsible for the chief glories of the castle. They include the Long Gallery (1590s), with its imaginative plaster work, and the Grand Staircase (*c*.1669) which rises majestically beneath vast murals illustrating the myths of the classical age. South of the castle lies the finest historical garden in Wales, and one of the best in Britain. In the 1670s, four terraces each 200 metres long were created on the slopes beneath the castle, work commissioned by William Herbert (d. 1696), the first earl of Powis, and the most prominent of the kingdom's Roman Catholic peers. Although planned by landscape gardeners from the Netherlands, the terraces

were inspired by the Renaissance gardens of Italy. From 1689 until his death, the earl was an exile in France, along with James II, who raised him to the marquessate and then to the dukedom of Powis. Work on the garden was resumed in the early eighteenth century, when it was embellished with lead statues and when fine wrought-iron gates were erected across the opening to the steps which lead to the terraces. The garden was neglected in the later eighteenth century, a period when its yew trees grew prodigiously. During renovation in the nineteenth century, the yew trees were only lightly cut back and they are now among the most enormous examples of topiary in Europe.

The sixth earl of Powis resides in the castle, although the building and the garden has been the property of the National Trust since 1952. The earl used to provide accommodation to Prince Charles when the prince was visiting Wales. However, as the earl is a devout Anglican (the family has long abandoned Roman Catholicism), he came to the conclusion that it was unseemly to welcome Charles to his home when the prince was accompanied by his mistress. By now, the prince has to be satisfied with his house near Llandovery – Llwynywermod, or Wormwood Scrubs.

In order to discover what Wales would look like if its development had frozen *c.*1790, Montgomery is the place to visit. The heart of the little town (1,256 inhabitants) is rich in buildings replete with fine detail – cornerstones, cornices, gables, door frames, windows, keystones – all of them clustering around the Town Hall (1748). The charm of the place is the result of its arrested development. In 1536, it was important enough to give its name to the new county of Montgomery, and it enjoyed considerable prosperity as the trading centre for the produce of the fertile soil of the borderlands. However, with the growth of travel on the River Severn, it was overtaken by Welshpool; later, the canal and then the railway came to Welshpool and Newtown, leaving Montgomery to doze in its remote green corner.

The size of St Nicholas's Church is evidence of the importance of medieval Montgomery. The glory of the church is the tomb of Richard Herbert (d. 1596), a man who had won a foothold in Montgomeryshire because of his kinship with the Herberts, earls of Pembroke, and the Somersets, earls of Worcester. Surmounting the tomb are the effigies of Richard and his wife Magdalen (although her body lies in London alongside her second husband John Danvers). Along its side are the effigies of their eight children, the poet, George Herbert, and the philosopher, Edward Herbert, among them.

The construction of the Herbert tomb belongs to a fairly recent era in the history of Montgomery. Conveniently located for the invasion of mid Wales, it has been a place of strategic importance for thousands of years. Evidence of Neolithic settlement has been found on Ffridd Faldwyn, where it is also possible to trace the double ramparts of an Iron Age hillfort. Its summit offers a splendid vista. To the north is the confluence of the Severn and the Camlad, the location of the Roman fort which safeguarded the road from Wroxeter to Wales. To the east is Offa's Dyke at its most formidable; the three-kilometre stretch near Montgomery is almost the only place where the present Wales/England border exactly follows the line of the dyke.

The view to the north-west is the most interesting, for it includes Rhydwhyman Ford (Rhyd Chwima is the correct spelling) across the Severn where substance was given to the concept of a Welsh polity. It was crossed by Roger, earl of Shrewsbury, in 1093, when he and his knights swept through Powys and Ceredigion down to the *cantref* of Penfro. Roger was a native of Sainte Foy-de-Montgomery in Normandy, and he named the motte built near the ford after his birthplace. The site is now known as Hen Domen, and recent work there has shown that it was a place of considerable significance. The Montgomery family rose in revolt in 1102, and the motte passed into the possession of Baldwyn de Bollers. It was the Cymricization of the name Baldwyn which gave rise to the Welsh Trefaldwyn.

It became accepted that Rhydwhyman was the place at which to discuss any disputes between the native Welsh rulers and the Marcher Lords, and between those rulers and the king of England. Meetings between Llywelyn ap Gruffudd and powerful barons such as Bohun, Mortimer and Audley were held there in December 1258, August 1259, August 1260 and July 1262. The most famous of the ford-side meetings was that in September 1267, when Llywelyn made homage to Henry III and when the document which recognized Llywelyn as prince of Wales was

sealed. Implicit in the status of prince was the territory, the principality, and the existence of the principality proved that thirteenth-century Wales had the potential to become a viable polity. For those who wish to celebrate the high point (so far) of Welsh independence, Rhydwhyman is the place to go.

Despite its border location, Rhydwhyman was wholly under the authority of the king of England. Although there was a garrison at Hen Domen, that stronghold came to have a secondary role compared with the castle, work on which began in 1223 on a hill south-east of the ford. By the mid thirteenth century, Montgomery Castle was the chief basis for the power of

the English king on the border between England and the lands of the native Welsh rulers. Llywelyn sought to challenge Montgomery by commissioning a castle at Dolforwyn, six kilometres to the west of the royal stronghold, a decision which added to the tension between the prince and the king of England. Henry III died in 1272, and was succeeded by Edward I. The prince's refusal to come to Rhydwhyman in January 1273 to do homage to the new sovereign further inflamed that tension – tension which led in 1277 to the undermining of what had been won by Llywelyn in 1267. Montgomery was therefore central to the apotheosis and downfall of the Welsh principality.

The way in which its designers made use of a difficult site makes Montgomery one of the most ingenious castles in Wales. It is believed that its plan was based upon that of Chateau Gaillard on the southern border of Normandy, which had been commissioned by Richard I in 1196. In the second half of the sixteenth century, the ruins of the castle came into the possession of Edward Herbert, father of the Richard Herbert whose tomb is in St Nicholas's Church. Edward's grandson – another Edward (1583–1648) – the first Baron Herbert of Cherbury, had an elaborate mansion built within the middle ward. He yielded the castle and the mansion to Parliamentary forces in 1644 on condition that his library would be unharmed. However, a few months after his death, the mansion was ransacked and the defences of the castle partly demolished. The entire complex disappeared under soil and brambles until the 1960s, when the site was cleared and the skill of its designers fully appreciated. The story is told in the delightful museum established in the old Bell Tavern.

Many people dwell above their workplace, but it is unusual for people to live beneath their workplace. That, however, was how it was for many of the nineteenth-century inhabitants of Newtown. With the woollen industry developing so rapidly, it was necessary to make the most efficient use of the limited land near the Montgomeryshire Canal, the waterway which reached Newtown in 1819. Having separate areas for buildings accommodating looms and for dwellings housing operators of looms was considered prodigal. The answer was to place the one above the other. This is what happened at Penygloddfa, an area

across the Severn from the original town. There, in the 1820s and 1830s, streets of three- and four-storey buildings were erected. The ground floor and first floor were dwellings and the upper floors were unpartitioned spaces accommodating looms. Until the 1970s, many of the buildings at Penygloddfa followed this pattern;

in that decade, some of them were demolished in a slum clearance campaign, but numbers 5–7 Commercial Street were renovated and became the location of Newtown's Textile Museum.

The museum offers an interesting portrayal of the lives of the weavers of the Severn Valley, but it is not the only place which is a reminder of the time when Newtown was the Bradford or the Rochdale of Wales. The need for a building in Newtown in which to sell the locally produced flannel became increasingly pressing in the 1820s when the town replaced Welshpool as the centre of the Welsh woollen industry. William Pugh of Brynllywarch, Kerry (1783–1842), financed the erection of the Weaving Exchange in Broad Street. An ambitious building with Doric pilasters, it opened in 1832. Auctions were held in it every other Monday, and merchants could be sure that they were not swindled, for the Exchange contained a machine which automatically measured the length of the cloth. The building is now the Regent Centre, home to a cinema and a nightclub.

The coming of the railway in 1861 led to the next development in the history of the local woollen industry. Through the initiative of Pryce Jones (1834–1920), Newtown acquired the world's earliest mail-order business. He played a role in persuading the Post Office to deliver parcels – the penny post established in 1839 only delivered letters. By the 1890s, he had over a hundred thousand customers receiving parcels from Newtown, Queen Victoria among them. The most famous of his wares was the Euklisia Rug, the predecessor of the sleeping bag, which was sold by the hundreds of thousands to the Prussian army. (An example of the rug is displayed in the Textile Museum.) Pryce Jones commissioned the building of the Royal Welsh Warehouse (1879, 1895), the huge bulk of which still dominates Newtown. In 1938, the business was sold to the Lewis Company of Liverpool; it now contains a miscellany of small shops – a symbol of the disappearance of Newtown's textile industry.

The most famous of the natives of Newtown was the pioneer of co-operation, Robert Owen (1771–1858), although he only spent the first ten years and the last year of his life in the town. He was buried in the cemetery of the parish church, a church that suffered so greatly from the Severn's floods that only its restored tower remains. Robert Owen's links with the town are commemorated by a monument in the churchyard (1902), a statue in the town centre (1953), and an interesting, if cramped, museum located in the building erected in 1902 to house the Free Library.

Near the museum stands one of the most intriguing places in Newtown. It is a branch of W. H. Smith; the shop was opened in 1927 and was demodernized in the 1970s in order that it should look as if it were at least eighty years old. (Incidentally, the statement in *Brewer's Britain and Ireland* that W. H. Smith established his first shop in 1792 and that it was located in Newtown is wholly untrue – one of the many errors in that interesting volume.) From the shop, it is a short walk to the main road (the A483/A489), where there is a large building constructed from particularly yellow bricks. It is St David's Church (1843–7), erected to take the place of the old parish church. Within it is what remains of the rood screen salvaged from the old church, the work of the same woodcarvers as were responsible for the masterpiece at Llananno.

St David's Church, Newtown

To the south and west of St David's Church are Garth Owen, Nantoer, Trehafren and Trerhandir, suburbs that caused the population of Newtown to increase from 5,517 in 1961 to 10,783 in 2001. The growth was the result of the decision to register Newtown as a new town under the New Towns Act of 1965. The earliest houses are uninspiring, but matters improved with the creation of Trehafren (1972–5) and Treowen (1974–80). Visitors to Newtown should stroll around those suburbs to appreciate their spaciousness and variety.

The 1960s and 1970s was the fourth time that constructing anew occurred on the banks of the Severn. There had been a new beginning with the coming of the canal, and another with the coming of the railway. The first occurred in 1279 when Roger Mortimer was granted permission by Edward I to create a *novo burgos*, perhaps to replace Dolforwyn, the castle and borough which Llywelyn ap Gruffudd had founded six kilometres to the north-east.

The remains of the motte of the *novo burgos* can be seen beyond the High Street. It came to be surrounded by the garden of Newtown House, the home of the oddest of all the residents of Newtown – John Pryce (d. 1761). As *The Dictionary of Welsh Biography* puts it: 'He was thrice married. His third wife refused to marry him until he removed from the bedchamber the embalmed bodies of the two wives who had preceded her.'

Of the five chief slate-quarrying areas of Wales (Penrhyn, Dinorwic, Dyffryn Nantlle, Blaenau Ffestiniog and Corris), Corris was the smallest. In the Corris area, among the smallest of the quarries was Llwyngwern, located across the Dulais River in Montgomeryshire. In its most successful year (1883), Llwyngwern produced 915 tons of slate, a year in which the Penrhyn Quarry at Bethesda produced over 100,000 tons. But now, Llwyngwern is perhaps the most renowned of all the slate quarries of Wales, for it was there, in 1974, that the Centre for Alternative Technology was established.

In 1974, the Green Movement had hardly begun. Admittedly, Rachel Carson's book, *Silent Spring* (1962), had been a dire warning, as were the comments of Fraser Darling in his Reith Lectures (1969). The Ecological Party of the United Kingdom, founded in 1973, nominated fifty candidates in the general election of 1979. Also in 1973, Leopold Kohr, a scholar whose ideas were rooted in the concept of sustainability, became a lecturer at the University College of Wales, Aberystwyth. Yet, the general view was that ecologists had bees in their bonnets, and twenty years would go by before their ideals became part of the general discourse. With public opinion so unsympathetic, the decision of the ex-soldier and old Etonian, Gerard Morgan-Grenville, to launch a venture on the waste of a Montgomeryshire

slate quarry was bold if not foolhardy. The venture was intended to be an experiment in sustainability, but within a quarter of a century, it became – to quote the centre's publicity material – Europe's chief eco-centre.

Arriving at the centre is an enjoyable experience. As it is thirty metres above the road, the only way to reach it when it first opened was to climb a steep and stony path. In the 1990s, a railway was built, with the weight of the 'down' carriage enabling the 'up' carriage to rise up the tracks. The 'down' carriage is heavier because water has been poured into its underside tank, to be released when the 'down' carriage reaches its destination. (The abundance of water on the site strongly appealed to Morgan-Grenville.) Water is then poured into the underside tank of the carriage that has reached the upper level, allowing the whole process to be repeated without the use of any extraneous power source.

On reaching the upper level, the first point of attention is the manure closet, where sewage is converted into sweet-smelling fertilizer. Beyond the closet is the information centre, a building constructed of mud walls; heated by the sun, the centre retains its heat through the insulation provided by sheep fleeces ('Insulate, insulate, insulate' is the Centre's prime message). Near the information centre is a video room, where visitors are informed

that mankind now uses in a year the same amount of energy as had been used in the vast era between the beginning of Greek civilization and the onset of the Industrial Revolution. From there, paths lead to a variety of interesting places, all fully-explained on bilingual billboards. (Whatever else may be said about the Centre, it is certainly didactic.) There is a theatre built of straw bales, a rather unkempt-looking organic garden, solar generators, water mills and plaques noting the major projects opened by Dafydd Elis Thomas, and the minor projects opened by Prince Charles. Dominating everything is the wind turbine which stands on a ridge above the Centre.

Work is not yet complete on the Centre's major project – the Wales Institute for Sustainable Education (WISE). The construction of its mud walls and its timber work sourced from sustainable woodlands is proceeding rapidly, and, when completed, the building will be the greenest in Europe. Much of the cost of £6 million has come from the Welsh Assembly Government and from Objective One funding, which means that the institute will be Welsh in more than name. This is a highly significant development, for there was a deep-seated belief in Wales that the concept of alternative technology was the preserve of incoming hippies. In the mid 1970s, the majority of the inhabitants of Wales were enjoying a measure of pleasurable consumerism for the first time, and were not prepared to be criticized by people who had traditionally had a privileged lifestyle. The readiness of the Assembly Government to be a partner in the WISE venture suggests that a change of historical importance has occurred. The promoters of the developments at Llwyngwern appear to have realized that, to judge by their readiness to learn lessons from the older generation of local farmers, themselves heirs to a long tradition of sustainable agriculture.

The influence of the Centre can be seen in much of the Dyfi Valley. (*Lyfidyfies* is the name adopted by some of the green enthusiasts of the area.) This is particularly evident in Machynlleth, but, before going there, it is worth visiting the Corris Railway Museum, which chronicles the history of the railway opened in the Dulais Valley in 1859. Nearby is King Arthur's Labyrinth; despite the dragon and giant nonsense

(very imaginative nonsense, it must be admitted), the underground river and waterfall are well worth seeing.

By now, the *Lyfidyfies* are responsible for much of Machynlleth's businesses – the wholefood café, the wholefood shops and the Aga store. The town's chief landmark is the clock tower, the most elaborate of the clock towers which are such a feature of the towns of mid Wales. Machynlleth's one-time Tabernacl Chapel is now the home of Museum of Modern Art, Wales.

There is one fairly contemporary reference (that of Adam of Usk) to a parliament held at Machynlleth in 1404, a reference which Jan Morris inflated into splendid enchantment. A building standing in Heol Maengwyn is centuries old; it certainly does not date back to 1404, but tradition has long associated it with Owain Glyn Dŵr and his Parliament. The building's trustees intend to ensure that it will be an interpretation centre comparable with those at Culloden and Bannockburn. May their admirable intentions be crowned with success.

In addition to being the name of a place, Aberystwyth is also the name of a mental condition – nostalgia which is more pleasant than the experience which gave rise to it. That, at least, is the claim made by Douglas Adams in his entertaining book, *A Dictionary Of Things That There Aren't Any Words For Yet*. So, it is worth going to Aberystwyth if only to find out whether one suffers from 'aberystwyth' after leaving. It is certainly an odd place. For example, it has an institution called the Aberystwyth London Welsh Society, a fact which is consistent with the notion that good Welshmen, when they die, go to Aberystwyth – to adapt Oscar Wilde's comments about Paris and good Americans. It is sometimes hailed as the capital of Welsh-speaking Wales, although it has a lower percentage of Welsh speakers than any of the other communities of Ceredigion apart from Llanbadarn Fawr.

Reaching Aberystwyth provides the same delight as does reaching Perth in Australia, the feeling of doing something exceptional – coming to a place of some size, at the end of the line, after long travelling through nowhere. But that is not the only delight Aberystwyth offers. The promenade is splendid – the second best in Wales after Llandudno. The cliff railway (1896) – the longest funicular railway in Britain – is also memorable, as is the camera obscura on the summit of Constitution Hill. (The praises of Aberystwyth's camera obscura are sung in the Alcázar at Jerez in Andalucia.)

But the great wonder is the Old College. It is said that Nikolaus Pevsner, the greatest of all architectural historians, on turning from New Street into Laura Place, shouted 'Good God' in disbelief. And, with its elaborate *porte-cochère*, its stair towers, its octagonal chimneys and its dormer gables, it is almost unbelievable. What can be seen from Laura Place is only part of its eccentricity. The view from there is of the structures erected in the 1860s, and the renovation following a fire in 1885. On the promenade, visitors should try to visualize what was originally built overlooking the sea – the house designed by John Nash in the 1790s for Uvedale Price, the prophet of the picturesque; alas, it was demolished in 1887 when the home of the University College of Wales was completed. Even stranger was the original design prepared by the architect, J. P. Seddon, in 1871, when the building was purchased from the bankrupt hotel promoter, Thomas Savin, by those seeking to establish a university in Wales. If the cluster of Castell Coch-like towers had been built, Pevsner would probably not have had an oath strong enough to express his astonishment.

The interior is also memorable, in particular the covered quadrangle, where some of the ablest young people in Wales gathered over the century and more that the quad was the heart of the University College of Wales. It contains statues of Thomas Edward Ellis and Lord Aberdare, and a recent poignant memorial to Gareth Jones, chronicler of the horrors of Stalinist collectivization, unveiled in 2006 by the Ukrainian ambassador to Britain.

Aberystwyth through the eye of the camera obscura on the summit of Constitution Hill

From the college, visitors should go to the castle, which was much mauled following the seventeenth-century Civil Wars. Now, it is difficult to appreciate that, with its concentric design and its powerful gatehouse, it was constructed as a worthy predecessor to the finest of the castles commissioned by Edward I in the north-west. A picture of the statue of the robust woman which adorns the war memorial once appeared on page three of *Yr Angor*, the local community newspaper.

As the promenade looks splendid from afar, and less so in close-up, the view of it from Constitution Hill or from the front of the college should suffice. There should be lamentation over the disappearance of the King's Hall (1934), Wales's second-best Art Deco building (Sully Hospital is the best). It was demolished in the 1990s, when it was discovered that it was far more strongly constructed than anyone had realized. (The inhabitants of Miami Beach, the capital of Art Deco, would surely have been delighted had it been reassembled there.)

In the rest of the town centre, there is much of interest, but little that is outstanding. Everything is painstakingly described in the Carmarthenshire and Ceredigion volume of *The Buildings of Wales*, and nerds have been seen wandering the streets with the volume in hand. Non-nerds should visit the Penglais campus, the development of which has been subject to six different plans (1929, 1930, 1935, 1957, 1965, 1974). This indecision has

produced some confused consequences, but some of the buildings have considerable appeal. Neuadd Pantycelyn (1948–60), an unexpectedly old-fashioned neo-Georgian structure, was the result of Percy Thomas's readiness to recycle a design he had already used at the County Hall in Carmarthen. The Great Hall is impressive, the campanile adjoining it is ingenious, and the starkness of Theatr y Werin (1973) has been mitigated by the completion of the Arts Centre. But, as the campus is inconveniently located on a steep slope, there is something unsatisfactory about the entire development. The migration to the slope is regrettable; how much better would it have been had *y coleg ger y lli* (the college by the sea) continued to be *y coleg ger y lli*.

The only wholly delectable building on the Penglais slope is the National Library. There was a time when the library stood alone; then, the view of it from the town bore comparison with the view of the Parthenon from the Agora in Athens. Those who have not been to the library for some years, should make their way there. It is much more interesting and lively than it used to be. In particular, the food has improved enormously.

Life in Aberystwyth: the Caban Café during a march by members of the Wales Social Forum

There is charm in Porthmadog, drama in Fishguard, and romance in Tenby, but there can be no doubt that Aberaeron is the most delightful seaside town in Wales, particularly now that its inhabitants have discovered paint.

By the last decades of the eighteenth century, there was some maritime trade on the banks of the Aeron estuary, and a hamlet had come into being around the bridge that crossed the river.

But, as the area was part of the parish of Llanfihangel Aberarth, it was hardly one of Cardiganshire's acknowledged communities. The land around the estuary was owned by Lewis Gwynne of Mynachdy, a mansion five kilometres inland near the village of Pennant. Lewis was a wealthy bachelor – the owner of £150,000, it was said – and, following his death in 1805, his wealth was inherited by his cousin, Alban Thomas, a clergyman who had already enriched himself by marrying the heiress of the Jones family of Tŷ-glyn in the Aeron Valley. (He added Jones and Gwynne to his surname.) In 1807, the Reverend Alban Thomas Jones Gwynne successfully sought an Act of Parliament authorizing him to develop Aberaeron harbour, authorization which led to the beginnings of a town and to the growth of the harbour as a centre of trade and shipbuilding and a launch-pad for sailors' careers. (The hundredth anniversary of the Act was much celebrated in 2007.)

The town was slow in developing; its centrepiece, Alban Square, not completed until the second half of the nineteenth century. It is not clear who designed the earliest streets – those on the north side of the harbour – but their style indicates the influence of John Nash. By the 1830s, however, it would appear that developments at Aberaeron were guided by Edward Haycock the elder, a Shrewsbury architect born c.1790. What is striking is the unity of plan and style of the streets from the era of Alban Gwynne (d. 1819) to that of his son, Colonel Alban Gwynne (d. 1861). Central to the charm of Aberaeron is the fact that its builders remained faithful to the Regency style for half a century and more, long into the period when the Victorians were favouring less elegant styles. The Aberaeron model found favour beyond the town's border, as houses at Llanarth and elsewhere bear witness.

The Mynachty estate leased building plots and provided the leases with building guidelines. It is interesting to wander around

the town looking for irregularities – evidence of lessees ignoring the estate's guidelines. Originally, the houses were roughcasted and there is no suggestion that there was an expectation that their outside walls would be painted. The stucco-painted walls are a twentieth-century development, and were celebrated by the shilling stamps issued by the British Post Office in 1970.

The town plan was not Haycock's sole contribution to the development of Aberaeron. He designed the town's Anglican church, and was probably also responsible for the Market Hall, which eventually became Cardiganshire's County Hall. By the 1960s, most of the council's offices were at Aberystwyth, a town which has never found favour among the rural inhabitants of the county. In 1989, plans were afoot to ensure that the bulk of the offices of the Ceredigion District would be at Aberaeron, plans which gained momentum after Ceredigion regained county status in 1996. The office buildings cluster around the octagonal council chamber on a hillside which provides superb views of Cardigan Bay.

According to the architect, Dewi-Prys Thomas, a visit to Aberaeron resembles a visit to Melitus, the city built by the Greeks at the mouth of the Meander River in southern Anatolia. The comments of the geographer, Harold Carter, were less fanciful. Alban Square, he noted, is a descendant of the *Piazza* or the *Grande Place* which is so much a feature of Europe's civic tradition. However, the square is occupied by a football pitch,

and the scale of the houses surrounding it are modest, proof, argued Carter, that European civic graces have not rooted wholly successfully on the coast of Cardigan Bay. But, to Geraint Evans, perhaps the most talented of twentieth-century Welsh artists, Aberaeron was a delight, and he sought to spend as much of his time as possible there.

From Aberaeron, it is a four-kilometre walk to Llanerchaeron, following the track of the railway which linked Aberaeron with Lampeter; the railway was opened to travellers in 1911 and closed in 1951, making it the shortest-lived passenger line in Wales. Recently, remains of a *taeogdref* (bond village) were discovered at Llanerchaeron, evidence that it had been the centre of an estate in the Middle Ages. In the 1790s, William Lewis commissioned John Nash to design a mansion at Llanerchaeron. (After William Lewis's death, Llanerchaeron came into the possession of his son-in-law, William Lewes.) Less imposing rooms adjoined the living quarters – the kitchen, the scullery, the dairy, the pantry, the brewhouse, and the rooms in which cheese was made and pigs were salted. Thus, under one roof, there was the combination of elegant mansion and self-sufficient household.

It was this combination which appealed to the National Trust in 1989, when J. P. Ponsonby Lewes died, leaving Llanerchaeron to it in his will. The Trust does not always welcome bequests, especially if they are not accompanied by a considerable endowment or when the property bequeathed needs expensive repair work. Lewes left no endowment, and, after decades of neglect, costs would inevitably be high. (The neglect was part of the appeal of the place, for everything within the mansion belonged to ages past.) Renovation had been completed by 2004, and Llanerchaeron now presents the fascination of a country house as well as rich parkland, fine gardens and a rejuvenated farm. In keeping with the concerns of the age, the farm is organic and those arriving at the property through their own exertions pay a reduced entrance fee. Does that apply to those who paddle a canoe along the Aeron?

While going from Tregaron to Pontrhydfendigaid along the B4343, the traveller crosses Pont Fflur. It was on the banks of Nant Fflur that the chief monastery of Deheubarth – the chief monastery of Wales in many respects – was founded in 1164. The founder was Robert fitz Stephen, a vassal of Roger de Clare (d. 1173), grandson of Gilbert de Clare who had seized Ceredigion in 1110. By 1164, Clare power in Ceredigion was waning rapidly. By 1165, Robert fitz Stephen was in prison and Rhys ap Gruffudd (the Lord Rhys) had regained Ceredigion for the royal house of Deheubarth. The Lord Rhys decided to relocate the monastery three kilometres to the north-east on the left bank of the Teifi. Building work had probably begun near Pont Fflur, and it is likely that remains of the proto-monastery lie beneath one of the fields of the farm of Hen Fynachlog (Old Abbey).

The Teifi-side monastery received its charter in 1184. The Lord Rhys endowed it lavishly, providing it with the resources which enabled its monks to establish daughter houses at Llantarnam and Aberconwy and a nunnery at Llanllyr. The mother house of Strata Florida was Whitland, and all the Cistercian monasteries of *Pura Wallia* sprang from Whitland, either directly or through her daughters. By the early thirteenth century, all the major territories under native Welsh rulers had a Cistercian house – Whitland (*c.*1157) in Dyfed, Strata Florida (1164) in Ceredigion, Strata Marcella (1170) in Powys Wenwynwyn, Cwm-hir (1176) in Maelienydd, Llantarnam (1179) in Caerleon, Aberconwy (1190) in Gwynedd and Valle Crucis (1201) in Powys Fadog. As the Cistercians – originally at least – were dedicated to asceticism, the Welsh may have considered their monasteries as a reassertion of the values of the Celtic Church, but perhaps more important for the native Welsh rulers was the fact that every Cistercian house was answerable to the authority of the head abbot; as he dwelt at Cîteaux in

Burgundy, he was not subject to the direct authority of the kings of England.

The monks of Strata Florida held their first service in their completed church on Whitsunday 1201. Apart from one splendid feature, little of that church survives. The splendid feature is the entrance in the western façade. It obviously belongs to the Romanesque tradition, but nowhere else is there a similar interpretation of that style. Architects of Romanesque buildings flanked entrances with pillars surmounted by capitals, but the entrance at Strata Florida has rows of continuous mouldings linked together by thirteen strips of stonework, all of them ending in neat scrolls. Perhaps the scrolls represent a bishop's crosier, or are based on the origin of the crosier – the shepherd's staff; if so, it was a suitable motif for a monastery dependent upon its flocks of sheep.

Although the monastery is much ruined, the ground plan is clear and is wholly in accordance with the austere style of twelfth-century Cistercian abbeys. Three chapels in the south transept have been given modern roofs in order to shelter a collection of the tiles which were laid over the whole of the floor of the abbey

church in the fourteenth century. Beyond the transept are the foundations of the chapter house and those of the northern side of the cloister – the southern side is buried beneath Mynachlog Fawr (Great Abbey), a house built in the late seventeenth century for the Stedman family, the post-Dissolution owners of Strata Florida.

The monastery suffered many blows – war damage in 1282–3, a strike by lightening *c.*1286, further war damage during the revolt of 1293–5, and serious misuse in the course of the Glyn Dŵr Rising. It is likely, therefore, that much of abbey was in a dire condition long before its dissolution in 1539 – which probably explains the fact that there is less to see at Strata Florida than at the other medieval monasteries of Wales. At Tintern, for example, it is possible to trace the location of the wall which enclosed the monastery, the gatehouse which gave access to it, and the remains of the Abbot's Hall, the infirmary, the kitchens and the guest rooms. Strata Florida undoubtedly had similar structures. The Department of Archaeology at Lampeter has established the Strata Florida Research Project in order fully to survey the site. The project's initial findings prove that the monastery, at its medieval apogee, was far larger than the present remains suggest. The Lampeter researchers are studying the abbey in the context of the extensive lands owned by the monks, research which includes field boundaries, the monks' links with the lead and silver mines of the area, and their method of administering the abbey's numerous granges. As the work

progresses, it is likely that it will become apparent that Strata Florida was even more important in the history of Wales than has traditionally been considered.

Even before the recent research, there was little doubt about the central role played by Strata Florida, particularly in the thirteenth century. It is the burial place of at least ten of the relations of the Lord Rhys. It is also the burial place of the greatest genius born in medieval Wales – the poet Dafydd ap Gwilym; in the 1950s, a bilingual (Welsh and Latin) memorial was unveiled to him in the north transept of the abbey church. In 1238, when Llywelyn ap Iorwerth, prince of Gwynedd, sought to ensure that all the native Welsh rulers would recognize his son, Dafydd, as his sole heir, it was at Strata Florida that the oaths of recognition were sworn. Above all, knowledge of the history of medieval Wales – particularly the crucial years 1175–1282 – would be slight but for Strata Florida, for there is virtually no doubt that the abbey's monks were responsible for *Brut y Tywysogyon*, the chief source for what happened to the Welsh people during the most exciting period of their history.

There is a pearl in the heart of Wales – Llananno church which squats between the River Ithon and the road from Llandrindod to Newtown (the A483). The building itself is of little interest; it is a small box erected in 1867 to replace its ruined medieval predecessor. The significance of the place arises from the fact that, during the rebuilding, great care was taken to ensure that the wooden screen that had stood between the nave and the chancel of the old church was placed in the new building.

The screen is a delight. The fashion of installing carved wooden screens in parish churches can be traced back to the fourteenth century, and it is likely that, by the eve of the Reformation, most of the thousand or so parish churches of Wales had some sort of screen. Parts of about three hundred of them are extant, but fewer than a dozen have survived in their entirety, most of them in remote places such as Llananno. There is a cluster in the parish churches around the Black Mountains – Llananno, Llanfilo, Llaneleu and Partrishow among them. Others include Betws Newydd and Llangwm Uchaf (Monmouthshire), Llanegryn (Merioneth) and Clocaenog (Denbighshire).

It is widely claimed that the finest of the screens of Wales is the one at Partrishow. Yet, although that is delightful, and although St Ishio's Church is fascinating (far more fascinating than St Anno's), the liveliness of the Llananno screen puts it in a class all of its own. Admittedly, the images of Christ, the twelve apostles and the twelve patriarchs are not the original ones, but the niches in which they stand are medieval. The most appealing features of the screen are the carvings on the beams above and below the niches. They are characterized by a splendid imaginative vigour; they include almost twenty different patterns representing a variety of plants (the 'true vine' in particular), patterns which are linked together by a carved band of wood issuing from the mouths of a pair of wyverns. The richness of the carvings makes them look more like jewellery than woodwork, and the visitor can do no more than stare at them, gobsmacked.

That, no doubt, was the experience of R. S. Thomas, whose poem about 'the serene presence' at Llananno is framed on the church wall.

The Llananno screen belongs to a tradition of woodworking which was wholly Welsh, and it may not be fanciful to consider that its inventiveness owes something to ancient Celtic art. It was the work of a school of woodworkers centred upon Newtown, and was characterized by more lively carving than the more restrained work seen at Llanfilo and Partrishow. The masterpiece of the Newtown school was the screen created for St Mary's, Newtown. That church was abandoned in 1840 because of flooding, but parts of the screen may be seen in Newtown's St David's Church.

In his book, *The Welsh Church*, Glanmor Williams paid tribute to Wales's medieval woodworkers: 'It is not a coincidence that the poets of Wales ranked the carpenters alongside themselves as artists… The canons of his craft and the requirements of his patron [obliged the carpenter, like the poet] to be confined to a limited number of highly stylized themes and patterns… The vines, the wyverns and the traceries of a Welsh screen could be as congenial an expression of Welsh medieval aesthetics as a *cywydd* or an *englyn*.'

From Llananno, a steep path leads to the remains of what the Ordnance Survey maps call Castelltinboeth, which can loosely be considered to mean hot-arsed castle. A more correct version of the name would be Castell Dinbaud; it probably commemorates Maud or Matilda de Breos, daughter and heiress of William de Breos, hanged by Llywelyn ap Iorwerth in 1230. Maud married Roger Mortimer (d. 1282), thus strengthening the Mortimer family's hold on what would be northern Radnorshire. Among the ambitions of Llywelyn ap Gruffudd (d. 1282) was the seizure of the Mortimer territories in the middle March, and the building of the castle may have been motivated by the desire to frustrate Llywelyn's ambitions. Located 420 metres above sea level, Castell Dinbaud is the second highest castle in Wales (Castell Dinas above Talgarth is the highest at 454 metres.) Virtually nothing of the stonework remains standing, but it is worth climbing to the summit, if only to see the deep trenches dug in the rock to reinforce the stronghold's defences.

From the summit, there is a splendid view of the valley of the Ithon, the longest of the tributaries of the Wye. To the north is St Padarn's Church, Llanbadarn Fynydd, which contains remnants of a screen in the same tradition as that at Llananno. To the south is St Cynllo's Church, Llanbister, one of the few Welsh parish churches containing a font for total immersion. To the west are the hills in which the River Lugg has its source, two kilometres before it forms the most attractively named waterfall in Wales – Water-break-its-neck. To the west lies the valley of one of the six Welsh rivers named Clywedog. In that valley are the ruins of Abbey Cwm-hir, where the headless body of Llywelyn ap Gruffudd was buried in 1282.

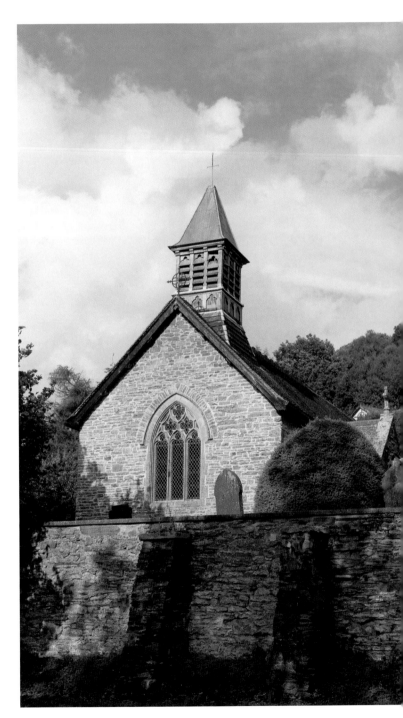

St Padarn's Church, Llanbadarn Fynydd

The A44 is the road which links Aberystwyth to Chipping Norton. The A488, which branches from it at Penybont, goes through Bleddfa but, before reaching that delightful place, it is worth turning on to a narrow road that leads to the foothills of Radnor Forest. About a kilometre from the main road, and, after opening and closing two gates, the traveller reaches one of the most interesting places in Wales – the Quaker meeting-house of The Pales. There is no grandeur there. Indeed, very little is there: a burial ground and a two-roomed thatched building – that is all. The meeting-house is always open and visitors can make themselves a free cup of tea. The tea should be drunk while sitting on one of the benches outside the meeting-house, there to enjoy the splendid views of the hills of Maelienydd.

Just as in the early years of the Celtic Church, the first necessity of the members of the Society of Friends was a place to bury the dead. The burial ground at The Pales was established in 1673, many decades before a meeting-house was built there. The name early Welsh Christians gave to their enclosed burial ground was *llan*, and it could be argued that The Pales, initially, was also a *llan*. Pales were the woven palisades erected around the *llan*. The Pales, therefore, has more or less the same meaning as *bangor*, which means wickerwork.

In 1717, the *llan* acquired a building, of which the present meeting-house is an adaptation. At present, Quaker meetings are held at thirty-one centres in Wales. Some of them take place in recent, purpose-built centres – at Bangor, for example – but most congregations hire a room. Of the structures in Wales specifically built for Quaker worship, The Pales is the oldest still in use. From 1857 to 1889, the Friends conducted an elementary school in the building, which was attended by up to forty children. Missionary work was undertaken between 1867 and 1891, and in 1876 a warden's residence was built near the meeting-house. The place languished from the First World War until the 1970s. In that decade, the meeting-house was reroofed, the wardenship was filled and a variety of activities were undertaken, among them discussion groups and campaigns central to the values of the

Friends, particularly matters relating to peace and justice. Although few people regularly attend the meeting held at The Pales at three o'clock on the third Sunday of the month, considerable numbers are present when a camp (vegetarian food, no alcohol) is held in a field nearby.

Wales is rich in places that have an aura of sanctity – the cathedral at St Davids, for example, or churches such as Partrishow, or ruins such as Strata Florida, or enchanted places such as Llanddwyn – but they are all outclassed by The Pales, which is replete with sanctity and tranquility. R. S. Thomas claimed that God is in the silence and that with the waiting comes worship. This is exactly the message of The Pales; it is hardly surprising that an essay by Waldo Williams is available there.

It is particularly interesting to wander around the burial ground, one of a cluster of Quakers' yards established in Radnorshire, a county whose inhabitants found the message of

George Fox more appealing than did the inhabitants of the other counties of Wales. Of the eighty-seven gravestones in the burial ground, the earliest was erected in 1838; those buried there during the first century of the ground's existence probably had no memorial stones. There are a number of Quakers' yards in Wales – for example, at Llanddewi Brefi, at Tabor above Dolgellau, and at Quakers' Yard near Treharris in the Taff Valley, and it is claimed that the yard at Cardiff lies beneath one of the platforms of the Central Station. The Pales is one of the very few which are still in use. The gravestones bear a limited number of surnames; the most prominent are Watkins, Jenkins, Owens, Drew and Brick, giving the impression that the cause was and is maintained by a few local kinship groups, some of whom lived in nearby farmhouses such as Rhonllwyn and Kilmanowydd. Bearing in mind that the Quakers spurn clergy, that their services are almost wholly lacking in ritual, that their beliefs were long regarded as heretical, and that the congregation at The Pales draws upon a very thinly populated area, the survival of the cause borders upon the miraculous. Some impression of the devotion of its members can be gained from the diary kept in 1900 by Thomas Watkins of Dolau (a diary edited for publication by a local vicar), in which he pleads 'with God not to turn His back on my dear Pales'.

A road leads from The Pales to Llandegley, a village which was once a spa; indeed, those wandering the banks of the Mithil Brook can still detect a whiff of sulphur. Thomas Phillips (1760–1851), founder of the Welsh Educational Institution at Llandovery, was a native of Llandegley. He sought to establish a Welsh boarding-school where the pupils would be taught through the medium of Welsh for at least an hour a day, an intention abandoned when A. G. Edwards, a native of Llanymawddwy, became headmaster in 1875. On the A44 near the village stands an official-looking sign directing travellers to Terminal One and Terminal Two of the Llandegley International Airport. The prospects of the airport were discussed in the House of Commons on 12 March 2003, but all attempts to find the terminals have proved unsuccessful.

Presteigne has one of the world's most appealing small museums, but more of that later. The town's name means the priest's border meadow, probably a reference to Presteigne's location on the banks of the River Lugg in a strip of Radnorshire that pushes out into the lowlands of Herefordshire. The place suffered several misfortunes. Llywelyn ap Gruffudd and Owain Glyn Dŵr attacked it; in 1262, Llywelyn destroyed its castle, causing Presteigne to be the only ancient border town to have little evidence of a medieval stronghold. The plague of the 1340s was a disaster and Presteigne suffered from pestilence time and time again. In 1681, many of the town's buildings were destroyed by fire, but it proved possible to renovate the finest of them – the Radnorshire Arms Hotel, originally built in 1616. It is one of the finest of Wales's black-and-white houses, and is almost as appealing as Nantclwyd House in Ruthin; there can be no higher praise than that.

Presteigne is situated to the east of Offa's Dyke, and only became part of Wales because of the successful campaigns of Gruffudd ap Llywelyn (d. 1063). The ecclesiastical parish remains part of the diocese of Hereford, which means that the inhabitants of Presteigne are among the few people in Wales who live in an area that has an established church. The origins of St Andrew's Church date from the time when the place was part of Mercia; indeed, the part of the church built in the tenth century is virtually the sole example in Wales of Anglo-Saxon architecture. The nave was rebuilt in the fourteenth century and within it is exhibited a tapestry of Christ entering Jerusalem, a splendid piece of work woven in Flanders in the sixteenth century. The chancel

The former Shire Hall, Presteigne

and the Lady Chapel date from the fifteenth century, and represent the Perpendicular Gothic style at its best. St Andrew's is the finest church in Radnorshire and one of the largest churches in mid Wales.

In the churchyard is the grave of Mary Morgan, a seventeen-year-old girl hanged in Presteigne in 1805 for murdering her newborn child with a pocket knife. The original gravestone quoted the comments of George Hardinge, the judge who condemned her to death – comments characteristic of the man who was central to the administration of the law in the counties of Radnor, Brecon and Glamorgan from 1787 to 1816. His inhumane attitude aroused so much antagonism that another stone was raised to Mary Morgan bearing a quotation from St John's Gospel: 'He who is without sin among you, let him first cast a stone at her.'

Strolling around the streets of Presteigne is a pleasant experience. Despite its small size (population, 2,463) – its inhabitants used to boast that it was the smallest county town

The Market Hall, Presteigne

in Britain – it has a distinctly urban feel. It is worth reading the posters advertising the varied activities of the inhabitants – art exhibitions, a musical festival and electric bicycle races amongst them. Broad Street was the site of the Newell family's ironmonger's shop, a business established in 1770. When the shop ceased trading in 1974, it was found to contain examples of two-hundred years of ironware production; almost all the objects in the shop were sold to the museum at St Fagans.

Busts at the Judge's Lodging Museum, Presteigne

The chief attraction of Broad Street – and the chief attraction of Presteigne – is the former County Hall. When Radnorshire was established by the Act of 'Union' of 1536, it was laid down that the location of the Court of Great Session should alternate between New Radnor and Rhayader. However, following the murder of a judge by the inhabitants of Rhayader, Presteigne was chosen as the judicial headquarters of the county, an arrangement which lasted until the twentieth century, although in 1889 Llandrindod became the seat of the county council. The County Hall was erected in 1829, a year before the Court of Great Session was replaced by the Assizes. Its architect was Edward Haycock of Shrewsbury, the man who is believed to have designed Aberaeron.

The practice of holding an Assize in all the thirteen counties of Wales came to an end in 1970. Since then, Crown Courts are held in seven locations, not one of which is in mid Wales; indeed, there is no judicial centre between Carmarthen and Caernarfon, or between Merthyr Tydfil and Mold.

The last court to be held in the County Hall was in September 1970. The empty building fell into decay and its demolition was mooted. Then, in the early 1990s, it was realized that in Presteigne there was a building admirably suited to throw light on the administration of the law in the nineteenth century. There are former prisons in Ruthin and Beaumaris, and a former courtroom in Brecon, but in Presteigne the prison and the courtroom are under one roof, and under the same roof are the judge's lodgings – not only the comfortable rooms of the judge himself, but also the drab rooms of his servants.

The old County Hall was opened as a museum in 1997, and was rapidly recognized as one of the most fascinating of museums. Among the features of the place is that everything can be touched, and that there is nowhere that is closed off. Listening in the court to the exact words spoken in a trial held over a hundred years ago is a memorable experience; even more memorable is a visit to the cells. None of the rooms contain anything that they would not have contained in the 1870s, as can be seen from the dishes and the glasses on the starched tablecloth of the judge's dining-room. The kitchen in the cellar where the food was prepared gives an impression of total authenticity. Beyond it are the servants' bedrooms; they also seem exactly as they were, although it should be noted that the rats have been exterminated.

In 2008, an exhibition on early Wales was opened at the National Museum. It contained many of the chief icons of Welsh history and prehistory – objects such as the skeleton of 'The Red Lady of Paviland' and the stone face of Llywelyn ap Iorwerth from Deganwy. Of them, the most memorable was a man's head, re-created by computer on the basis of a skull of *c.*3500 BC. The skull was found in the Penyweirglodd chambered tomb south of Talgarth, and the man's features show that human faces have not changed at all in over five-thousand years. The tomb also contained the most ancient sheep bone to have been found in Wales; a Neolithic musician had attempted to turn the bone into a whistle.

The Penyweirglodd tomb is one of a cluster of fascinating monuments. Three-quarters of the chambered tombs of Wales were constructed less than two kilometres from the sea, in places such as Anglesey, Ardudwy, Pembrokeshire and Gower, and it is believed that they were the work of people who sailed the western sea-routes. Northern Breconshire in the only area in Wales where there is an inland group of such structures. Why did people in the fourth millennium BC build at least sixteen such monuments around the Black Mountains?

The centre of the cluster is Talgarth, one of Wales's most attractive villages. Indeed, on its website, someone has written: 'If it were possible to bottle Talgarth, there would be a market for the bottles'. It has the air of being more than a village. With its Town Hall, its banks, its rugby club and its fire brigade, it has the swagger of a town. It developed from the 1860s onwards following the opening of the Brecon to Hereford Railway, but the greatest impetus to its growth was the opening of the Mid Wales Hospital (1900) and of the Tuberculosis Sanatorium (1913–20). Indeed, perhaps a higher proportion of Talgarth people work in health care than in any other place on Earth.

Those who have not recently been to Talgarth should go there. The opening of the bypass has transformed the place; lorries trying to navigate the horrendous bends in its streets are now but a memory, although a building on the square still bears the notice: 'Car transporter driver Do not hit this house'. Opposite the notice is one of Breconshire's two tower houses (the other is in Scethrog). The tower now houses a visitors' centre, further proof of Talgarth's urban ambitions.

Talgarth was wholly central to a highly significant chapter in the history of Wales. On hearing the preaching of Pryce Davies, vicar of Talgarth, in 1735, Howel Harris had the religious experience which caused him to spend the rest of his life as an evangelist. The event took place in his parish church – the church of Gwenddolen, a substantial building dating from the later Middle Ages which commemorates one of the many daughters of Brychan Brycheiniog. In 1737, on hearing Harris preaching in St Gwenddolen's churchyard, a student intent on medical studies

The notion of *y teulu* baffled William Williams, Pantycelyn. He wrote: '*Pam y treuliaist dy holl ddyddiau yn creu ryw fynachlog fawr, / Pan y tynnodd Harri frenin mwy na mil o'r rhain i lawr?*' (Why did you spend all your days creating a large monastery, / When King Henry destroyed more that a thousand of them?)

One of the neo-Gothic windows of Trefecca College

– William Williams of Pantycelyn – had an equally profound experience. It could therefore be claimed that Talgarth was the cradle of the Calvinistic Methodist denomination. Harris was buried near the altar of St Gwenddolen, and the inscription on his tomb describes him as 'the first itinerant preacher of redemption in this period of revival'. Another Harris, Joseph (not Howel's brother), has a far more elaborate memorial in the church, but the most delightful is that to William Vaughan (d. 1631), carved by Aaron Brute, a member of a family responsible for many lively epitaphs in the churches around the Black Mountains.

The road which leads from Howel Harris's home at Trefecca Fach to St Gwenddolen's Church passes College Farm, the academy commissioned by the countess of Huntingdon in 1768 in order that the students could benefit from the presence of Howel Harris. By then he was living in Trefecca Fawr, which is now the Presbyterian Church of Wales's centre for the training of lay people. It was built in 1752 to house *y teulu* (the family) – the spiritual *kibbutz* which became Harris's main interest in the last decades of his life. Harris himself may have designed the building. It was only in 1750 that work began on Horace Walpole's Strawberry Hill, the house that is considered to be the birthplace of the neo-Gothic style in Britain. It is striking therefore that, two years later, Harris chose the same style at Trefecca Fawr. (Harris's spiritual family inspired those who named the Trevecca Nazarene University at Nashville, Tennessee.)

Knowledge of the whereabouts of the residences of the rulers of Wales in the early Middle Ages is scanty. According to tradition, the royal seat of Gwynedd was at Aberffraw, of Powys at Mathrafal and of Ystrad Tywi at Dinefwr. Knowledge of the seat of the rulers of one of the smallest kingdoms – Brycheiniog – is more reliable.

In its entry for the year 916, the Anglo-Saxon Chronicle records that Aethelflaeda, Lady of the Mercians (daughter of Alfred the Great), sent an army to Brecenan Mere which seized the wife of the king of Brycheiniog. Brecenan Mere was undoubtedly Llangorse Lake (Llyn Syfaddan), the largest natural lake in the south. The court of Brycheiniog was probably located on the crannog which rises from the water a few metres from the lake's northern shore. A crannog is an artificial island created by piling stones, planks and brushwood in shallow water. The building erected upon it would have been conical in shape, with a roof of reeds. (There is a recent re-creation of such a building in the leisure centre at the lakeside.)

The Llangorse crannog is the only known example in Wales. They are numerous in Ireland, and the fact that there is one in Brycheiniog adds to the evidence of links between it and Ireland. The Brycheiniog dynasty had Irish origins, and within the kingdom several stones were erected bearing inscriptions in Ogam, a script devised in Ireland. As these can also be found in

Dyfed, another kingdom with a dynasty of Irish origin, the Roman road – now the A40 – which linked the river basins of the Tywi and the Usk must have been important in ensuring that south-west Wales was in contact with the south-eastern parts of the country.

The Brecknock Museum at Brecon contains objects found at the crannog; the woven material in particular is proof that the material culture of the rulers of Brycheiniog attained a considerable level of sophistication. After Aethelflaeda's attack, the kingdom came increasingly under the control of Deheubarth, and it was while seeking to retain Brycheiniog as part of his territories that the last king of Deheubarth, Rhys ap Tewdwr, was killed in 1093. Almost a hundred years after his death, Giraldus Cambrensis noted that the birds of Llangorse Lake sang only to the heirs of Deheubarth.

The inhabitants of the crannog undoubtedly depended upon the riches of the lake for much of their food. Giraldus waxed lyrical about the pike, perch, trout, tench and eels of its waters. A pike from the lake is the heaviest fish (one hundred and fifty kilograms) ever to be caught in the inland waters of Britain. One of the poems of Lewys Glyn Cothi mentions the 'monster' of Llangorse Lake. Thus, along with Nessy and Tegi, there was also Gorsy. A giant pike rising from the water is the most likely explanation for the Gorsy legend.

The lake is within easy reach of some of the most attractive villages in Wales. A particularly enjoyable walk is that from Llangorse to Llanywern, a journey which passes the track of the railway which used to link Hay with Merthyr Tydfil. Theophilus Jones, the historian of Breconshire, commented upon the water-logged churchyard of Llanywern; he was sad to think of the

The re-created crannog dwelling on the bank of Llangorse Lake

Equally interesting is Scethrog, where there is a fifteenth-century tower house, one of twenty in Wales. (There are hundreds in Ireland and Scotland, proof that in the later Middle Ages the inhabitants of those countries had themselves to provide the security that the state failed to provide.) The Scethrog tower house was once the home of George Melly, founder of the Brecon Jazz Festival. From Scethrog, the A40 takes the traveller passed Newton, the birthplace of the poet, Henry Vaughan (1621–95), to Llansantffraed, where he is buried. The gravestone bears the famous epitaph: *Henricus Vaughan Silures servus inutilis peccator maximus gloria miserere* (Henry Vaughan Silurian, useless servant, greatest of sinners, glory, mercy).

From Llansantffraed, it is worth crossing the bridge over the Usk to Talybont, where activity on the Brecon-Abergavenny Canal is at its busiest, and where the canal, a river (Afon Caerfanell) and a one-time railway add to the attractive landscape. Talybont is the best place at which to start walking the Taff Trail; the journey from the Talybont reservoir to that of Taf Fechan is among the most delightful in Wales.

St Gastayn's Church, Llangasty Tal-y-llyn

bodies in their boggy beds, and suggested that the churchyard should be drained so that the departed could 'all moulder dryly, snugly and comfortably together'.

The most attractive village in the area is Llangasty Tal-y-llyn, where an attempt was made to realize one of the ideals of mid-nineteenth-century High Churchmen – the integration of worship and schooling. Robert Raikes, who lived in the mansion of Treberfydd nearby, commissioned a church, a rectory, a school and a headmaster's house in accordance with the principles of the Oxford Movement. The group of buildings, with its superb lakeside location, is unique in Wales, although similar principles underlie an attractive cluster of buildings at Towyn near Abergele.

Turning off the A40 east of Bwlch and travelling along the A479 is a delectable experience. The road goes up the valley of the river which has the most appealing of all Welsh river-names – Afon Rhiangoll (the Lost Maiden). Shortly after leaving the A40, the A479 reaches Tretower, the best place in which to study the evolution of the dwellings of the powerful families of medieval Wales. The story begins *c*.1100, when Picard, one of the knights assisting Bernard de Neufmarché in the task of destroying the kingdom of Brycheiniog, commissioned the building of a motte near the Rhiangoll. Then, *c*.1150, a curtain wall was built around the motte; the rooms erected within the walls are among the best examples in Wales of the use of the Romanesque style in a non-ecclesiastical context.

The next development came in the 1230s; the curtain walls were demolished and the motte was surmounted by a tall masonry tower similar to that erected at Bronllys, 14 kilometres to the

The western façade of Tretower Court viewed through the gatehouse

north. The most extensive building work at Tretower was that undertaken between 1457 and 1470 for Roger Vaughan, half-brother of William Herbert, who became earl of Pembroke in 1468. The work had a twofold significance. It was built for a Welshman, not for a member of a Marcher family, an indication that the era of the Marcher Lords was coming to an end. Furthermore, it was a hall house, a dwelling lacking fortification, a fact of the greatest significance. As Peter Smith put it: 'The distinction between a military castle, safe behind battlements, and a peasant class, living in undefended cottages, started to fade, and the main stream of domestic architecture began to flow in quite another direction, in the direction of dwellings undistorted by the necessities of war.'

Tretower Court is the best example in Wales of a fifteenth-century gentry house. Although its timber work lacks the splendour of that at Bryndraenog (Beguildy) – Wales's finest timber building – the whole structure is hugely attractive. Its centrepiece is the Great Hall, but some of the rooms are more intriguing, among them the mess of Roger Vaughan's indentured soldiers, who perhaps included the poet, Guto'r Glyn. After the era of Roger Vaughan, the court was much revamped, but what is visible today is the result of Cadw's efforts to return the building to its fifteenth-century state. In the garden south of the building, nothing has been planted that would be unfamiliar to Roger Vaughan and his contemporaries.

Tretower Court's lack of fortification has been stressed, but, bearing in mind that it was built less than fifty years after the Glyn Dŵr Rising and that late medieval Brycheiniog had tower houses at Scethrog and Talgarth, it is hardly surprising that one part of the Court does contain defensive features. That is the gatehouse, which has slits for arrows and bullets. Yet, according to Peter Smith, these are merely 'mild defensive gestures'; thus, the court belongs essentially to a new era.

The medieval garden at Tretower Court

South of Tretower, a mansion was built for a very different kind of landed proprietor. He was Joseph Bailey (1783–1858), who had made his fortune at the Nantyglo ironworks, and had spent it buying 9,000 hectares in Breconshire – the best example in the history of Wales of an individual amassing a large estate in a single generation. Glanusk was built for him, an enormous mansion that was demolished in 1954. It was he, in 1852, who financed the construction of Penmyarth church, a building dominated by his tomb.

North of Tretower the road leads to Llanfihangel Cwmdu, the home of Thomas Price (Carnhuanawc, 1787–1848), early-nineteenth-century Wales's greatest patriot. A historian, a musician, a naturalist, a linguist and a pan-Celticist, he founded a Welsh-medium elementary school at Cwmdu, a venture which aroused the scorn of the compilers of *The Report on Education in Wales* (1847). In the 1990s, Cymdeithas Carnhuanawc (the Carnhuanawc Society) unveiled a plaque on the building in which the school was held. Carnhuanawc could turn his hand to

almost anything, and it is likely that he had a part in the rebuilding of the church in the 1830s and in building the rectory in which he lived. From his death until the beginning of the Second World War, his tomb in the burial ground of St Michael's Church was a place of pilgrimage for the Welsh-language enthusiasts living in the south-eastern borderlands. Pilgrimages resumed in the 1990s under the patronage of Cymdeithas Carnhuanawc, the movement which in 2002 regilded the inscription on his tomb.

Further up the Rhiangoll Valley, the A479 comes under the shadow of Mynydd Troed (609 metres), which seems to swing to the right and to the left as the traveller climbs towards it. Across the valley from Mynydd Troed stands Castell Dinas, Wales's highest castle (454 metres above sea level). It is believed that Castell Dinas was Owain Glyn Dŵr's stronghold after he broke through to the south during the winter of 1400. It is likely, therefore, that Glyn Dŵr's first southern campaign was to lead his forces down the Rhiangoll Valley to attack Tretower Castle.

Tretower Castle

From the Middle Ages until the nineteenth century, many Welsh boroughs bordered upon being city states, with their own territories, their own patricians, their own plebeians, and their own resources. Among the most prosperous of those boroughs was Brecon.

The founding of Brecon is a textbook example of the colonising methods of the Normans. Bernard de Neufmarché, who held extensive lands in Herefordshire, saw an opportunity, in the early 1090s, to break into Wales. He moved slowly across the 25 kilometres from the point where the Wye flows into England to the confluence of the Honddu and the Usk, consolidating his authority, step by step, through commissioning the building of motte-and-bailey castles. He chose the rising land on the west bank of the Honddu for his castle, his fortified town and his church – the trio central to the power of the Lords of the March.

Watton Mount, Brecon

Brecon's earliest church was probably built within the walls of the castle bailey, but it was soon relocated to the north of the castle within its own fortifications. It was a Benedictine church, a priory of Battle Abbey in Sussex. Lavishly endowed, it became one the most splendid of Wales's medieval churches. It has an essentially Romanesque plan, a sanctuary of *c*.1200, a transept of *c*.1250, and a nave of *c*.1350. Surprisingly, its conventual buildings survived in a usable condition. Thus, when the church became the cathedral of the diocese of Swansea and Brecon in 1923, diocesan meetings could be held in the old chapter house, and the dean could take up residence in the prior's house. That house may have been the home of John Price, who gained possession of the priory buildings following the dissolution of the monasteries; if so, it was there that the earliest Welsh book to be published (*Yn y lhyvyr hwnn*, 1546) was compiled.

St Mary's Church, Brecon, surrounded by visitors to the Brecon Jazz Festival

The centre of Brecon is no longer in the vicinity of the priory and castle. Brecon spread eastwards – an exception to the general rule that urban centres tend to drift westwards (Paris, London and Edinburgh, for example). The need for a place of worship in the eastern extension had been realized by the sixteenth century when St Mary's Church was completed. Its church tower became the focal point of the town. Brecon's ability to erect and sustain two large churches is evidence of the patronage of the lords of Brycheiniog, who were, from the time of the de Breos family in the twelfth century, to that of the dukes of Buckingham in the early sixteenth century, among the most powerful families in the kingdom.

The Acts of 'Union' of the sixteenth century not only recognized Brecon as the county town of the newly-formed Breconshire, but also as the headquarters of one of the circuits of the Courts of Great Session. It was therefore the capital of one of the four 'quarters' of Wales. In addition, it was situated at the junction of the south's main east-west road and its main north-south road, and consequently there was a considerable demand for the services of its hoteliers and ostlers.

Following the industrialization of districts beyond the Brecon Beacons, Brecon became the home of the middle class which came into being because of the growth of ironworks such as Dowlais and Cyfarthfa, for it was the bankers and lawyers of Brecon who serviced the iron industry. Furthermore, Brecon was the first market town in Wales to have a canal link (1800), a crucial element in the growth of its economy.

At least five-hundred architectural features in Brecon are listed in the conservation register, far more than in any other Welsh market town. According to David Verey, author of *The Shell Guide to Mid Wales* (1950), the staircases of its major town houses are its greatest glory; he lists a dozen houses, but acknowledges that there are scores of others, and he emphasizes that they are proof that Brecon was once replete with remarkably skilful carpenters and joiners.

It is only rarely, if at all, that opportunities arise to appreciate these splendours, and some effort also has to be made to visit another of the attractions of Brecon – the chapel of Christ College, the only friary chapel in Wales which is still in use.

Although much renovated in the 1860s, the chapel is still, in its essentials, the place of worship used by the Black Friars (the Dominicans) in the fourteenth century. The Memorial College (1869), named to commemorate the Dissenters persecuted following the Restoration of the Stuart monarchy in 1660, has had a less fortunate fate. It is now a block of flats. The barracks houses the museum of the South Wales Borderers Regiment, and there are more military buildings at Dering Lines. Indeed, a visitor to Brecon may get the impression that it is as much a garrison town now as it was in the era of Bernard de Neufmarché. Brecon's most confidently solid building is the one-time County Hall (now the Brecknock Museum), the finest neo-Grecian building in Wales since the demolition of the Town Hall at Bridgend in 1971.

The most delightful place in Brecon is the canal basin, where the imaginative can conjure up in their minds the barges which brought new life to the town in 1800. The best spur to such imaginings is to read the forthcoming English translation of Janet Davies's novel, *Amser i Geisio*.

In the north-east, there is a wealth of large Iron Age hillforts such as Dinorben, Ffridd Faldwyn and Moel Hiraddug, but they are rare in the south-west. That region has scores of forts and cliff castles hardly more than half a hectare in extent. Consequently, the notion arose that the Demetae, the Iron Age inhabitants of the south-west, lived peacefully in small homesteads. It was argued that they were not subject to centralizing oppressive forces – for there can be hardly anything more oppressive than a governing class with the authority to force others to undertake the back-breaking work of building hillforts.

In the territory which would later be Deheubarth, there are

Spectators at the unveiling of the memorial to Gwynfor Evans at Garn Goch

only about a dozen hillforts more than two and a half hectares in extent, but among them is the largest hillfort in Wales – Garn Goch near Llangadog. The larger of the Garn Goch hillforts is eleven hectares in extent, and it is adjoined by a round four-hectare fort. The existence of Garn Goch raises doubts about the notion that the Demetae lacked any form of central authority. Furthermore, the recent discovery that the largest auxiliary fort built by the Romans in Wales was sited near Dinefwr challenges the belief that the invaders expected very little opposition from a tribe so lacking in centralized power as it was believed was the case with the Demetae.

It is worth walking the eight hundred metres around the larger of the Garn Goch forts in order to examine the eight openings, all of which have upright stone slabs on both sides, slabs which originally, no doubt, sustained the heavy gates across the openings. The scale of the stone ramparts is especially impressive, particularly on the western side, where they are twenty-five metres across and are, in places, up to seven metres high. As the interior of the fort is covered with bracken, it is difficult to trace anything there. However, a Bronze Age cairn was found near the northern rampart, one example, among many, of a later age – the Iron Age in this case – making use of the locations chosen by an earlier one.

The chief glories of Garn Goch are the vistas it provides. The splendours of the valleys of the Tywi and the Sawdde are at its feet, and above it rises the Black Mountain, now part of the Fforest Fawr Geopark.

Gwynfor Evans's ashes were scattered at Garn Goch, and near the ramparts a monolith was raised to commemorate him. The hillfort – the symbol, perhaps of the sovereignty of the Demetian people – was his favourite place; the hillfort's significance and the splendid views it offers inspired Gwynfor's tireless efforts – the dedication which made him twentieth-century Wales's greatest patriot.

He also delighted in another even more splendidly located monument – Carreg Cennen Castle, located about five kilometres south of Garn Goch. There are Welsh castles located at considerably higher elevations, but, as Carreg Cennen stands on a limestone ridge which rises almost 100 metres above the bed of the River Cennen, it is the most dramatically sited of all the castles of Wales.

As the ridge is so conspicuous, it is hardly surprising that there is evidence that the people of the Iron Age, as well as the Romans, made use of it. Carreg Cennen became the caput of Cennen, the southernmost of the three commotes of Cantref Bychan. The descendants of the Lord Rhys had a castle there by the early thirteenth century. Thus, Carreg Cennen was originally a Welsh castle, although nothing that might have been commissioned by members of the House of Dinefwr can be seen there now. What is visible is work undertaken between the Conquest and 1322 for John Giffard, who was granted the castle by Edward I in 1283.

In addition to its location, the castle has other appealing features, including the complex passage between the outer and inner wards, and the tunnel which leads to a natural cave in the limestone cliff. The size of the inner ward is striking, as is the size of the domestic buildings within it; as so remote a stronghold would have been home only to a castellan, the scale of those buildings is surprising. It is highly unlikely that John Giffard, who had a more accessible castle at Llandovery, would have spent much time there, and it is certain that the castle was never the residence of his successors, the Despenser and the Lancaster families.

When Henry Bolingbroke, duke of Lancaster, seized the English throne in 1399, Carreg Cennen became a royal castle. It was targeted by Owain Glyn Dŵr; indeed, the era of the Glyn Dŵr Rising was the only exciting era in the castle's history. It was under siege in 1403, when its castellan, John Skydmore, wrote a letter which is one of the most revealing documents relating to the Rising. Glyn Dŵr seized the castle, and, after the failure of the Rising, considerable sums were spent on its renovation. The castle was seized again in 1461, this time by the Yorkists, and efforts were made to demolish it. Sufficient remained standing for it to be an object of delight to the early Romantic artists; J. M. W. Turner painted a picture of it in 1798. In 1804, it became part of the estate of the Campbell family, earls of Cawdor. In the 1970s, the castle farm was sold to its tenant and through some strange confusion, the castle was included in the sale. It is worth going to the farm's delightful café to hear the castle's owner, Bernard Llewelyn, tell the story.

It is necessary to go to Carmarthen to appreciate the merits of Llandeilo. The view from the bridge over the Tywi at Carmarthen towards the road that climbs the hill surmounted by the County Council offices is disappointing; the view from the bridge over the Tywi at Llandeilo towards the road that climbs the hill surmounted by the tower of St Teilo's Church is enchanting. The tower dates from the late fifteenth century, but most of the rest of the church is the result of mid-nineteenth-century rebuilding work. There was undoubtedly a church at Llandeilo in the sixth century, for all the later evidence stresses that it was the centre of the *clas* of St Teilo. By the thirteenth century, there were twenty-five parish churches in Wales dedicated to Teilo, but the one in the Tywi Valley was the only Llandeilo Fawr (Great Llandeilo). Teilo was probably buried there, but, to satisfy the ambitions of Llandaff, which claimed him as a founder, and to please Penally, his birthplace, providence arranged that there should be three Teilo corpses.

The chief attraction of the church is the exhibition opened in February 2006, an exhibition which seeks to explain the significance of *Llyfr Teilo*, also known as the Lichfield Gospels or the Book of St Chad. The book, written in the ninth century,

has been kept at St Chad's Cathedral, Lichfield, since *c.*1000, but it is believed that its original home was Llandeilo, where it was probably compiled. It consists of the Latin text of the gospels of Mathew and Mark and part of that of Luke. (It is believed that there was a second volume containing the rest of the gospels, a volume which disappeared from Lichfield in the seventeenth century.) It contains 236 pages, eight of which are illuminated – the portraits of Mark and Luke are particularly striking. Within it is a note stating that it was a gift to God on the altar of St Teilo, a statement which may apply to Llandaff. However, on the margins of some of the pages there are references to land in the vicinity of Llandeilo – Meddyfnych (Llandybïe), for example – which tend to confirm the view that it was intended for the altar at Llandeilo Fawr, not for that at Llandaff. The marginal notes are the book's greatest fascination, for they are the earliest surviving examples of written Welsh.

Llandeilo has a special charm. The view of the Tywi Valley from Crescent Road is magnificent, but the town's chief characteristic is the profusion of its luxury shops. The days when its drapers' windows displayed old-fashioned corsets have long gone. The boutique is now dominant. With its wine bars, its fine hotels and its delicatessens, Llandeilo mirrors the change that has overtaken the inhabitants of the Tywi Valley, both native and incoming.

Its closeness to Dinefwr is one of the main virtues of Llandeilo. Although there is no surviving reference to Dinefwr before the 1130s, the fact that the Romans chose it as the location of their largest fort in the south-west proves that its potential as the site of a stronghold has long been appreciated. It is probable that Dinefwr was the chief centre of the kingdom of Ystrad Tywi, a kingdom which probably came into existence during Teilo's lifetime.

From the 1130s onwards, there are increasing references to the status of Dinefwr. The Welsh Triads stress the threefold character of Welsh kingship, with Aberffraw the symbol of the sovereignty of Gwynedd, Mathrafal of that of Powys and Dinefwr of that of Deheubarth. The status of Dinefwr is clearly proclaimed in a letter from Llywelyn ap Iorwerth to Henry III, in which Llywelyn describes the place as *caput Suthwallie*. Very little is visible above ground at Aberffraw and Mathrafal, but the ridge at Dinefwr is crowned by a substantial castle built for the rulers of Deheubarth in the twelfth and thirteenth centuries. In consequence, Dinefwr is the only place where Welsh sovereignty can be seen embodied in stone.

The most prominent feature of the castle is the round keep built either for the Lord Rhys's son, Rhys Gryg (d. 1234) or for his grandson, Rhys Mechyll (d. 1244). Rhys Mechyll's grandson, Rhys Wyndod, was obliged to yield Dinefwr to the English king in 1277, and, over the following centuries, the castle fell into ruin. Gruffudd ap Nicolas leased Dinefwr in 1440, and his descendants, the Rhys or Rice family – a family which received the title Baron Dynevor in 1780 – owned the place until the 1980s. Through the marriage of the great-grandson of Rhys ap Nicolas, Gruffudd ap Rhys, to the heiress of Abermarlais, their descendants could claim that their ancestry went back to the Lord Rhys, a factor which has caused some Welsh royalists to claim that the Rhys family of Dinefwr is the lost royal family of Wales.

A belvedere was built on the top of the keep *c.*1660, but little was done to save the structure from total ruin. It is probably to Dinefwr Castle that John Dyer (1699–1757) was referring in the lines in his poem 'Grongar Hill', the earliest topographical poem in the English language:

> And ever and anon there falls
> Huge heaps of hoary moulder'd walls.

Cadw came to the rescue in the 1990s and, by now, Dinefwr is a model of careful conservation.

There was a Welsh borough on the slopes near the castle, but it fell into decline following the establishment of an English borough – Newton – about half a kilometre to the north. That borough has also disappeared, but Newton House, a building first erected in the later Middle Ages, still stands. It is owned by the National Trust and contains an interesting museum that recalls the history of Dinefwr. The exhibition pays particular attention to Dinefwr's chief glory, the park – landscaped in the eighteenth century – with its white cattle, which, it was claimed, were brought from the underworld by the Lady of Llyn y Fan Fach.

Cardigan, states *Brut y Tywysogyon* in its entry for the year 1200, is 'the key to all Wales'. The comment is difficult to fathom, for Cardigan is hardly a location of enormous strategic importance. Perhaps the chronicler was overstressing its significance in order to express his anger towards Maelgwn ap Rhys, who had sold the favourite home of his father, the Lord Rhys, to King John for a pittance.

The first reference to the area comes in the context of Roger de Montgomery's attack upon Powys, Ceredigion and Dyfed in 1093. He commissioned the building of a castle near the Teifi estuary, a stronghold which was abandoned after 1110 when a new castle was built for Gilbert de Clare above the chief crossing of the river. That castle was seized and destroyed by the Lord

Rhys in 1165, but, five years later, the castle was rebuilt, of stone and mortar as the *Brut* put it – the first reference to a masonry castle in Wales. It was the location of the literary and musical contests held under the patronage of the Lord Rhys at Christmas 1176, a festival generally considered to be the earliest national eisteddfod of which a record has survived.

In the early decades of the thirteenth century, Cardigan Castle was frequently held by Llywelyn ap Iorwerth, but, after his death in 1240, it came permanently into the possession of the English crown. Around it, the original county of Cardigan coalesced, a county which, after the 1280s, came to consist of the entire ancient kingdom of Ceredigion. The castle was revamped under Henry III, and what can be seen there today are essentially the ruins of what existed in the 1240s.

In 1940, after centuries of neglect, the castle came into the possession of Barbara Wood, who took up residence in a house built in 1827 adjoining the north tower. Very few people were allowed entry to the castle, and as its owner aged (she was born in 1918), the structure became increasingly unstable. The National Eisteddfod was held at Cardigan in 1976, and the fact that no one attending it was allowed to visit the place where the Lord Rhys had presided over a national gathering eight-hundred years earlier was the cause of much resentment. Part of the castle's curtain walls collapsed into the roadway and the authorities had to erect scaffolding to protect the traffic. The inhabitants of Cardigan gave vent to increasing anger, and the local paper, the *Tivy-side* [sic] *Advertiser*, launched a vigorous campaign. On 14 February 2003, Ceredigion Council gained possession of the castle through compulsory purchase. (The price was rumoured to be £250,000.) In 2004, the castle reached the final round of the BBC's *Restoration* competition, and it was estimated that £3.5 million needed to be spent on the place. It is therefore hardly surprising that the authors of the Carmarthenshire and Ceredigion volume

Dydd Sadwrn Barlys (the last Saturday in April) at Cardigan

Members of the Welsh Folk Dancing Society performing on the bank of the Teifi

(2006) in *The Buildings of Wales* series expressed the opinion that Ceredigion Council's purchase was a remarkably courageous venture.

Centuries have passed since the castle was central to the life of the town. Over the greater part of those years, the most important factor in the history of Cardigan was its location on the Teifi estuary. By the early nineteenth century, both banks of the river were lined with warehouses. In 1816, three-hundred ships were registered at the port, more than in any other port of Wales apart from Milford Haven. By the end of the century, however, the river was silting up and the town had been linked with the railway network through *Y Cardi Bach* (1885). The port went into rapid decline and now only pleasure boats sail in the estuary.

Before the prosperity waned, Cardigan acquired two of its most interesting buildings, the Market Hall and the Town Hall. The ground floor of the Town Hall, with its squat round pillars sustaining pointed arches, looks like something that has wandered from a medieval cellar; its upper floor, with its panelled roof, is also appealing. The façade of the Town Hall, a building inspired by the ideas of John Ruskin, includes bands of Cardigan brick. (The area was one of a great many places in Wales in which brick was produced, a building material that can be seen everywhere in the town centre.) For a time, part of the hall was home to the Cardigan Grammar School, the only school established during the Protectorate which survived the Stuart Restoration.

Explorers of Cardigan should visit St Mary's Church, which was established as a Benedictine priory *c.*1100. However, nothing survives of the original building. From the thirteenth century onwards, the priory profited from its effigy of the Virgin Mary with her candle which burned without consuming its wax, profits which financed the rebuilding of the church in the fifteenth century; only a few features of that church survived further rebuilding in the eighteenth century. (The candle and the cult of the Virgin Mary have found a home in Cardigan's Roman Catholic church, Our Lady of the Taper, the location of Wales's National Marian Shrine.) The conventual buildings of the priory were adapted as a house following the dissolution of the monasteries, a building which was the home of Katherine Philipps, 'the matchless Orinda'. In 1788, it was rebuilt in accordance with plans by John Nash, but that building was swallowed by Cardigan's Memorial Hospital in 1922, 'a sad story', state the authors of the volume on the buildings of Carmarthenshire and Ceredigion of 'civic zeal overwhelming architecture'.

Foel Drygarn is Wales's best example of a palimpsest. The term originally meant a parchment on which new writing had been imposed upon a previous text. By now, it tends to mean a place on which a newer generation has made its mark where an earlier generation had left its mark. This is a perfect description of Foel Drygarn.

Foel Drygarn is located about two kilometres west of Crymych; a path rises about 120 metres from the road to a summit crowned by a wealth of monuments. The summit is 363 metres above sea level, and the splendid views it offers extend to Foel Cwmcerwyn, the highest point of the Preseli Hills (536 metres). Those enjoying the vista will be immediately aware that everything visible from the hilltop is a palimpsest. That is probably true of any landscape, but the realization that landscapes have been created by people placing layer upon layer of their labour on the land over many millennia is more apparent in the Preseli Hills than almost anywhere else.

The most obvious features of Foel Drygarn are the three cairns which stand in a row on its summit. Three metres high, they are the tallest cairns in Wales apart from the astonishing Gop near Trelawnyd in Flintshire. They were erected *c*.1500 BC. About a

thousand years later, they were surrounded by a three-hectare enclosure defended by stone ramparts. Within the two main enclosures are the remains of a hundred and forty platforms – areas that have been levelled in order that dwellings may be built upon them – and other platforms lie beyond their confines. The hillfort had inhabitants from the Iron Age until the Roman era, although it is doubtful whether every platform represents the foundations of a house occupied throughout that period. The most fascinating feature of Foel Drygarn is the evidence it offers of the apparent desire of Iron Age people to live in the vicinity of Bronze Age graves. Did they feel that those graves – the graves of their ancestors, perhaps – somehow sanctified this part of the Preseli Hills?

It is a walk of about two kilometres from Foel Drygarn to Carn Menyn or Carn Meini, a place which perhaps offers a key to one of the great mysteries of prehistory. Where did the so-called bluestones of Stonehenge originate? If the Preseli Hills were the source, the place must have been held in great reverence in order to induce the builders of Stonehenge to transport four-ton stones a distance of 385 kilometres to Salisbury Plain. It has been suggested that some of the bluestones came from Carn Meini,

and it is claimed that they were taken from there in the middle of the third century BC, a supposition that has gained some credence from the recent research of Geoffrey Wainwright, a Welshmen who became the chief archaeologist of English Heritage. Carn Meini is an exposure of igneous rock which has been riven by frost action into natural columns, some of which look similar to a few of the bluestones of Stonehenge. Geoffrey Wainwright maintains that Bronze Age peoples believed that the stones of Carn Meini – a place supposedly surrounded by health-giving wells – could cure the sick, and that it was their therapeutic power that caused them to be transported so far. Others – Professor Richard Atkinson, for example – have argued that the Preseli Hills were the highest summits seen by those who sailed to Ireland from the Severn Sea, and that, as a result, they came to have an aura of sanctity. How the stones were transported remains a mystery, for contemporary efforts using Bronze Age technology have ended in abject failure. It has to be admitted, however, that there are respected authorities who adhere to the notion that the bluestones, derived from various rock outcrops in north Pembrokeshire, arrived at Salisbury Plain as a result of glacier movement.

Carn Meini is only about two kilometres from the village of Mynachlog-ddu. From the path to the village Carn Gyfrwy and Craig Talfynydd are visible, both of which are worth a glance in order to appreciate the wall of hills that sustained the poet, Waldo

Williams, '*ym mhob annibyniaeth barn*' (in all independence of mind). These are the words quoted on his striking memorial on the road from the village to Glynsaithmaen, the location of one of the numerous clusters of menhirs in the vicinity of Mynachlog-ddu.

The most intriguing standing stone in the area is the gravestone in the cemetery of Bethel Baptist Chapel. It commemorates Thomas Rees, who dwelt at Carnabwth, a cabin reputedly built in one night. Twm Carnabwth is believed to be the first Rebecca – the leader of the attack on the Efailwen tollgate on 13 May 1839, an attack which was planned, tradition maintains, in the barn at Glynsaithmaen. There is no evidence that Twm played any further part in the Rebecca Riots. Although he lived until 1876, he is remembered only for his role on 13 May 1839 and for his epitaph – the most whimsical epitaph in Wales. It states:

> *Nid oes neb ond Duw yn gwybod*
> *Beth a ddigwydd mewn diwrnod.*
> *Wrth gyrchu bresych at fy nginio,*
> *Daeth angau i fy ngardd i'm taro.*

(Only God knows what can happen in a day. While harvesting cabbage for my dinner, death came to my garden and felled me.)

Gazing through the gaps between the upright stones that support the capstone of Pentre Ifan cromlech, when the sun is disappearing into the waters of Newport Bay, is a memorable experience. The view is magnificent, and the eye can feast on more remains of ancient times than anywhere else in Wales – the cairns on Mynydd Carningli, for example, or the Iron Age fort at Castell Mawr or the menhirs at Tafarn-y-bwlch.

But the wonder is Pentre Ifan itself. It is Wales's most recognizable monument, and the earliest to receive state protection. As its 16-ton capstone seems to float above the tapering uprights beneath it, it appears to defy the laws of gravity. It would be pleasing to think that its builders deliberately sought to create the elegance which would delight people five millennia later, but, in fact, the capstone and the five uprights which support it were originally buried under a pile of soil and stones which extended for thirty-six metres. That is now difficult to appreciate, but aerial photography shows that, when erected, the stones stood under an enormous covering which, over the ages, has been almost wholly eroded.

There are at least a hundred and fifty known *cromlechi* in Wales; it is likely that there were once many more. Most of them are near the sea, and, since they have similarities with structures in coastal locations from Portugal to Scotland, they are assumed to be the work of peoples who sailed the western sea-routes in the centuries between 4000 and 2500 BC. The most obvious part of Wales that pushes out into the sea is the south-west, and it is hardly surprising, therefore, that many of Wales's surviving *cromlechi* are located in the ancient kingdom of Dyfed.

To the archaeologist, the cromlech is a chambered tomb, but that is only half the story. Bodies were certainly placed in them, but that was only one aspect of their function. Part of the intention of their builders was to make their mark on the landscape, and to create a place where those dwelling in the vicinity of the monument could hold rituals in the presence of their ancestors. Bearing in mind the technology available to the builders, the raising of the Pentre Ifan capstone was an enormous task. Despite the fact that suitable stone was at hand, it is estimated that it would have been the work of at least a dozen men over several months using creepers as ropes and tree trunks as rollers. Such technology would later be improved and used in the building of classical temples and medieval cathedrals. The skills needed to create such structures prove that there is no basis to the proverb that necessity is the mother of invention. The true mother of invention is ritual.

It is worth walking the six kilometres from Pentre Ifan to visit another prehistoric monument – Castell Henllys. The path follows the boundary of the farm of Fachongle Isaf, where John Seymour wrote books which persuaded many discontented dwellers in the suburbs of England to resettle in rural Wales. It also passes one of the four residential centres of the Urdd, a stone building adapted in the early 1990s from the gatehouse of the demolished mansion of Pentre Ifan. It should be visited if only to admire its roof's splendid rafters.

Part of the path from Pentre Ifan to Castell Henllys follows the valley of Nant Duad, one of the tributaries of the River Nyfer. On a slope above the valley stands Henllys, a farmhouse built *c.*1850 near the site of the dwelling occupied by George Owen (d. 1613), the historian of Pembrokeshire and the first to describe the Pentre Ifan cromlech. Further up the slope stands Cwmglöyn; in about 1790, a local poet, Ioan Siencyn, wrote verses to the squire of Cwmglöyn, verses which, in the opinion of Saunders Lewis, were proof of the longevity of the tradition of Taliesin.

Taliesin's work opens a window on the Iron Age, and the best place in Britain to get to grips with that age is Castell Henllys. In the last centuries of the pre-Christian era, a fortified village was

The reconstituted Iron Age village at Castell Henllys

Nevern – vie for the accolade of Wales's finest example. There are only ten panels on the cross at Carew and the link between the shaft and the head is clumsy. The interlacing on the Llantwit Major cross is monotonous, and that is also true of the one at Penally. Thus, it can be stated with confidence that the community of Nevern has the most recognizable of all Welsh prehistoric monuments, Wales's most interesting Iron Age village, and Wales's finest Celtic cross. That is quite remarkable for a community that only contains 822 inhabitants.

built on a promontory above Nant Duad. In 1982, archaeological work began on the site and it was discovered that it contained the foundations of a number of round houses, some of which were then rebuilt using the same resources – timber, wattle, clay and reeds – as had been available to the original builders.

The rebuilding carries conviction, and the site was chosen by the BBC in 2001 to film the series *Surviving the Iron Age*. (The houses in the Celtic Village at St Fagans look equally convincing, but, as they were not built on foundations constructed over two-thousand years ago, they do not have the same degree of authenticity.) By now, a grain store and four houses – one of them having a diameter of twenty-six metres – have been reconstructed. Castell Henllys is well-known for its archaeological courses, and its Visitors' Centre has been much praised.

A visit to this delectable part of the world should end by following the Nyfer to the village of Nevern. There, in the burial ground of St Brynach's Church, stands a splendid Celtic cross. It was carved *c.*1030 and has over twenty panels of stone interlacing, almost all of them with their own distinct patterns. Four Celtic crosses – at Carew, Llantwit Major, Penally and

A hundred places are discussed in this book. If only five were under discussion, they would be St Davids, Blaenavon, Portmeirion, St Fagans and a toss up between Pont Cysyllte and Newport's Transporter Bridge.

The journey to St Davids along the A487 from Fishguard and through Croes-goch can seem to be a journey to the end of the Earth; indeed, that was the view of the authors of the classical world for – to quote Ptolemy, AD *c.*150 – the road leads to Octopitarum Promontorium (the Promontory of the Eight Perils).

Although St Davids strikes modern travellers as being remote, it was, in the sixth century, much frequented by those who sailed the western sea-routes. Indeed, with a dynasty of Irish origins then in power in Dyfed, the Irish language may well have been as audible as the Welsh language on the banks of the River Alun, the stream which flows into the sea at Porthclais. The most sheltered part of the Alun Valley is Vallis Rosina (the Vale of the Little Swamp), and it was probably there, *c.*550, that David established a monastery which followed more ascetic rules than those associated with earlier pioneers such as Dyfrig and Illtud.

In David's era, Vallis Rosina probably had a small church and a number of monk's cells, all in the monastic tradition that had been developed by the Eastern Church. Nothing of David's settlement remains, and the only objects surviving from the early centuries are a few pieces of carved stone. Rhygyfarch of Llanbadarn compiled a life of David *c.*1090; most of the content of the *Vita* was repeated in a manuscript purporting to be the work of Giraldus Cambrensis and further material was gathered by the Llanddewi anchorite in 1346. It is Rhygyfarch who describes David's best known miracle – the hill rising beneath his feet at Llanddewi Brefi, although it is difficult to think of a more uncalled-for miracle in view of Ceredigion's multiplicity of hills. By 1300, about sixty of Wales's parish churches had been

dedicated to St David, but the locations of those churches offer very doubtful evidence of the precise places which experienced the power of his ministry.

Nevertheless, the numerous dedications, the extensiveness of the diocese of St Davids and the failure of all efforts to move the cathedral to a more accessible place suggest that the saint's fame was based on traditions relating to a figure remarkable for his holiness. He was a hero to the Normans as well as to the Welsh, and it was Bernard, (d. 1148), the first Norman bishop of St Davids, who initiated the campaign to elevate the diocese to an archbishopric, a campaign amongst the most patriotic in the history of Wales. Bernard also commissioned a new cathedral at St Davids, a building which was demolished in 1182, when the construction of most of what can now be seen in Vallis Rosina was begun. Gifts offered by pilgrims probably helped to finance the construction work, gifts that increased following the Pope's

Sculpture at the Bishop's Palace, St Davids

155

recognition that the spiritual benefits of two visits to St Davids equalled those conferred by one visit to Rome. As the Latin verse put it: *Roma semel quantum / Bis dat Menevia tantum.*

It is the bogginess of Vallis Rosina which explains the oddest feature of the late twelfth-century building – the fact that the Romanesque pillars of the nave seem to be leaning westwards, as if the whole structure was about to slide down the Alun Valley. The nave has a wooden ceiling, and therefore lacks one of the finest features of many English cathedrals – stone vaults that seem to rise heavenwards. But the ceiling has its glories; with its bosses and its 144 panels gorgeously carved in bog oak in the early sixteenth century, it is a masterpiece of 'almost Arab sumptuousness'. One unexpected feature of St Davids is the *pulpidum*, which virtually closes the nave off from the crossing. That makes the interior of the building look more like cathedral interiors in Spain than in England or France, where there is almost always an uninterrupted vista from the west door through to the high altar. Visitors should see the splendid bishop's throne (the *cathedra* which gives a cathedral its name), the tomb which it is claimed is that of the Lord Rhys, and the statue of Giraldus Cambrensis with the mitre he never received at his feet.

The Bishop's Palace is almost as attractive as the cathedral.

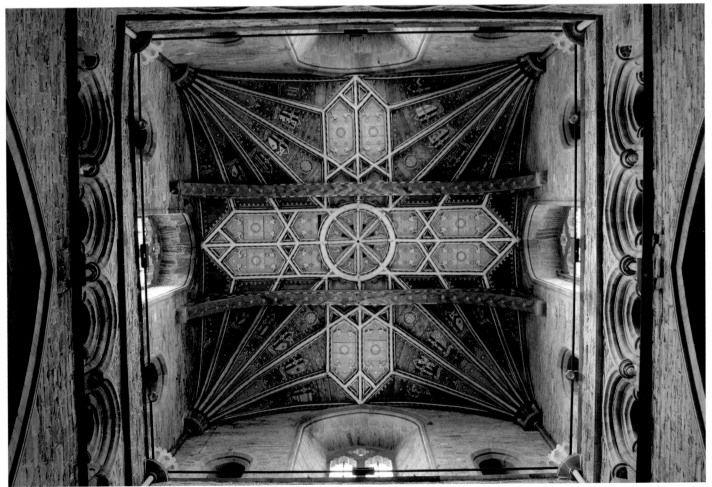

The wooden vault of the cathedral crossing

After climbing the thirty-nine steps from the cathedral to Porth y Tŵr, visitors have the curious sensation of being at the same level as the parapet of the cathedral tower. The walk through the town (a city since 1994) offers little of interest apart from Oriel y Parc, a splendid post-modern visitor centre built in 1999 and enlarged in 2007–8. But the surrounding area is replete with places of interest – chambered tombs, forts, medieval chapels, ancient farmhouses and the promontory of Penmaendewi. The visit should end where the story begins – in St Non's Chapel, where, according to tradition, David was born on an appallingly stormy night.

An effigy of c.1380 claimed to be that of the Lord Rhys (d. 1197)
The statue of the Virgin Mary at St Non's Well (right)

It was commissioned by Henry de Gower, bishop from 1328 to 1347. Its most prominent features are its arched parapets, an architectural subtlety visible in another of the residences of the bishops of St Davids – the palace at Lamphey. Such parapets can also be seen at Swansea Castle, the work, perhaps, of the builders Gower was employing in Swansea in 1332 at the Hospital of the Blessed David. The rose window of the palace's Great Hall is especially memorable. The hall, which is 36 metres in length, is the second longest to be built in medieval Wales. (That at Conwy Castle, 38 metres in length, is the longest.) As part of his campaign to move the cathedral to Carmarthen, William Barlow, bishop from 1536 to 1548, sold the lead of parts of the palace roof, and the building lay desolate until the Ministry of Works came to the rescue in 1932.

In the vicinity of St Davids

A measuring rod of the size of a medieval town was the number of parishes it contained. Shrewsbury had five, but virtually all the towns of Wales had only one, and some important places – Denbigh, Ruthin and Caernarfon, for example – had to be content with mere chapels-of-ease. There were two parishes in medieval Cardiff and three in Haverfordwest – St Mary's, St Martin's and St Thomas's. A parish was an area sufficiently populated and wealthy to maintain a church and a priest. As there were more parishes in Haverfordwest than in any other medieval Welsh town, it could be considered to be the largest town in the Wales of the Middle Ages, but the records do not wholly confirm the supposition. In 1281, there were 423 burgages or urban plots in Cardiff and 360 in Haverfordwest. If each burgage were occupied by a resident family – and that is a big if – Cardiff in 1281 was larger than Haverfordwest. The following centuries

were kinder to Haverfordwest than to Cardiff, and, by the end of the Middle Ages, the contest to be the largest town in Wales was between Haverfordwest and Carmarthen. Both towns attained county status, but Haverfordwest was the only Welsh town to have an MP all to itself, and the only town in the territories of the English crown to have its own lord lieutenant.

Its location was the key to Haverfordwest's prosperity. The town stands at the lowest point at which the Western Cleddau can be forded; it was the ford which was crossed by *hæfer* (goats) which gave the place its name; west was added to avoid confusion with Hereford. The Western Cleddau is navigable up to Haverfordwest, and so great was the trade on the river that numerous warehouses were built along Quay Street. (A picture by the Brothers Buck [1744] gives the impression that the river at Haverfordwest was as busy as the Pool of London.)

The remains of Haverfordwest's Augustinian Priory

Haverfordwest was the chief centre of the colony of Flemings planted in the commote of Rhos in the early twelfth century. Although the lordship of Haverfordwest was held to be answerable to the authority of the *comitatus* which had its headquarters at Pembroke, its more central position allowed it to become a larger town than Pembroke, and to be the natural choice as Pembrokeshire's county town when that county was fully recognized in 1536.

A visit to Haverfordwest should start with the castle. A very steep hill leads to it; indeed, the historian R. T. Jenkins considered that Bangor, compared with Haverfordwest, hardly had any hills at all. Haverfordwest was first built for Tancred, one of the leaders of the Flemings, but what is now visible dates in the main from the last decades of the thirteenth century. Owain Glyn

Dŵr attacked the castle in 1405 and it changed hands several times during the seventeenth-century Civil Wars; after those wars, it was partially demolished. Only a shell remains today, but, because of its elevated site, it can be seen from all parts of the town. A gaol was built in the outer ward in 1790; between 1808 and 1866 part of the gaol was used as a mental hospital, the only one in Wales at the time – a matter of gratification in view of the dreadful treatment meted out to the patients. It became the Pembrokeshire Record Office, but that will soon be located elsewhere.

The hill which faces the one on which the castle stands is crowned by St Thomas's Church. The dedication is interesting, for the Thomas is not the apostle; he is St Thomas Becket, a martyr whose dedications are rare in Wales. St Martin's Church,

The remains of Haverfordwest Castle

A street corner at Haverfordwest, with St Mary's Church in the background

erected in 1774. With its stucco walls gleaming with paint and the elegant curve of its chief façade, it is a building to enjoy – although R. T. Jenkins confessed that he fled from it in terror. Tabernacle was originally a Calvinistic Methodist chapel, but, after much dispute, its members joined the Congregationalists. Haverfordwest played a prominent role in the Methodist Revival; John Wesley visited the town on fourteen occasions and Howel Harris preached at the limekilns of Prendergast. Perhaps the most interesting revivalist linked with Haverfordwest was John Gambold (1711–71), a prominent adherent of the Moravian Brethren in the Britain of his day. (There was a Moravian chapel in Haverfordwest until 1961, the last to survive in Wales.) Gambold, a native of Puncheston, wrote a number of Welsh-language hymns, but, according to David Mathias, a Pembrokeshire man who was a Moravian missionary in Caernarfonshire, they failed to receive acceptance there because the high standard of Gambold's Welsh meant they were useless in the north.

The tower of St Martin's Church, Haverfordwest

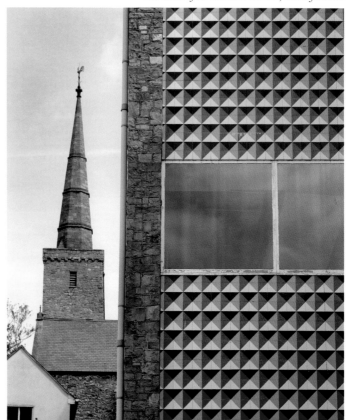

whose slender tower is one of the landmarks of the town, also has a hilltop site. The finest of Haverfordwest's churches is St Mary's, which contains some of Wales's best examples of early Gothic. Among its many interesting features is the tomb of John Philipps (d. 1764) of Picton Castle, patron of Griffith Jones, Llanddowror.

The town's Dominican friary, founded in 1246, stood near St Mary's Church, but nothing of it has survived. The Augustinian priory has proved more resilient. It can be seen on the west bank of the Western Cleddau under the shadow of the bulky offices built for the Pembrokeshire County Council in 1999. The priory was founded *c.*1210, and following its dissolution in 1536, it was, for centuries, a quarry for the inhabitants of Haverfordwest. Substantial parts of the church still stand, and, following work by Cadw in the 1980s, the ruins have been made safe and visitors can appreciate the layout of the cloister and its surrounding rooms.

Haverfordwest is a town of chapels as well as churches. The most splendid of them, and possibly the most striking chapel in Wales, is Tabernacle, the revamping in 1874 of a building first

Pembroke Castle was the only one in the south-west that was never seriously threatened by Welsh forces – the key to the fact that invaders held unbroken authority in southern Dyfed from the 1090s onwards. In 1093, Roger de Montgomery, earl of Shrewsbury, swept through Powys, Ceredigion and Dyfed. A palisade of stakes and turf was erected across a promontory that pushes out into one of the backwaters of the Milford Haven Waterway; it was commissioned by Arnulf, the son of Roger, and behind it the most powerful stronghold of the south-west was built.

Following a revolt in 1098, the lands of the Montgomery family were confiscated and Pembroke eventually came into the possession Gilbert de Clare (d. 1148). It was from Pembroke that Gilbert's son, Richard ('Strongbow', d. 1176) sailed to Ireland with his Cambro-Norman force, there to open a sad chapter in the history of the Irish. Pembroke was held by the Clares and their descendants, the Marshal, Valence and Hastings families, until the late fourteenth century.

The chief glory of Pembroke – the round keep of the castle – belongs to the era of William Marshal, who held the lordship from 1186 until 1219. Standing 23 metres in height, with a diameter of 15 metres, it is the largest round keep to be built in Britain in the early thirteenth century, when such keeps represented the most fashionable form of military architecture. It was probably William Marshal who also arranged for the borough of Pembroke to be surrounded by walls. The town was one long street with no side streets, and that is precisely what may be discerned within the surviving walls today.

William Marshal's successors commissioned further building work at the castle – the Great Gatehouse, for example, built when William de Valence was earl of Pembroke (1247–96), and the Great Hall, erected for Aylmer de Valence (earl, 1296–1324). The Great Hall provides access to a cave beneath the castle which has yielded evidence of the Mesolithic Age. Following the extinction of the Hastings family in 1389, the lordship was granted to a series of relations of the English king. In 1452, it came into the possession of Jasper Tudor, half-brother of Henry VI, and it was in Pembroke Castle in 1457 that Jasper's nephew, Henry Tudor (Henry VII), was born. His birthplace, it is claimed, was a room in the tower immediately west of the Great Gatehouse, where waxwork figures portray the birth. (As Pembroke Castle is the property of the Philipps family of Picton Castle, interpretive material there has a flamboyance which is absent from monuments under the direct care of Cadw.)

The townspeople of Pembroke supported Parliament in the first of the seventeenth-century Civil Wars, and the Crown in the second. Cromwell himself led the seven-week siege of the castle in 1648, a siege which was followed by attempts to make the building militarily unusable. Although it had a long history as a stronghold, the town did not enjoy great prosperity; Haverfordwest became the seat of county government and Pembroke was replaced as a port of significance by Tenby.

The development which gave new life to the area was the decision of the Admiralty in 1810 to establish a naval shipyard at Pater, three kilometres west of Pembroke. The decision led to the first town in Wales to be built under government auspices since the activities of Edward I in the late thirteenth century. The work of erecting a wall around a 33-hectare yard began in 1814, the year the first ship was built at Pater – or Pembroke Dock as it came to be known. The venture was beneficial to Pembroke itself, and it is significant that houses of the early nineteenth century dominate the original town's centre. As the decades passed, the new Pembroke outgrew the old. By the mid nineteenth century, Pembroke Dock had twice the inhabitants of Pembroke.

The Clock House, Pembroke

A street in Pembroke Dock

unemployment there was far higher than in most of the towns of the south Wales coalfield, the places generally considered to have been the main victims of the depression of the inter-war years. New jobs came to the town during the Second World War, but the war also brought further suffering. Fires caused by the bombing in 1940 lasted for eighteen days, the longest-lasting fire in Britain since the Great Fire of London in 1666.

Since the Second World War, the fortunes of Pembroke Dock have fluctuated. The Royal Air Force came and went, the same has been true of phone centres, but the place is home to the car ferry linking Britain to the southern parts of the Irish Republic. The town has also been important in Welsh cultural life, for it was there, in 1949, that *Dock Leaves* was founded, the journal which became the mouthpiece of the second wave of Anglo-Welsh literature which was such a significant factor in the life of Wales in the second half of the twentieth century.

Payday, 1907

Pembroke Dock is quite unlike any other town which came into existence in nineteenth-century Wales. The grid of its streets is more rigid than in any other place in Wales, and the forts that defend the yard, in particular the Defensible Barracks (1842–5), create a townscape that has no parallel. The intention was to build wooden sailing ships for the British navy, copper-bottomed by copper sheeting from Swansea, but, in the later nineteenth century, with the Admiralty demanding iron ships powered by steam, Pembroke Dock – a place far from iron production and coalmining – became increasingly redundant as a shipbuilding centre.

A total of 280 ships were built there, among them some of the largest wooden ships of the day. The yard made virtually no contribution to the ships which proved their worth during the First World War; it was closed in 1926. When *The Local Unemployment Index* was first published in 1928, unemployment among the adult insured males of Pembroke Dock was 38.1 per cent. It rose to 58.3 per cent in November 1932, when

For the Pope, the place to which to retreat is Castel Gandolfo, some 24 kilometres from the Vatican. The bishops of St Davids had to travel further, for their Castel Gandolfo – Lamphey – was at least 50 kilometres from the Bishop's Palace adjoining the cathedral. It was doubtless a delight to leave the windy promontory of Pebidiog for a sheltered place in the pleasant land of southern Dyfed. Lamphey has a special tranquillity, and wandering there at dusk, when the medieval walls throw long shadows over Cadw's well-kept lawns, is a memorable experience.

It is not known when Lamphey came into the possession of the bishops of St Davids but it was certainly part of the estates of the successors of St David long before the coming of the Normans. Legend links St Tyfai, the patron saint of Lamphey's parish church, with his alleged uncle, Teilo, a native of Penally, and it is possible that Lamphey was one of the seven bishops' houses of Dyfed mentioned in early documents. In about 1212 Giraldus Cambrensis referred to the bishop's house at Lamphey, a building which is now perhaps represented by the ruin known as Old Hall, which may have been built for Geoffrey de Henlaw, bishop of St Davids from 1203 to 1214.

The building of the Western Hall, probably for Richard Carew (bishop, 1256–80), a relation of Giraldus Cambrensis, was a much more ambitious project. It contained an extensive first floor hall, with an outside stairway and basement storage rooms. It was there, no doubt, that Bishop Carew entertained his guests. The hall had plastered walls, the plaster decorated with paintings of flowers – a rare feature in the thirteenth century.

It was a later bishop, Thomas de Gower (bishop, 1328–47), who was responsible for Lamphey's finest building – the hall which is adorned with arched parapets of a pattern similar to, but showing less craftsmanship than the arched parapets at the Bishop's Palace at St Davids. Lamphey acquired a fifteenth-century chapel, the most appealing of all the buildings in this enchanting place. In the territories of the English kings, the later fifteenth century was the era of the Perpendicular Gothic style of architecture. Apart from the east window at Gresford, the splendidly complete tracery of the window in the chapel at Lamphey is Wales's best example of that style.

In 1546, the bishop of St Davids was obliged to yield Lamphey to Henry VIII, who granted it to Richard Devereux. Richard's son, Walter (d. 1576), the first earl of Essex, spent long periods there, as did Walter's son, Robert, who was executed in 1601 for rebelling against Elizabeth I. Thereafter, the palace deteriorated until it was taken into the care of the Office of Works in 1925. In about 1821, the 1,850-hectare Lamphey estate came into the possession of the Mathias family, who commissioned the building of Lamphey Court, one of the finest Greek Revival houses in Wales.

From Lamphey, it is only six kilometres to Manorbier, a journey worth making in order to visit what Giraldus Cambrensis described as 'the pleasantest place in Wales'. Manorbier Castle was originally built *c.*1110 as a motte-and-bailey structure for Odo de Barri, Giraldus's grandfather, and perhaps some of the castle's stone walls had already been erected by the time Giraldus was born there *c.*1146. The eastern curtain wall which glares down from a ridge is particularly impressive, and within the walls there is a house available to holidaymakers. (Apart from Ruthin Castle, Manorbier is the only place in Wales where visitors can spend a night within the walls of a medieval stronghold.) It is interesting to speculate what Manorbier would be like today if Thomas Phillipps (1792–1872) had fulfilled his ambition of placing a roof on the inner ward and placing beneath it his collection of sixty-thousand books and manuscripts – the Book of Aneurin among them. If Aberystwyth is considered a rather remote location for the National Library, what would be the reaction if it were at Manorbier? Before leaving the environs of the castle, visitors should see the medieval dovecote, the largest in Wales apart from that at Barry.

The village of Manorbier is very attractive. Virginia Woolf, who spent her childhood holidays there, thought it was a delightful place. Her biographer considered that it was in a wild and remote area, although, as Giraldus stressed, it was a heartland of arable agriculture, where people grew corn and ate bread. The village website is evidence of the village's vibrant social life and its occasional waspishness. A path from the village leads to the church, the earliest parts of which predate anything visible in the castle. The walk from the church to the promontory on which the King's Quoit cromlech stands is delectable. The promontory offers a fine view of the beach, where Giraldus's brothers made sandcastles; predictably, he used the sand to build churches and cathedrals.

The round tower, Manorbier Castle

There is grandeur in Llandudno, dignity in Aberaeron and charm in Morfa Nefyn, but there can be no doubt that Tenby is Wales's most attractive seaside resort. At least fifteen-hundred years ago, a small fort (*din bych*) was built on the promontory above Carmarthen Bay. That was the *addfwyn gaer* (the gentle fort) praised in 'Edmyg Dinbych', a poem included in the Book of Taliesin. The poem mentions the lord of the fort, Bleiddudd, a member of the Dyfed dynasty, and the cell in which *ysgrifen Brydain* (the writings of the Britons) were kept. It is evident that the place was in the mainstream of Welsh culture and sovereignty a millennium and a half ago. The Laws of Hywel Dda mention the rights of the *maer* of *Dynbyc*, and about two kilometres south-west of the fort lies Penally, the birthplace of

The fort (1868-70) on the summit of St Catherine's Island

St Teilo and the location of one of Wales's finest early Christian monuments.

The situation changed in the 1090s, when the *cantref* of Penfro came into the possession of Arnulf de Montgomery. The invaders could feel secure, largely because of the strength of their castle at Pembroke. The defences built in the rest of the *cantref* were slight. Arnulf's followers are believed to have built a timber and turf castle which destroyed all evidence of the fort praised by the ninth-century poet. A stone castle was erected in the later twelfth century, probably as a reaction to the attack of the Lord Rhys and his brothers in 1153.

Llywelyn ap Gruffudd led an attack on Tenby in 1260, and it is probably that attack which led to the decision to surround the borough with walls. About half the original walls still stand, and the townspeople take pride in the fact that they dwell in a walled town. In 1989, it is they who founded the Walled Towns' Friendship Circle, a society which by now has been joined by almost a hundred and fifty towns, twelve of them in Wales. Its logo is the Five-Gate Barbican, the most striking surviving part of Tenby's walls and a structure described by Tenby's best-known

son – Augustus John – as 'a piece of cheese gnawed by rats'.

Despite the need to defend the town against the Lord Rhys, Llywelyn ap Gruffudd and Owain Glyn Dŵr, Tenby was more Welsh in character than is often assumed. Its lively trade with the southern shore of the Severn Sea attracted a number of English immigrants, but Flemish immigration was slight in the *cantref* of Penfro, and it has been claimed that Welsh-language influences can still be discerned in the dialect of the southernmost parts of Pembrokeshire. By the later Middle Ages, the number of Welsh names among the town's merchants and officials was increasing rapidly; it was they, no doubt, who added the words *y pysgod* (of the fishes) to Dinbych, probably to avoid confusion with the other Dinbych (Denbigh). Giraldus Cambrensis drew attention to the wealth of fish in Tenby's coastal waters, and the eleven payments made between 1328 and 1431 to improve the town's quays indicate that the activities of the port were central to the borough's prosperity. It was from the port that Jasper Tudor and his fourteen-year-old nephew, Henry, sailed into exile in 1471,

after hiding, so the story goes, in a tunnel located beneath Boots the Chemists.

It is delightful to wander in search of evidence of medieval Tenby – the remains of the walls, the fifteenth-century Merchant's House and, above all, St Mary's Church, among the largest and finest of the parish churches of Wales. The wealth produced by the port in the later Middle Ages was responsible for the church's glories, in particular the fine roof of the nave and the dramatic steps that rise to the chancel. The building is rich in memorials, including that to Thomas White, who assisted the escape of Jasper and Henry; White's elaborate tomb is evidence of the reward he received following Henry's seizure of the English crown in 1485. The most interesting memorial is of a later date; it commemorates Robert Recorde (d. 1558), a native of Tenby who invented the equals sign (=), and was erected in 1908 on the 350th anniversary of his death.

Although what remains of medieval Tenby is memorable, the town's main appeal is the result of its growth as a seaside resort.

From the 1780s onwards, doctors waxed lyrical about the benefits of thalassotherapy – the health-giving advantages of bathing in salt water. As Tenby has four kilometres of shoreline bordered by clean sea water, it was obviously the place to go. In 1805, William Paxton settled in Tenby, where he financed the building of baths that offered indoor salt water. By his death in 1824, the old town was full of buildings in the sober style of the late eighteenth and early nineteenth centuries. On the whole, the medieval street pattern was maintained and the result is a higgledy-piggledy townscape rich in dignified unostentatious houses. Every corner offers views of the splendid beaches or of the islands of Caldey, St Margaret and St Catherine. As the inhabitants have discovered paint, the stucco buildings are cheerfully colourful. To the perceptive German writer, Peter Sager, Tenby is 'magically, coolly, Celtically Mediterranean', although it could also be seen as a rather rococo version of Aberaeron.

As the town and its surroundings are so attractive, Tenby has not suffered from the changes in the habits of holidaymakers that have undermined the prosperity of places like Rhyl. It benefits from the mild climate of southern Dyfed, and is a resort worth visiting at any time of the year, although perhaps it is best avoided on those occasions when it lives up to its reputation as the capital of hen and stag parties.

Most of the manuscripts of the Welsh Laws begin like this: 'Hywel the Good by the grace of God son of Cadell king of all Wales… summoned unto him six men from every commote in Wales… to the place known as y Tŷ Gwyn in Dyfed.' The introduction states that those summoned laboured for six weeks imposing order on the Law of Wales, and some manuscripts suggest that the completed text was taken to Rome to receive the blessing of the Pope. The choice of *y Tŷ Gwyn* (Whitland) as the location of the meeting was hardly surprising. Hywel Dda (d. 949) had inherited Seisyllwg (Ystrad Tywi and Ceredigion), the southern part of the kingdom of his grandfather, Rhodri Mawr (d. 878). By marrying the heiress of Llywarch ap Hyfaidd, the king of Dyfed, he had also gained possession of Dyfed. Whitland was on the border of Dyfed and Seisyllwg. Assuming that there were differences in legal practices between the one kingdom and the other, the choice of a place on the border to sort out those differences is wholly intelligible. The meeting was probably held in the 930s, and it is possible that there was a further meeting after 942, when Hywel's authority was extended to Powys and Gwynedd.

The Lawbooks that have survived belong to a period at least three centuries later than the age of Hywel Dda, and they are the only documents which link Hywel with Whitland. Nevertheless, the references to Whitland have inspired the creation of what is perhaps the finest memorial in Wales – the Hywel Dda Memorial Garden opened in 1984. It was designed by Peter Lord, and abounds with the work of artists in enamel, slate, glass and iron. It has six sections, each illustrating an aspect of the Law – the Law of Women, the Law of the Court, the Law of Ownership and so on. With its shady trees and its splendid interpretation centre, the garden is a place of enchantment.

The railway came to Whitland in 1854, and, by the end of the nineteenth century, the place was a junction of some importance.

Its good communications and its location at the heart of Wales's dairying country caused it to be home to one of the largest milk factories in Europe. By the 1960s, the factory dealt with over half a million litres of milk a day, the produce of more than three-thousand farms. Its closure in 1994 was a disastrous blow to the local economy.

From the Whitland on the banks of the River Taf, visitors should go to the Whitland on the banks of the River Gronw. There, a band of monks from Clairvaux in Burgundy, the most important daughter of the monastery at Cîteaux, the mother house of the Cistercian order, arrived *c*.1157, and founded the monastery of Domus Albus. By 1157, there were already four Cistercian monasteries in Wales – Neath, Basingwerk, Margam and Tintern – all of them founded under the patronage of Marcher Lords. Whitland may also have begun as an Anglo-Norman foundation, but as the Lord Rhys strengthened his

authority in the south-west, it was brought into the mainstream of Welsh life. As it came to have daughters at Strata Florida, Cwmhir and Strata Marcella, and granddaughters at Llantarnam, Llanllyr, Cymer, Aberconwy and Valle Crucis, it was the mother house of the Cistercian abbeys of *Pura Wallia*. Even after the area had been obliged to recognize the authority of Marcher Lords, the monks of Whitland retained their links with the native Welsh rulers. Indeed, *Cronica de Wallia*, which is believed to have been compiled at Whitland, is the most comprehensive source for the activities of the descendants of the Lord Rhys. In the centuries following its dissolution in 1536, the site fell into ruin, and now little more than the footings of the abbey church survive.

From Whitland, it is a mere eight kilometres to St Clears, where there was a small borough and a riverside port. The journey follows the much improved A40 (Wales should be grateful for the desire of the Irish to get to England.) The road passes Pwll-trap, a significant place in Welsh history, for it was there, after a few protests in 1839, that the real Rebecca Riots began.

The chief reason for visiting St Clears is to see the sole example of Romanesque architecture in Carmarthenshire – a twelfth-century arch that is part of the church of Mary Magdalen. From 1150 to 1414, the church was a priory of the order of Cluny, answerable to the monastery of St Martin-des-Champs in Paris. (That monastery is now the Musée National des Techniques and houses Foucault's Pendulum.) The carving on the arch is cruder than work of a rather earlier period at Chepstow and Llandaff, but there is something attractive about its robustness.

South-east of St Clears lies Trefenty, where two Welshmen were using a telescope to study the craters of the moon at the same time as Galileo was examining the moons of Jupiter. It is even a shorter walk to Llanddowror; on any list of a Welsh patriot's indispensable pilgrimages, the grave of Griffith Jones at St Teilo's Church, Llanddowror, must be close to the top.

Writing of Wales in 1586, William Camden described Carmarthen as 'the chiefe citie of the country'. By then, it could claim almost fifteen-hundred years of history as an urban centre. Indeed, signposts on its peripheries state that it is the oldest town in Wales. There may be substance to the statement, although no inscription has been found there which indubitably asserts Carmarthen's early civic status. (Such an inscription has come to light at Caerwent.)

However, archaeological work carried out since the 1960s tends to confirm that status. It is believed that *c*. AD 78 a Roman fort – Moridunum – was built west of the later site of St Peter's Church. A civil settlement developed east of the fort. By the mid second century, as the Demetae – the inhabitants of south-west Wales – had accepted Roman rule, it would seem that the fort had been abandoned while the civil settlement had grown. The settlement was laid out in accordance with Roman traditions, and its shape can be traced in the present pattern of Carmarthen's streets – its northern boundary along Richmond Terrace, its southern along the Parade, and the western gateway linked to the eastern gateway along Priory Street. A civic settlement or *vicus* developed outside almost every Roman fort, but it was generally an organic, unplanned township. The orderliness of what was constructed at Moridunum suggests that the Romans deliberately created a town there, perhaps to ensure that the Demetian *civitas* – the territory of the Demetae – had a focal point or capital. The town walls enclosed thirty-three hectares (compare the eighteen hectares within the walls at Caerwent). Adjoining the walls was an amphitheatre – one of seven such structures in Britain – which may well have been the meeting place of the Demetian elders.

Moridunum means the fort by the sea. Over the years, the name contracted to *myrdin* or *myrddin*, and acquired the prefix *caer* (fort or town), giving rise to the place-name Caerfyrddin. There were no doubt stories concerning Myrddin or Merlin long before the 1130s, when Geoffrey of Monmouth wrote his *Historia Regum Britanniae* (History of the Kings of Britain), the book which linked Myrddin to Caerfyrddin and which incorporated him in the Arthurian legends as a wizard.

But, in the six centuries following the fall of the Roman Empire, the main development in Carmarthen was the establishment in the Roman town of a church, allegedly associated with Teulyddog, a disciple of St Teilo. Then, *c*.1109, Henry I, king of England, ordered the building of a castle on the ridge above the Tywi. Around the castle, some distance from the Roman town and St Teulyddog's Church, the settlement of New Carmarthen developed. Like the Roman town, it was surrounded with walls; thus Carmarthen has the remains of two fortified towns.

The castle was the most prominent feature on the ridge above the Tywi until the Carmarthenshire County Hall was rebuilt (1938–56). The hall is something of a throw-back to a French château, and its architect, Percy Thomas, recycled the plan when designing Neuadd Pantycelyn in Aberystwyth. More survives of the castle than is often assumed and recent work by Cadw has made the ruins more accessible. The largest surviving part is the gatehouse, erected in the fourteenth century and renovated following the Glyn Dŵr Rising. The gatehouse adjoins Nott Square and the Town Hall (1777), a remarkably interesting building and the scene of some of the most dramatic events in the history of Wales – the victory of Gwynfor Evans in 1966 among them.

Nott Square leads to Lammas Street, the width of which is indicative of the fact that it was, for centuries, the site of Carmarthen's chief market. The town is rich in fine chapels; the finest of them – the English Baptist Chapel (1870) – is attractively sited in a cul-de-sac off Lammas Street. Carmarthen is even richer

in attractive houses built in the eighteenth century, an era when the landowning families of Carmarthenshire felt the need to have a house in the county town. The large one in Spilman Street was where the earl of Cawdor resided on his visits to Carmarthen.

Spilman Street leads to St Peter's Church, which looks rather odd since its tower (c.1500) has been limewashed. The nave of the church is a mixture of medieval and nineteenth-century building work, and is crowded with monuments. The most interesting is the tomb of Rhys ap Thomas (d. 1525), the chief Welsh ally of Henry Tudor, a tomb removed from the Franciscan friary when that was dissolved in 1538.

From the church, visitors should walk to Brewery Road to see the old-time Carmarthen workhouse, erected in 1908 following the destruction by fire of the original workhouse erected in 1837. In June 1843, the 1837 building was the scene of the most dramatic episode in the Rebecca Riots, when it was sacked by a crowd of more than two-thousand people enraged by deprivation and oppression.

The walk from Brewery Road to the banks of the Tywi takes the visitor past some of the key places in the history of Wales. At the bottom end of Priory Street stood the Augustinian Priory where the Black Book of Carmarthen, the oldest surviving collection of Welsh poems, was probably compiled. The road goes on to the Parade, where the cradle of liberal theology in Wales, the Carmarthen Presbyterian College, once stood. King Street was the location of the printing press of the Spurrell family, long the most important publishers in Wales. The Ivy Bush Hotel in Spilman Street was the place where in 1819 Edward Williams (Iolo Morganwg) grafted the Gorsedd of the Bards of the Isle of Britain on to the eisteddfod movement. From there, the wanderer should walk down to the Tywi and try to imagine the river when it was full of ships, the basis of the trade which for centuries enabled Carmarthen to be the largest town in Wales.

The pedestrian bridge (2006) crossing the Tywi

Carmarthen railway station

In 1893, Wales acquired its national university, in 1907 it acquired its national museum and national library, and in 1946 it acquired its national opera company. At the end of the twentieth century, there was much discussion of what institutions a self-confident nation should have. The great achievement was, of course, the creation of the National Assembly, but there were those who felt that priority should not be given to specifically political institutions. The most prominent among them was the artist, William Wilkins, the most talented cultural entrepreneur

Wales has ever had. He wanted Wales to have a national botanic garden, as Scotland had had since 1670, and Ireland since 1795. By a sheer act of will, he brought a botanic garden for Wales into existence.

The garden is in Carmarthenshire, the home of Wilkins's ancestors (he is a descendant of the Physicians of Myddfai), a county which, until the opening of the garden in 2000, had not had its rightful share of national institutions. Wilkins was impressed by the valley of Nant Gwyno, a stream which flows into the Tywi at Llanarthney. Several hundred hectares of the valley had been bought in 1789 by William Paxton, a businessman who had made a fortune in India. The estate was known as Middleton after previous owners, members of a younger branch of the Myddelton family of Chirk.

Paxton commissioned the building of Middleton House, which was designed by S. P. Cockerell, the probable designer also of Wilkins's house at Trapp near Carreg Cennen Castle. In addition, Cockerell was responsible for Paxton's Tower, one of Wales's most attractive landmarks, which was intended as the climax of the view from Middleton. Paxton was obsessed with water – his great ambition was to develop Tenby as a centre for thalassotherapy. He sought to establish a spa at Middleton and arranged for Nant Gwyno to be dammed in order to create a succession of lakes.

The Middleton estate came into the possession of the Carmarthenshire County Council in 1931, the year in which the mansion was destroyed by fire. In the 1980s, Cadw saw few merits in the place, but, by 1989, Wilkins had seen its possibilities and was beginning to infect other people with his enthusiasm. It was not everyone who agreed that Wales needed a national botanic garden, and even those who did were not unanimous that it should be at Middleton; John Redwood, secretary of state for Wales from 1993 to 1995, proved skilful in confusing the issue by suggesting other sites. But Wilkins and his friends stood firm. A grant of £21.7 million was obtained from the Lottery Fund, support was forthcoming from Prince Charles, and the Carmarthenshire County Council leased 237 hectares at

Middleton for a pepper-corn rent. (Scotland's botanic garden initially consisted of 13 hectares and Ireland's of 19.)

When opened in 2000, Wales's National Botanic Garden was the first to be established in western Europe for a century and more, an important consideration in view of the fact that the rest of western Europe's national gardens had come into existence before the current concerns of ecologists had come to the fore.

The most prominent feature of the garden is the 110-metre-long glasshouse, the largest building of its kind in the world. Designed by Norman Foster and Partners, it contains an ingenious ravine and a collection of plants characteristic of a Mediterranean climate. The glasshouse is only one of the garden's attractions. It is delightful to follow the meandering stream that accompanies the path up to the glasshouse; it is gratifying to see that the chief

remaining part of Cockerell's work – the stable court – has been excellently renovated; it is pleasing to see the wide range of plants in the double-walled garden; it is an informative experience to learn about the chronology of Wales's geology through the stones which line the Broadwalk. Those who have not visited the garden since its early days should go there again; the plant growth of a decade can be revolutionary.

The strength and weakness of the garden is that it came into existence as the venture of enthusiasts who received no certainty that there would be funds available to run it. The Lottery money was earmarked for its establishment, not for its maintenance, and it is unlikely that visitors' entrance fees will ever be adequate to finance so ambitious a project. The garden suffered a financial crisis in 2006, when some of its plans had to be curtailed, those

dealing with sustainability and threatened plant species in particular. However, the fact that the garden exists at all is a miracle, although, as that can be said about any Welsh national institution, there is nothing particularly unusual about the history of Middleton.

It would be a pity to leave the area without visiting another of the achievements of William Wilkins. It is only eight kilometres from Middleton to Aberglasney, a journey which offers views of Dryslwyn Castle and of Grongaer, the hill on which John Dyer was inspired to write his topographical poem. The story of the garden at Aberglasney is even more exciting than that of the garden at Middleton. As the entire Aberglasney site is only 600

metres at its widest, it is easier to appreciate its layout than is the case with the botanic garden. The delight felt by William Wilkins on 1 April 1995, when his Trust finally obtained possession of the place, can be readily imagined. And to crown it all, images of the two men who commissioned the original glories of the place – Anthony Rudd (d. 1616) and his son Rice Rudd (d. 1664) can be seen nearby on a charming tomb in Llangathen church.

Llanelli was the location of the bloodiest industrial conflict to occur in twentieth-century Britain. Llanelli has the grave of the only Wesleyan Methodist minister in the world whose portrait appears on a beer bottle. The first Welsh-medium primary school maintained by a local authority was opened at Llanelli in 1947. In the mid twentieth century, Llanelli was the largest town in the world the majority of whose inhabitants claimed to be able to speak a Celtic language. In 1945, the Labour candidate at Llanelli (James Griffiths) won the largest majority in the history of British parliamentary elections (34,117). The Llanelli Rugby team is the only local team in Britain to defeat New Zealand's All Blacks (1972). Llanelli is the only town in Europe whose name contains two voiceless alveolar lateral fricatives (the grandiose term for the Welsh pronunciation of the double l). Llanelli is the only town in Wales in which a leader of the British Conservative Party was brought up, namely Michael Howard.

No more of Llanelli's merits (if they are indeed merits) should be listed, lest those visiting the place are disappointed. Little is left of the interweaving of streets and works which was characteristic of Llanelli in the mid-twentieth century. Most of the works were involved in tinplate making. Llanelli was indeed Tinopolis, with up to ten-thousand people in the town and its vicinity working in the industry. By now, the number is not a tithe of that, but as

production at Trostre exceeds the entire output of the numerous old works, Llanelli today produces more tinplate than ever before in its history.

The working-class streets of the town, the details of whose houses enchanted the authors of *The Shell Guide to South-West Wales* (1963), have lost much of their appeal following the removal of chimneys and the coming of tiles, uPVC and false stone cladding. The dignified buildings of Buckley's Brewery fell into ruin after they were bought and closed by Brains of Cardiff. But the town is full of places of worship – thirty-nine according to a survey made early in the twenty-first century – although the condition of many of them is cause for concern. An interesting day could be spent gazing at chapel façades, and, if possible, at some chapel interiors, especially Capel Als, where David Rees, 'The Agitator', was minister from 1829 to 1868. It originally followed the design of that prolific minster, Thomas Thomas, the architect of hundreds of chapels; it was revamped in 1894 by Morris Roberts of Porthmadog, and the fine interior is the result of his efforts. The façade of Zion Baptist Chapel is the finest in Llanelli. It was there that Jubilee Young, the most popular preacher of his day, was minister from 1931 until 1967. Zion is to be converted into a theatre with a grant of £25 million from the Welsh Assembly Government.

It is also worth visiting the parish church, if only to see the grave of the Reverend James Buckley (of beer-bottle fame) and the tombs of the Stepney family. The Stepneys were Llanelli's chief landlords, a position they obtained following Thomas Stepney's marriage *c.*1691 to the heiress of one of the numerous branches of Carmarthenshire's Vaughan family. The family home, Llanelly House, is the most interesting building in the town. Completed in 1714, it has been described as the finest house built in Wales in the early years of the eighteenth century, although at its core is the house built for the Vaughan family in the

BRACE'S - PROUD TO BE WELSH

LLANELLI

GOALS	TRIES	POINTS
2	1	9

SELANDNEWYDD

| 1 | | 3 |

BRACE'S
Bread

wrw
construction

A detail at Llanelly House

seventeenth century. It received publicity throughout Britain in 2003 on reaching the final round of the BBC *Restoration* programme. Although it failed to win, resources have been found to ensure that the façade is a thing of beauty but years of work are needed on the interior.

Visitors should not leave Llanelli without seeing something of its surroundings. At Penclacwydd, purposeful buildings have been erected which provide excellent views of the large number of waders and other birds that are attracted to the site. Felin-foel Brewery is the only survivor of the many brewery buildings which existed in nineteenth-century Wales. Its ingenious use of gravity makes it one of the most important buildings of its type in Britain. It is worth going to the Llanelli Museum in Parc Howard,

if only to see examples of the superb porcelain produced in the town between 1839 and 1922 and to gaze at the world's oldest spare tyre. From the museum, it is only a short journey to the striking furnace at Furnace and to the home of the Mansel Lewis family, Stradey Castle, a fascinating building completed in 1875. It was one of the first dwellings in Wales to be wired for electricity and the family still uses the original voltage. Wanderings should end at the Visitors' Centre near the North Dock, an inventive building which tells the story of Llanelli's maritime history. It was erected in the wake of the opening of the Millennium Coastal Park, the largest land reclamation scheme ever undertaken in Britain.

In order to gain the best overall impression of Swansea, the city centre should be avoided in favour of going to the summit of Townhill in order to look down upon the splendid expanse of the bay. No other city in Britain, or in Europe, offers such a panorama. (Donostia – San Sebastián – is perhaps a competitor, but that city lacks Swansea's expansiveness.) In the early 1920s, when the Swansea Corporation won prizes for its pioneering work in housing working-class families on Townhill, the view from the hill included the old Swansea – the town which existed before the appalling bombing of 19, 20 and 21 February 1941. Old though I am, I would like to be older – old enough to remember the old Swansea.

But the bay is still there, and from Pantycelyn Road, Townhill, it is possible to delight in the half circle of golden sand and azure sea which starts at the islets off Mumbles Head and ends with the massive walls built to enclose the harbour which serves Port Talbot steelworks. Walter Savage Landor spent some time at Swansea in 1796 and 1813, and, years later, when an exile in Italy, he yearned for the glories of Swansea Bay.

From Pantycelyn Road, a steep street leads down to central Swansea at Kingsway, the best place to discover how unimaginative were those responsible for the first phase of the post-war rebuilding in central Swansea. Of that rebuilding, the only structure worth visiting is the market, designed by Percy

From the market, the explorer should visit the Royal Institution of South Wales (now Swansea Museum), a delightful Greek-revival building erected in 1841. Around the institution are a number of buildings – particularly Jernegan's Assembly Rooms (1821) – erected in the first half of the nineteenth century, a period when Swansea was incontestably the most important urban centre in Wales. (Cardiff has virtually no buildings of that period.)

Thomas and completed in 1961. There had been a market at Swansea from the earliest days of the town – originally an open-air market held every Wednesday and Saturday. In 1651, the market acquired a building situated south of the castle; it was relocated to Oxford Street in 1828. The market destroyed by the bombing of February 1941 was that of 1895, designed by Glendinning Moxham, an architect whose work is almost as evident in Swansea as is that of William Jernegan. Although the present building is by no means as large as Moxham's, it is the largest indoor market in Wales. As Swansea is within easy reach of a wealth of sea food from nearby coasts and seas, of the dairy products of Carmarthenshire and of the fruit and vegetables grown in the fertile fields of Gower, there can hardly be a market in Britain which can compete with that of Swansea in terms of the variety and freshness of the food on sale. Swansea market is an object lesson for those concerned about food miles and the impersonal character of supermarket service. Almost every stall is run by a local family and almost everything on sale comes from adjacent seas and farms. This is merchandizing at its most civilized.

The banks of the Tawe provide evidence that Swansea has become far more ambitious architecturally than it was in the 1950s. The beginnings of SA1, a sophisticated mixture of industry, apartments and leisure facilities, augur well. What has been achieved in the Maritime Quarter to the south is proof that Swansea has regained its confidence. Adjoining the quarter is the National Waterfront Museum, opened in 2005. It is a successful attempt to ensure that what is essentially a large shed looks memorable. The museum is proud of its multimedia exhibits which are as tactile as possible, but it is pleasant to meet some old friends, particularly the replica of Trevithick's engine which once graced the Welsh Industrial and Maritime Museum at Cardiff.

Visitors should not leave Swansea without at least glancing at the most intriguing place in the city. In passing the place, a glance is the sole option, for, from the highway, the only view on offer is that of a neat, rounded hillock. The highway is the A483 and the hillock is located across the road from Amazon's vast depot.

Beneath the hillock is one of the most alluring of places. It is Swansea's Waste Water Treatment Plant, which deals with the water and sewage flushed down the lavatories used by 180,000 people in Swansea and its surroundings, and all the water flowing from the city's roofs and down its gutters. Open days are held in the plant, where the workforce of about half a dozen remarkably welcoming people are eager to ensure that members of the public appreciate the miracles which they achieve daily at the plant. One of the consequences of its effectiveness is that the beaches of Gower – once infamous for the sludge which polluted them – are now among the cleanest in Europe.

I had expected a place overrun by rats, smelling disgustingly and featuring water covered by blobs of excrement. But there were no rats and no disgusting smells. Watching the extraction of grease, hair, rags and condoms, and the process which ensures that most of the particles of excrement sink to the bottom of the water can be an enchanting experience. The use of micro-organisms and ultraviolet light is particularly ingenious. Seeing the foam on the liquid brought back memories of visits to Scottish whisky distilleries. It was particularly exciting to go to the summit of the tower on the top of the hillock and to look out at the buoys some

One of the buildings at SA1

four kilometres away in the Severn Estuary, buoys which mark the place at which the water is released into the sea. I became convinced that the water was among the purest in the world; I offered to drink a glass of it, but was advised to stick to the admirable products of the Tŷ Nant Company.

Three Cliffs Bay

Of the views of Swansea available from Pantycelyn Road, Townhill, the most appealing is the view of Mumbles. The headland is the starting point for an exploration of the coast of south Gower, which includes glories such as Three Cliffs Bay. The coast has long been inhabited; indeed, the Palaeolithic remains discovered at Goat's Hole Cave at Paviland are proof that there were people in south Gower long before there was water at the bottom of the cliffs. Evidence from later periods includes Penmaen Burrows chambered tomb, the Penmark Bronze Age hoard, the Iron Age hillfort at Rhossili and the remains of a Roman villa at Oystermouth. The area was also associated with the 'saints' of early Christian Wales, as place-names such as Ilston (Llanilltud Gŵyr) and Bishopston (Llandeilo Ferwallt) indicate.

The most interesting building in the vicinity of Mumbles is Oystermouth Castle. In 1106, Henry I authorized Henry, earl of Warwick, to seize the commote of Gower, and – in accordance with Norman practice – the earl consolidated his conquest by commissioning the building of castles at Swansea, Llandeilo Tal-y-bont, Loughor, Penmaen, Pennard and Oystermouth. Although Swansea was the *caput* of the lordship of Gower, it would seem that Oystermouth was the favourite home of the earl's successors, especially during the ascendancy of the de Breos family (1203–1322).

Oystermouth Castle is one of the most delightful of the castles of Wales. It does not have the menace of Harlech, nor is it a statement of power like Caernarfon, nor an affirmation of wealth like Raglan. It is neatly compact and the refined detail that survives suggests that it was a comfortable dwelling rather than a stronghold from which to attack. Approaching from the south, the first structure that comes to view is the gatehouse. The concave walls on either side raise an interesting question. Are they the northern halves of towers whose southern halves have been demolished or are they the northern halves of towers the southern halves of which were never built? If there is truth in the supposition that the work on the gatehouse began when the Marcher Lordships were under threat from Llywelyn ap Gruffudd and was completed after the threat had vanished, it is likely that the gatehouse was never flanked by completed round towers.

The inner court was surrounded by rooms built in the late thirteenth century, which were occupied by members of the de Breos family during their visits to Gower. The chapel, the windows of which still have remarkably complete stone tracery, is particularly attractive. In 1461, the castle, which by then was falling into ruin, came into the possession of the Herbert family. In 1927, a Herbert descendant, Henry Somerset, tenth duke of Beaufort, presented it to the Swansea Corporation.

Among other appealing buildings in the vicinity of Mumbles is the lighthouse which stands on the outermost of the two islands off the promontory. (There may be substance to the belief that Mumbles was initially a name restricted to the islands, and that it had its origin in the mumbling noise made by the sea as it flowed

between them.) The lighthouse, completed in 1793, was designed by William Jernegan, the most prolific of Swansea's architects. With its internal and external octagons, it is among the most remarkable lighthouses in Britain.

By 1793, a village had come into being west of the islands – a dense network of small streets on the slope rising from the sea. It was considered to be a place apart, the probable origin of the verse:

Mumbles is a funny place,
A church without a steeple,
Houses made of old ships wrecked
And most peculiar people.

The village's original inhabitants were fishermen, but, by the 1790s, Mumbles was becoming increasingly industrialized, the result of the development of coalmining in the Clyne Valley. To convey the coal to the port of Swansea, Mumbles was, in 1804, linked to the port by iron rails along the edge of the bay. In 1807, the horses which pulled the coal-carrying wagons began also to pull carriages carrying passengers. As the line followed a track that was not part of a highway, it was considered to be a railway rather than a tramway, and won recognition as the earliest passenger railway in the world. The line closed in 1960.

The beginnings of the conveyance of passengers along Swansea Bay coincided with the emergence of Swansea's ambition to become a fashionable seaside resort. Although the rapid growth of heavy industry undermined the town's hope of becoming 'the Brighton of Wales', Mumbles became increasingly associated with tourism and leisure activities. The 'Mumbles Mile' – the promenade with its countless public houses – became a paradise for revellers, Dylan Thomas allegedly among them. The best-known of the 'Mile's' public houses – the Mermaid – changed its name to Dylan's Tavern. It later caught fire but was reopened in 2007 as an ambitious restaurant. Indeed, by now, Mumbles's chief attraction is its restaurants, at least twenty of them. Swansea is twinned with Kinsale, Ireland's gastronomic capital. Originally, there were those who believed that Swansea was unworthy of being the gastronomic partner of its twin; any visitor to Mumbles today would undoubtedly disagree with that belief.

The walk along Mumbles promenade offers splendid views of Swansea Bay, but the village has links with more savage aspects of the sea, as the history of the Mumbles lifeboat amply proves. The best place to appreciate the courage of Mumbles's lifeboat men is All Saints Church, Oystermouth. It has Tim Lewis's stained-glass window (1989) which commemorates the eight men – the entire crew of the lifeboat – who were drowned in 1947 while seeking to save the crew of the *Samtampa*. It is among the most moving memorials in Wales.

In the second half of the eighteenth century, when the industrialization of Wales was gathering pace, only one individual gave any thought to the planning of the industrial settlements which were multiplying so prodigiously. That individual was John Morris (1745–1819), the son of Robert Morris, a Shrewsbury man who became the chief owner of the Llangyfelach copperworks in 1727. In 1768, John Morris inherited his father's properties and in 1773 he commissioned the building of what Gwallter Mechain (Walter Davies) called a 'castellated mansion' to house twenty-four of the families of colliers who worked for him at Tre-boeth. He employed a cobbler and a tailor to serve the families and ensured that his tenants had allotments on which they could grow their own food.

It is often claimed that Morris Castle is the world's earliest example of an employer commissioning a block of flats for his employees. The welfare of his workers was not John Morris's sole motivation for castle-building. He was involved in the construction of a luxurious mansion at Clasemount for himself and his family, and believed that the view from the mansion would be enhanced if it included a striking construction. Morris Castle was built on the highest point of Cnap-Llwyd Common, and consisted of a three-floor central block with a four-floor block at each of its four corners. In some ways, it belonged very much to the Swansea of the 1770s; bricks made of copper slag were used in its construction, perhaps the first use around Swansea of a building material which would eventually become very popular in the area. On the other hand, as the blocks were crowned with battlements, the castle was the earliest example in Swansea of a building erected in the neo-Gothic style, a style in which the lords of Copperopolis would increasingly delight.

Some elements of Morris Castle are still visible. Parts of two blocks survive above Salem Street in Plas-Marl, and it is possible to trace some of the soil banks which divided the allotments.

However, nothing remains of Clasemount, a dignified Palladian mansion completed c.1776. It was located slightly to the east of where the Driver and Vehicle Licensing Agency now stands, and was demolished in the 1820s after John Morris the second (1775–1855) moved to Sketty Park House.

John Morris was the last of the lords of Copperopolis to migrate from the sulphuric smoke and stink of the Lower Swansea Valley. The Morris family was still there in the late eighteenth century and it was, in part, the desire of John Morris the first to have additional eye-catching structures to view from Clasemount that explains his decision to establish Morriston. It is remarkable that one individual's desire to have picturesque views from his front door should result in the creation of a town. Founded in 1779, Morriston was certainly meant to be a town; fifteen hundred people lived there in 1811, a year in which Cardiff had fewer than 2,500 inhabitants. The growth of Morriston is described in one of the best studies of an industrial landscape ever published – Stephen Hughes's *Copperopolis* (2000). Morriston consisted of two grids of streets, the larger with Woodfield Street at its centre, and the smaller with Globe Street as its backbone. The latter adjoined the Forest Copperworks, another of John Morris's ventures and led to the bridge across the Tawe designed in 1748 by William Edwards, the Pontypridd bridge-builder. Edwards was also the designer of the grids, but the smaller of them lost its coherence when the Swansea Canal was driven through it between 1794 and 1796.

It is the larger grid which gives Morriston a coherent structure. Its centre is the point where Morfydd Street crosses Woodfield Street/Martin Street. An island at the crossing is the site of St John's Church, completed in 1789 and rebuilt in 1862. Nothing survives of Morriston's original buildings, but William Edwards's plan continues to give the place an air of intended importance. Other lords of Copperopolis imitated John Morris's

The interior of Tabernacl Chapel

example. Between 1803 and 1813, forty dwellings were built to house employees of Pascoe Grenfell, owner of the Upper and Middle Bank copperworks. What survives of Grenfelltown can be seen around Taplow Terrace and Rifleman's Row, south of Bon-y-maen. (Grenfell's leases obliged tenants to collect their urine and to deliver it to their workplace.) Trevivian was a more ambitious project; it was begun in 1840 by John Henry Vivian (1785–1855), owner of the Hafod copperworks. The project had been completed by 1878, when there were hundreds of houses on the site.

The Morrises were staunch Anglicans – John Morris rejoiced that his son, Thomas, was an Anglican clergyman – and it was John, no doubt, who ensured that the centrepiece of Morriston should be an Anglican church. But his descendants lived to see his town wholly overshadowed by a Nonconformist building – Capel Tabernacl (1872–3). With seating for 1,450 people, it is claimed that it is the largest chapel in Wales. As Wood Street Chapel, Cardiff (2,900 seats) and the Albert Hall Chapel, Swansea (2,600 seats) have been demolished, the claim is probably correct. Tabernacl was designed by John Humphrey, whose architectural education did not go beyond his apprenticeship as a carpenter; the masterpiece he designed for the Congregationalists of Morriston represents the pinnacle of the tradition of ministerial architects which is such a feature of the chapels of Swansea. Gazing at the façade of Tabernacl, with its three high arches and its echoes of the finest of the buildings of the classical and Renaissance eras, is a memorable experience. The chapel interior, with its enormous organ and the dip in the line of the gallery which guides the eye to the pulpit, is equally memorable. The climax is that rare feature of a Nonconformist chapel – a steeple. Forget about the Morrises. Morriston is a town at the foot of John Humphrey's steeple.

Generations of carvings at Tabernacl Chapel

During the first phase of the Industrial Revolution, the south Wales coalfield was the world leader not in one, not in two, but in three metal industries – iron, copper and tinplate. In many ways, the chief of those industries was copper; in 1788, Britain's output of copper was valued at twice that of iron. By 1810, Wales was responsible for 54 per cent of the world's output of copper. The centre of the industry was around Landore and Llansamlet in the Lower Swansea Valley. That might be considered to be an odd development in view of the fact that there was no mining of copper ore within the south Wales coalfield. But, in the mid eighteenth century, the ore was not the bulkiest of the materials necessary for the making of copper. Then, the smelting of one ton of copper ore involved the burning of three tons of coal. Thus, it was more economical to transport the ore to the coal than the coal to the ore. Originally, Britain's chief source of copper ore was Cornwall and the nearest coalfield to Cornwall was that of south Wales. The coalfield contained few areas where coal-bearing land was accessible by ship. The most important of such areas was the Lower Swansea Valley, where the Tawe's five kilometres of navigable water was central to the development of the copper industry. Furthermore, the ships carrying ore from Cornwall could return carrying coal from Swansea, a commodity much in demand to power the steam pumps which prevented the flooding of Cornish mines.

Swansea's thirteen copperworks were all sited on the banks of the Tawe in a four-kilometre strip from the Upper Forest works near Morriston to the White Rock works near Foxhole. The earliest was Llangyfelach (1717); thereafter, the most important to be established were the Cambrian (1720), White Rock (1737), Upper Forest (1752), Middle Bank (1755), Upper Bank (c.1757), Hafod (1809) and Morfa (1835). All the works belched out poisonous fumes. By the mid nineteenth century, the Lower Swansea Valley annually released 92,000 tons of sulphuric acid into the atmosphere, depriving the soil of its fertility and ensuring that most copper workers did not survive much beyond their mid thirties. The fire and brimstone fitted the traditional notion of hell. As the old verse put it:

> It came to pass in days of yore
> The devil chanced upon Landore.
> Quoth he: 'With all this smoke and stink,
> I can't be far from home, I think.'

Growth in production led industrialists to comb the world for copper ore, and, by the late nineteenth century, most of the ore smelted in the Lower Swansea Valley came from Chile, Cuba and Australia. The cost of transporting ore over vast distances and the desire of exporting countries to develop their own copper-smelting industry caused the future of smelting in the Tawe Valley to become increasingly bleak. Of the chief works, White Rock closed in 1924 and Upper Bank in 1928; although

Hafod/Morfa continued in production until 1980, its later years were a story of lurching from crisis to crisis.

Following the demise of copper smelting, Swansea inherited the largest area of derelict land in Europe – 360 hectares of ruins and toxic soil. The train journey from Cardiff to Carmarthen involved going into Swansea's High Street Station and then backing out of it on the same track. Thus, travellers saw dereliction when arriving and departing, and thereby gained a depressing impression of Swansea. The Lower Swansea Valley Project was launched by University College Swansea in 1961 – a multidisciplinary study of the challenge represented by the dereliction. By now, people should visit the Lower Swansea

The ruins of the canteen and the power-house at the Morfa Copperworks, with the Liberty Stadium in the background

Valley in order to appreciate the miracle that has been achieved since 1961 – the fertile soil, the sweet pastures, the flourishing copses and the unpolluted lakes.

But there should be another reason for visiting the place – to have an opportunity to understand the enormous contribution made by the area to the story of world industrialization. Sadly, the opportunity is not there. As Stephen Hughes put it: 'The clearance of the largest area of dereliction in Europe made no provision for the retention of significant historic copper-smelting plant.' The fact seems almost a matter of celebration at Swansea's Waterfront Museum, where the visitor is informed that 'there are now few remains of the old industries of the Swansea Valley'.

That is not true. As Stephen Hughes shows in his *Copperopolis*, a wealth of evidence survives. The problem is gaining access to it and understanding it. The promise to construct a trail through the valley has not been honoured. There was a suggestion in 2005 that the remains of the Middle Bank works would become an interpretation centre, but nothing has come of it. In his *Real Swansea* (pp. 186–95), Nigel Jenkins describes his frustration when seeking to understand the significance of what survives in the valley, an experience familiar to all who want to find out more about the unique history of the Lower Swansea Valley. (Help may be at hand. In 2010, the Economic and Social Research Council offered a grant of £95,000 to bring 'back to life' the dilapidated Hafod works.)

It is not only evidence of the copper industry that has suffered neglect. Landore offers nothing commemorating the fact that it was there that Wilhelm Siemens developed the open-hearth furnace, a development which transformed the steel industry throughout the world. With the corrugated steel sheets of Landore at hand, the Lower Swansea Valley became one of the chief centres of tinplate production, but the evidence of that industry is also sparse. However, intriguing building work is afoot in the valley. It is worth wandering around Hafod Street and Aberdyberthi Street; there, a tympanum is being erected above every front door, thus bringing something of the elegance of the Renaissance to the streets of Landore.

The engine-house at the Hafod Copperworks

Since the opening of the A48 bridge (1966) across the River Neath, and even more so since the completion of the M4 bridge (1993), it is easy to forget that Neath exists. But it is worth visiting the place, if only to admire the way in which St David's Church (1869) – John Norton's masterpiece – dominates the town. (Norton performed the same service for Pontypridd and Ebbw Vale.) South of the church stands the Mechanics Institute (1847) designed by the distinguished naturalist, Alfred Russel Wallace. (A plaque on the institute records his association with the building.) To the north stands the Castle Hotel, where the Welsh Rugby Union was founded in 1881; the room in which the event took place has been preserved exactly as it was in 1881.

These are recent happenings in the history of Neath. Visitors should start by crossing the River Neath to the community of Blaenhonddan where the Nidum Roman fort is situated. Built of timber and earth c. AD 75, it was important enough to be one of the three forts in Wales mentioned by the Roman historian, Tacitus. (Burrium [Usk] and Isca [Caerleon] were the other two.) It was rebuilt in stone c. AD 120, and was abandoned c.150, when it was probably believed that the native inhabitants of the area had accepted the Roman yoke. (Most of the fort lies under Twr-y-felin School.)

The local inhabitants proved less willing to accept the Norman yoke. A motte-and-bailey castle was erected on the left bank of the Neath c.1129. It was probably commissioned by Richard de Granville, a knight who was given the task of defending the westernmost parts of the lordship of Glamorgan by Robert fitz Henry, earl of Gloucester. The castle was besieged by the Welsh in 1185 and was destroyed by Llywelyn ap Iorwerth in 1231. It was rebuilt, but was seriously damaged during the Revolt of Llywelyn Bren (1316) and the troubles which sprang from the ambitions of Hugh Despenser, lord of Glamorgan. What can be seen today are the ruins of a castle commissioned by Despenser in the early 1320s. The pair of towers defending the gatehouse stand with dignity near the Neath Canal, the best preserved of the canals of the south Wales coalfield.

On the other side of the Neath is another canal – the Tennant Canal, dug to link Aberdulais with the port of Swansea. That canal offers reflections of the most interesting of Neath's medieval ruins. Neath Abbey was founded c.1129 as a house of the order of Savigny, which merged with the Cistercian order in 1147. Its founder was Richard de Granville, who granted the monks some 3,250 hectares between the Neath and the Tawe, land that he urged the monks to seize from the Welsh. Austere buildings were erected there in the early twelfth century, and there was much rebuilding in more elaborate styles between the late twelfth and the early fourteenth centuries. However, what is visible from

Neath Abbey

197

the entrance are the remains of a substantial late sixteenth-century structure – a building with large oblong windows which have straight mullions and transoms, a far cry from the pointed arches characteristic of the golden age of monasticism. The windows are part of a mansion constructed of stone taken from the dissolved abbey. It was built for Richard Williams, who adopted the surname of his mother's father, Walter Cromwell. (Oliver Cromwell was Richard's great-grandson.) Because of the stone

robbery, it is difficult to envisage the splendours of the abbey – the finest in Wales according to John Leland, and the monastery at which Abbot Leyshon Thomas presided over Welsh monasticism's Indian summer. Little survives of Neath Abbey church; it was completed at much the same time as Tintern's abbey church and was only slightly smaller than that magnificent building – it had a length of 62 metres compared with the 72 metres at Tintern. The only part of the complex which has survived in its entirety is the dormitory's vaulted undercroft, a room of great dignity.

The fate of the buildings after the era of Richard Williams is unclear, but it would seem that they had been abandoned by 1792 when an ironworks was established nearby. What remains of the works are among the most important industrial ruins in the world, particularly the 20-metre-high south furnace (1793), which was fed with iron ore, coke and limestone from the summit of the rock which stands behind it. Among the owners of the works was the Quaker, Joseph Tregelles Price, founder in 1815 of the world's first peace movement. Near the abbey stands the house where he lived; it bears a plaque to his memory.

Visitors to Neath should not leave without exploring Gnoll Park, the best example in Wales of the ingenious adaptation of the landscape for aesthetic purposes. The Gnoll was the residence of Humphrey Mackworth (1657–1727), the pioneer of the copper industry at Neath and a leading patron of the Society for the Propagation of Christian Knowledge, but only the foundations survive of the ambitious house erected for Mackworth's descendants. Humphrey's son, Herbert, delighted in waterfalls, and the 55-metre cascade constructed for him in the 1740s is a marvel. Herbert's son – another Herbert – delighted in follies; the Ivy Tower at Tonna was among his commissions. It takes about two hours to wander around Gnoll Park. There can be few other places in Wales where so many eccentric sites may be visited in so short a time.

Neath Abbey reflected in the Tennant Canal (right)

In terms of the geography of Wales, Margam is the coccyx – the bone at the bottom of the spine. The mountain which rises from Wales's northern coast above Abergwyngregyn is part of a chain which extends southward across the country and reaches the southern coast at Margam. From the summit of Mynydd Margam, it is possible to walk for 250 kilometres along Wales's watershed to Ffridd Ddu above Abergwyngregyn, following paths which are almost always at least 307 metres (1,000 feet) above sea level.

Climbing the mountain is one motive for visiting Margam. Another is to see the most delightful structure erected in Wales during the second half of the eighteenth century – the Orangery built in the 1780s to provide winter shelter for a collection of orange and lemon trees. It extends for almost 100 metres, the longest such building in Britain. Its chief façade has seventeen bays characterized by superb stonework. The Orangery was commissioned by Thomas Mansel Talbot (1747–1813), great-nephew of Bussy, fourth Baron Mansel (d. 1750). Bussy was a descendant of Rhys Mansel (d. 1559), who bought Margam's Cistercian abbey from the crown in the 1540s.

The abbey church is particularly interesting, if only because it is the sole Cistercian abbey church in Wales that is still a place of worship. Almost nothing survives of the abbey churches of Grace Dieu, Llantarnam, Strata Marcella and Whitland, and very little of that of Conwy; only ruins survive at Basingwerk, Cwmhir, Cymer, Neath, Strata Florida, Tintern and Valle Crucis. But services are held at Margam. Admittedly, they are not held in what were once the splendours of the crossing, the transepts or the sanctuary, for those parts of the abbey church have long fallen into ruin. They are held in the westernmost part of the nave. Margam's nave is the only complete piece of Cistercian architecture in Wales that provides evidence of the order's early tradition of austerity. The surviving fragment of the abbey church houses a rich array of monuments. It contains tombs from the sixteenth to the nineteenth centuries which are almost comparable with the wonderful collection of tombs in St Mary's Church, Abergavenny. The most striking is that to the last of the Talbots – Theodore Mansel Talbot, the gifted High Church heir to the family's entire fortune – who died childless in 1876 at the age of 37.

The only other substantial surviving part of the abbey is the chapter house. In 1799, its vault was allowed to collapse, for why should those who delighted in the neo-classicalism of the Orangery worry about the fate of a remnant of Gothic barbarism? Even in its ruined state, the elegance and detail of the chapter house are highly appealing.

Further proof of the Talbots' respect for the neo-classical tradition was their readiness to ensure the future of the banqueting hall of their ancestors, the Mansels. The façade of the hall (c.1670), with its two wholly Roman arches and its Ionic and Composite fluted columns, was carefully demolished in 1835 and re-erected near the Orangery. But, by then, it was impossible to resist the neo-Gothic tide. The castle commissioned by

Christopher Rice Mansel Talbot in the 1830s was a massive exercise in Tudor Gothic. C. R. M. Talbot was one of the few individuals who could afford such an extravaganza; he was the owner of Glamorgan's largest landed estate (13,760 hectares). The rents of his farms, the royalties paid by his industrial tenants, the dividends from his investments in railways and the profits of the docks named after the family at Port Talbot, meant that he was acknowledged as Britain's richest commoner. (It is unlikely that he received any financial returns from the role for which he was best known – his sixty-year membership of the House of Commons [1830–90].)

Margam Castle was designed by Thomas Hooper, who was also the architect of Penrhyn Castle. (The fact that Hooper was working on a Romanesque spectacle at Penrhyn, while at the same time designing a Tudor-Gothic building at Margam, proves that the architects of the era had little that could be called their own distinctive style.) Margam Castle is particularly significant, for it was the subject of the earliest datable Welsh photograph (1841). The castle is now owned by the Neath-Port Talbot County Borough Council, and its park, with its peacocks, deer, sculptures and trees, is delightful. The castle has suffered from decades of neglect, and was damaged by fire in 1977. When the restoration is complete, it is hoped that it will house Wales's museum of photography.

Of all the attractions of Margam, the most fascinating is a collection of objects far older than the abbey, the Orangery and the castle. They can be seen in a modest building located north of the abbey church. It houses the Stones Museum, which contains about twenty inscribed stones, many of them dating from the sixth to the tenth centuries. They came to light at Margam or in the vicinity, proof that Margam was a spiritual centre long before 1147, the year in which Robert fitz Henry, earl of Gloucester, founded the Cistercian abbey.

About thirteen-hundred years after the carving of the first of the inscriptions in the Stones Museum, Margam acquired one of Wales's most intriguing places of worship – the Beulah Calvinistic Methodist chapel. It was built in 1838 and was financed – and perhaps designed – by C. R. M. Talbot. It was located on the route selected for the M4, and in 1976 was demolished and rebuilt on the outskirts of Port Talbot. Beulah is the sole octagonal chapel in Wales, a sufficient reason for making an effort to visit it.

The façade of the ground floor of the Margam Banqueting House

It is not easy to think of a profoundly interesting place within the confines of the Bridgend County Borough. Yet, as the county borough is home to 128,645 people – almost 5 per cent of the inhabitants of Wales – some effort should be made. Between 1974 and 1996, when the local government unit was the Ogmore District, the choice would have been obvious; it would have had to be Ewenny, but Ewenny was transferred to the Vale of Glamorgan in 1996. St Grallo's Church, Coychurch, and St Mary's Church, Bridgend, are attractive buildings, but the area's finest structure – Bridgend's Town Hall, a splendid Greek revival building completed in 1843, was demolished in 1971. Charm is evident in the 'Old Parish' (Llangynwyd), and the public buildings of Maesteg have a monumental dignity. Coety Castle was subject to a dramatic siege and Island Farm was the location of a remarkable escape. These are all places worth seeing, but – to quote Dr Johnson on Giant's Causeway – they may not be worth making a special effort to go to see them.

However, there is one place in the county which is worth going to see, if only because everyone is intrigued by the idea of lost cities. The castle and town of Kenfig were established in the early twelfth century. By 1349, the town had 144 burgesses, which possibly indicates that it had a population in the region of a thousand – a substantial figure for a town in Wales at that time. In the following decades, Kenfig was buried by sand sucked out of the bowels of the Severn Sea by apocalyptic forces. Stones from Kenfig church were used to build a new church at Pyle, further inland and therefore in a more secure location. When Leland visited the area in the 1530s, he noted that ruins could still be seen at Kenfig, but they probably disappeared as a result of the damage caused by the storm (or the tsunami?) of 1606/7. When excavation began in 1924, nothing of Kenfig was visible on the surface, but today visitors can see walls revealed by the excavators. Most of the site is still covered by sand, and, as the excavators'

website puts it: 'It is quite a thought that as you walk around those areas near the castle, where there are no high dunes, there are probably medieval artefacts lying only inches below your feet.' Excavation has restarted and there may yet be exciting discoveries. Although the town disappeared, the notion that there were Kenfig burgesses did not. Indeed, the special electoral rights of Kenfig's burgesses lasted until 1918.

From Kenfig, the explorer should walk to Sker House, the ruins of which used to loom eerily above the sea. The restoration of the house was completed in 2003. Iolo Morganwg's anecdote concerning the place became the basis of a credible story written by Isaac Hughes (*Y Ferch o Sger* [1902]). R. D. Blackmore's *The Maid of Sker* (1872) is far less convincing.

Sker House is within easy reach of Porthcawl, home from 1948 to 2001 of that remarkable institution, the Miners' Eisteddfod. Like other coastal resorts in Glamorgan – Barry, for example, or Penarth – Porthcawl's origins were industrial, for the place came into being following the construction of a tramroad from Maesteg to Sandy Bay. A small dock came into operation at Porthcawl in 1866, but, in the following years, work at the dock became secondary to the employment offered by leisure activities. By now, with the well-off reluctant to spend their holidays in such places, Porthcawl has become a town to which to retire. (In 2001, 29.3 per cent of its inhabitants were pensioners, the highest percentage in Glamorgan.) It still attracts the less well-off, as the vast caravan park at Trecco Bay amply proves.

Porthcawl is located between the two areas of the Bridgend County Borough that have been overwhelmed by oceanic forces. Kenfig Burrows lies north-west of the town and Merthyr Mawr Burrows to the east, and it is claimed that the burrows form Europe's largest shifting sand-dune system. Wanderers on the burrows on a hot summer's day can imagine they are in a Near Eastern desert – indeed, much of the film, *Lawrence of Arabia*, was shot on the dunes. Candleston Castle, on the edge of Merthyr Mawr Burrows, has not yet been buried, but there is every prospect that it will be in the near future.

The chief reason for visiting the Merthyr Mawr Burrows is that they provide access to the village of Merthyr Mawr, an attractive group of thatched cottages. The area offers further delights – the opportunity to walk along the stepping-stones across the River Ewenny, to visit Ogmore Castle and to dine luxuriously at The Pelican in its Piety.

Stepping stones across the Ewenny River near Ogmore Castle

For those enchanted by Romanesque architecture – and they are a growing breed – Ewenny Priory is the place to go. It is not the earliest of Wales's Romanesque buildings. Work was afoot at St Mary's Church, Chepstow, before 1071, but, as that church has experienced so much revamping, it does not offer the sense of solidity which is so much a part of the experience of viewing Romanesque architecture. A Romanesque building gives the impression that it has been carved out of an enormous lump of stone, a marked contrast with the succeeding style – Gothic – which emphasizes the skeletal. Several buildings containing Romanesque elements survive from early twelfth-century Wales – St Woolos Cathedral (Newport), and Llandaff Cathedral, for example – but more than elements survive at Ewenny. Its priory church is the finest Romanesque building in Wales, although, if the Welsh border were to extend slightly to the east, Wales would include Kilpeck, a worthy competitor.

Dating Ewenny church is no easy task. It seems to have been built in accordance with a unified plan, and therefore doubt has been cast upon the suggestion that there were several periods of building. The church was commissioned by the castellan of Ogmore Castle, William de Londres. William died in 1126, and work at Ewenny is wholly consistent with the notion that it was undertaken in the 1120s. However, it is evident that the parish churches built in the Vale of Glamorgan in the twelfth century were much smaller than the church at Ewenny. In 1141, William's son, Maurice de Londres, granted Ewenny to the Benedictine monastery at Gloucester, with the intention of ensuring that the church should become a priory for monks dependent upon Gloucester. It is difficult to believe that a church on a scale suitable to be a priory was built before the building had attained a degree of monastic status, and the present tendency is to assert that it was rebuilt in the 1140s in a style – by then rather old-fashioned – which had been pioneered at Gloucester during

the rebuilding which occurred there between 1089 and 1100.

St Michael's Church, Ewenny, consists of two parts – one for the monks (the chancel, the presbytery and the south transept; the north transept is in ruins) – and one for the parishioners (the nave). The division reflects the fact that the priory was a colonial institution. As Glanmor Williams put it: 'Nothing could symbolize with more forbidding massiveness the barrier between foreign monk and conquered native than the tremendous chancel wall cutting off the monks' choir from the parishioners' nave.' The abbot of Gloucester was aware that he was sending monks into hostile territory, and advised them to 'strengthen the locks of your doors and surround your house with a good ditch and an impregnable wall'. Indeed, the 'impregnable wall' is the most prominent feature of Ewenny. It stands 4.5 metres high and encloses two hectares; three of its towers still stand and evidence of a portcullis can be seen in the chief gatehouse.

Although the wall is the most prominent feature of Ewenny, the most delightful is the vault of the presbytery, the subject of a

watercolour painted by J. M. W. Turner in 1797. The painting stresses the solidity of the building, and the inclusion of hens and a dog suggest that, by the 1790s, there was little respect for what had been the monks' place of worship.

Ewenny came to an end as a priory following the dissolution of its mother house at Gloucester in 1539. In 1546, it was bought by Edward Carne for £726 6s. 4d. As he was a fervent Catholic (he was chosen by Mary Tudor to go to Rome to pledge the queen's loyalty to the Papacy), it was perhaps inconsistent of him to benefit from the destruction of monasticism, one of Catholicism's central features – although he was not alone in such inconsistency. His son became a Protestant, and the Carne family dwelt at Ewenny until the death of the last of them, John Carne, in 1741. His heir, also John, died in 1700 at the age of fifteen years, ten months and eleven days. His memorial, which declares that the death of 'Ewenny's hope, Ewenny's pride' was 'The ruin

of this worthy family', is particularly moving. The finest memorial in the church is that to the founder of the priory, Maurice de Londres – a splendid example of thirteenth-century sculpture. After the extinction of the Carnes, Ewenny passed by marriage to the Turbervilles, who still live in the adjoining mansion.

From the priory it is but a short stroll to the village of Ewenny, where Matthews Ewenni (Edward Matthews) was the Calvinistic Methodist minister from 1852 to 1864. He was the author of one of the most popular Welsh-language books of the time (*Hanes Bywyd Siencyn Penrhydd*), and was among the last of the preachers who delighted congregations in the attractive Welsh of the Vale of Glamorgan. The most interesting building in the village is the pottery. It was founded in 1610 and is still owned by descendants of its founder. When its four-hundredth anniversary was celebrated in 2010, it had been in existence two years longer than had the priory.

'ONID OES AWDURDOD I'R CROCHENNYDD AR Y PRIDDGIST, I WNEUTHUR O'R UN TELPYN PRIDD UN LLESTR I BARCH, AC ARALL I AMMARCH?' RHUFEINIAID 9-21

HATH NOT THE POTTER POWER OVER THE CLAY OF THE SAME LUMP TO MAKE ONE VESSEL UNTO HONOUR, AND ANOTHER UNTO DISHONOUR?

Examples of the products of the Ewenny Pottery

On the coast of Glamorgan lies the small creek where the River Col-huw flows into the sea. It is perhaps the most significant place in the history of the spread of Christianity among Celtic-speaking peoples, for it was there in the fifth and sixth centuries that pilgrims landed on their way to Illtud's monastery two kilometres inland. That monastery may be considered to be the axis of early Celtic Christianity; it had contacts not only with other parts of Wales and with Brittany and Cornwall, but also with the world of the Gaelic-speaking Christians of Ireland and Scotland. (It would appear that it was Irish, rather than English, influences which transformed Illtud into Twit.) The monastery was located in south Wales, a unique area of western Europe, for it was the only part of the Western Roman Empire not to be overrun by invaders from beyond the imperial frontiers.

Nothing survives of Illtud's monastery, which probably consisted of little more than a timber church and a group of individual monks' cells. (The Celtic Church followed the eremitic practice of the Eastern Church – monks living alone; coenobiticism – monks living communally – is a later practice associated with the western tradition of St Benedict.) In fact, Llantwit Major offers more evidence of earlier ages – for example, the Castle Ditches and the Summerhouse promontory forts, both dating from the Iron Age, and the remains of a second-century Roman villa.

Walking up the narrow Col-huw Valley is a pleasant experience, although the pleasure declines as the village of Llantwit Major comes into view. In the twentieth century, the village grew more rapidly than almost any other one in Wales. It had 1,113 inhabitants in 1901 and 9,687 in 2001, and today the village's most conspicuous features are its savage traffic calmers. (Llantwit Major is now considerably larger than Cowbridge, or Llantwit Minor as the Llantwitians call the one-time capital of the Vale of Glamorgan.) However, the scene improves on reaching the centre of the village with its wealth of sixteenth-century buildings, among them the Town Hall, the Old White Hart Inn and the Old Swan Inn, the thatched To-hesg and the dignified and multi-chimney-stacked Great House.

The glory of the place is the church. The earliest parts still standing are six-hundred years later than the era of Llantwit Major's original renown. They include the Western Church and the adjoining roofless Galilee Chapel. (Plans are afoot to restore the chapel as a centre for Celtic Christian studies.) The Western Church is now no more than the ante-chamber of a later church built to its east, a building replete with fascinating features. They include a thirteenth-century sculpture of the Jesse Tree, a handsome fourteenth-century reredos, and murals dating from every century of the later Middle Ages.

Inscribed stones at St Illtud's Church, Llantwit Major

Above all, the church contains a collection of inscribed stones which prove that Llantwit Major played a major role centuries after the age of Illtud. Chief among them is the 'Houelt Stone', a memorial raised by Hywel 'for the soul of Rhys his father'. It is likely that Hywel was the Hywel ap Rhys mentioned by Asser, the biographer of Alfred the Great. Hywel was the king of Glywysing (the territory between the Rhymney and the Tawe), who feared that his kingdom would be seized by the acquisitive descendants of Rhodri Mawr. The 'Houelt Stone' belongs to a sculptural tradition which flourished in the ninth century, particularly in Ireland – evidence for the belief that Llantwit Major's links with Ireland lasted long after the age of Illtud. The links were maintained by those who sailed the western sea-routes, voyages which explain why there is a church dedicated to Illtud in Llanelltyd at the furthermost navigable corner of the estuary of the River Mawddach. Although knowledge of the ancestors of Rhys and Hywel is sketchy, they gave rise to a dynasty which united Glywysing and Gwent, thus creating, perhaps for the second time, the kingdom of Morgannwg.

There are two intriguing buildings in the vicinity of the church. One of them is a dovecote, a smaller version of the splendid culverhouse at Barry. The other is a structure probably built as the dwelling of the priest who prayed daily in the chantry chapel of the Ragland family, which was added to the church in the late fifteenth century. (The prayers of chantry priests allowed souls to avoid long periods in purgatory; by 1500, members of the family of the elector of Saxony had amassed two million years' credit, credit which was lost when the elector, under the influence of Luther, abandoned his belief in purgatory.)

The priest's dwelling, with its two floors, fireplaces and lavatory, looks as if it would have been remarkably comfortable, and brings to mind the cells in the cloister of that magnificent building – the Carthusian monastery at Pavia.

Before leaving Llantwit Major, the explorer should visit Boverton Place, one of the largest buildings erected in sixteenth-century Wales. There were rumours in 2007 that the ruins had been sold for £55,000 – a remarkable price in a village where few houses change hands for less than £300,000 – but it appears that the cheque bounced. Thus, the chance to restore the huge pile is still available. North of Boverton lies Bethesda'r Fro, where Thomas William was minister from 1806 until his death in 1844, and where he wrote his renowned collection of hymns, *Dyfroedd Bethesda* (1824). The surroundings of the chapel, which is almost embedded within the St Athan military camp, would have been very alien to Thomas William, but the chapel itself, with its open fire and its candlelight, has hardly changed at all since it was completed by Thomas William's flock in 1807.

The chapel at Bethesda'r Fro

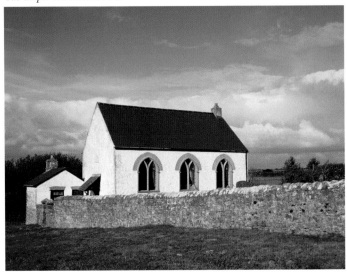

The rapid nineteenth-century industrialization of Wales led to an equally rapid urbanization. Of all Wales's urban centres, the one which grew most prodigiously was Barry. In 1881, only 85 people lived in the parish of Barry, but by 1901, the Barry Urban District, established in 1894, was home to 27,000 people. Thus, Barry is the chief marvel in the history of Welsh urbanization.

Something does survive of the old Barry – evidence of a Roman building at Cold Knap, for example, and the remains of a pilgrimage chapel on Barry Island. There are medieval features in St Cadog's and St Dyfan's, the churches of parishes which were partially absorbed by Barry in 1894. The most attractive medieval monuments are Barry Castle in Romilly Park, a small fortified mansion built in the fourteenth century, and the remarkably complete thirteenth-century dovecote at the end of Gladstone Road – the largest culverhouse in Wales.

But the main story is that of the docks. In 1883, Cardiff's Bute Docks dealt with 8.2 million tons of goods, 4.8 million tons more than they had handled in 1874, the year of the opening of Roath Basin. Cardiff had undergone no dock expansion between 1874 and 1883. That period was one of increasing delay and congestion, much to the frustration of the coal exporters, especially David Davies of Llandinam, owner of some of the most important collieries in the Rhondda. (Much of Davies's anger arose from the hostility of a self-made man and a Liberal towards a Conservative aristocrat, the third marquess of Bute.) In 1883, parliamentary permission was sought to build a dock at Barry, despite the fact that the Bute estate authorities had vowed to complete a large dock at Cardiff by 1887.

After one of the longest battles in the history of Parliament, the Barry Bill was passed in 1884, and Barry's first dock was opened in 1889; its second followed in 1898. Compared with Cardiff, Barry had several advantages. It was not located on an estuary and was therefore not burdened with the cost of constantly scouring shipping-lanes. The entrance channel's depth of water was sufficient to allow entry to the docks regardless of the height of the tide. (In that facility, Barry was alone among the ports of the Severn Sea.) Barry was designed to accommodate the

The former offices of the Barry Dock and Railway Company, and the statue of David Davies, Llandinam

building was rapidly constructed between 1898 and 1900 is proof of the confidence in Barry in the last years of the nineteenth century. (It is claimed that the office is a rare example of a 'Calendar Building' with 4 chimneys [seasons], 52 rooms [weeks] and 365 windows [days].) In front of the building – which is now one of the offices of the Vale of Glamorgan County Council – stands a statue of David Davies (1893) holding the plans of the docks; there is a replica of the statue at Llandinam.

To the bulk of the inhabitants of Glamorgan, Barry is not a dock town but a holiday town. This is also a role that has declined, as can be seen from the closure of Butlins and the demolition of the Lido. (However, Barry Island Pleasure Park, closed in 2009, reopened in 2010.) The political traditions of Barry have also declined, traditions evident in the town's prominence in movements such as the Workers' Educational Association, trade unionism and the Labour Party, and its significance as the birthplace of Gwynfor Evans.

But Barry has a future. It came into being to compete with Cardiff; indeed, David Davies prophesied that Barry's success would cause grass to grow in the streets of Cardiff. But, by now, Cardiff is the salvation of Barry, for it is refugees from the high prices of houses in the capital that are likely to revive the town in the next generation.

largest ships then afloat; unlike Cardiff, where there were unpaid debts arising from the costs incurred by docks that had long ceased to be useable, Barry was not burdened by redundant expenditure. Above all, the Barry company owned not only the docks but also the railways which served them. These advantages had become increasingly apparent by 1901, when Barry replaced Cardiff as the largest coal port in the world.

Cardiff had its advantages too. It was there that all the legal, financial and administrative work arising from the coal trade was undertaken. The offices of shipping companies and coalowners, long-established at Cardiff, all stayed there. Thus, the greater the increase in Barry's coal exports, the more numerous the working-class jobs available there, and the more numerous the middle-class jobs available in Cardiff. This explains why Barry was almost as much a working-class town as were the settlements of the coalfield.

Barry reached its apogee as a port in 1913 when it exported 11 million tons of coal. As it dealt with almost nothing else, its decline was inevitable as depression hit the south Wales coalfield.

It is difficult for the inquisitive explorer to gain access to the docks. For those eager to understand Barry's unique role, the place to go is the Docks Office, a dominating building owing something to Christopher Wren. The fact that the enormous

Those seeking the beginnings in Wales of the Renaissance style of architecture have only one place to go – Old Beaupre in the heart of the Vale of Glamorgan. (Beaupre – the fair meadow – is a suitable name for the place, although the word is pronounced as if it were the title of a company offering health insurance.) The walk across the fields from Howe Mill Farm offers a view of Beaupre Castle – a large ruin with walls which stand almost to full height, but which do not sustain a roof. Its southern part has been adapted as a dwelling and offers no access to the public. Old Beaupre, a mansion rather than a castle, is believed to have been built for the Bassets, a incoming family which bound its fortunes to Glamorgan for centuries. The grave of Richard Basset (d. 1849) in St Hilary's churchyard states that he was 'the last of the male heirs of the ancient Basset family of Beaupre'. He represented the eighteenth generation of the Bassets who succeeded each other at Beaupre.

The visit to those areas open to the public begins at the gatehouse which bears the date 1586 and the letters R B (Richard Basset) and C B (his wife, Catherine Basset). If there were nothing much else to see at Beaupre, it would hardly be worth a visit, but across the court from the gatehouse is a sight which leaves the visitor dumb-struck.

The remarkable sight is the Tower of the Orders, a gateway added in 1600 to the castle's fourteenth-century Great Hall. Its façade has three sections. The opening is flanked on either side by a pair of pillars, each surmounted by a Doric capital (a round cap surmounted by a square abacus). At the centre of the section above the opening are the arms of the Bassets, flanked by pairs of pillars, each surmounted by an Ionic capital (a cap bearing scroll-like ornaments). The uppermost level had a central window, now blocked, flanked by pairs of pillars, each surmounted by a Corinthian capital (a bell-shaped cap bearing ornaments based on acanthus leaves). Doric, Ionic and Corinthian are the three main orders of classical tradition, and the elegance and sophistication of the capitals is astonishing. Other stone carvers working for Richard Basset were responsible for sculpting classical motifs – on the north wall of the gatehouse, for example – but their work is generally crude. With the Tower of the Orders we can see for the first time in Wales work that fully reflects the architectural genius of the Renaissance. The central section with its Ionic pillars is the most appealing part of the structure. Beneath the family arms is the motto of the Bassets: 'Gwell Angau na Chywilydd' (Death rather than Dishonour), the motto adopted by the Welch Regiment. The carvings on the friezes are charming, particularly the ox heads; the ribbons hanging from their horns resemble those on the red hats of cardinals.

Towers of the Orders had been built at least half a century before Richard Basset commissioned the tower at Beaupre. One was built at Château d'Anet in Normandy in 1546, and,

in succeeding decades, English landowners were eager commissioners of such structures. It seems that the tradition came to an end with the building of the Tower of the Five Orders (Tuscan and Composite as well as Doric, Ionic and Corinthian) at Oxford in 1620. What is remarkable is that a minor squire in the Vale of Glamorgan insisted on acquiring what was the most exalted architectural fashion of his era. He deserves our gratitude.

The Jones family, heir of the Bassets, abandoned Old Beaupre and settled at New Beaupre, a kilometre and a half to the north. (Daniel Jones [d. 1841] of New Beaupre supplemented the profits of the Gwent and Glamorgan Eisteddfod of 1834 in order to finance the building of Cardiff's Gwent and Glamorgan Hospital; there is a plaque to his memory near Newport Road.)

Little of distinction is evident at New Beaupre. It is more interesting, after wandering around a roofless sixteenth-century building, to visit a structure dating from that century which still has its roof. Three kilometres west of Old Beaupre stands Llanmihangel Place, an early Tudor manor house. Its owner runs it as a guest-house, and staying there is a memorable experience.

The most intriguing aspect of the house is the defensive features it contains. At the end of the seventeenth century, the mansion's owner was Humphrey Edwin, a Congregationalist and the Lord Mayor of London in 1697; he attended chapel in full lord mayoral livery, much to the distress of his Tory contemporaries. However, there is nothing puritanical about his tomb in St Michael's Church.

Two kilometres south of Old Beaupre lies Flemingston. No journey through the Vale of Glamorgan would be complete without visiting the village. Its chief glory is Flemingston Court, a remarkably well-preserved early sixteenth-century mansion. Flemingston's main interest lies in its links with Iolo Morganwg (Edward Williams), who came to live there when a child and who maintained contact with the village until his death in 1826. His house stands at the centre of a neat row of cottages. It is intriguing to imagine what it was like at his death, when every room contained piles of manuscripts rising to the ceiling – a collection which has been a quarry and a quandary to scholars ever since. Iolo was buried in Flemingston church, and, in 1855, peeresses with Glamorgan connections, the marchioness of Bute and the countess of Dunraven among them, paid for a plaque in his memory. It is fascinating to read the long tribute, which omits all reference to his skill as a forger. Flemingston is now home to some of the richest people in Wales. One wonders what Iolo, a radical democrat and a republican, would have made of that.

There are some very odd buildings in Wales – Gwrych Castle, for example – but the oddities of Cardiff Castle place it in a class all of its own. It had its peculiarities from the very beginning. The Romans constructed not one, not two, not three, but four forts on the site, each one on top of the other. The last, built *c.* AD 280, was of stone, a rarity among the three dozen Roman auxiliary forts in Wales and its Marches. Sixteen centuries later, the ruined walls were rebuilt, and, consequently, Cardiff is virtually the only place in Europe where it is possible to see a more or less believable replica of a third-century Roman fort.

A century or two after the completion of the fourth fort, King Arthur came to Cardiff. That, at least, is what Geoffrey of Monmouth tells us, although he may have been inventing a story in order to please his patron, Robert fitz Henry, earl of Gloucester (d. 1147), who was lord of Cardiff when Geoffrey was writing his *Historia Regum Britanniae* (The History of the Kings of Britain) in the 1130s. There is more substance to the belief that in 1081 Robert fitz Hammo, father-in-law of Earl Robert,

commissioned a motte within the ruins of the Roman fort, although the height of the motte – at 10.87 metres, the highest in Wales – may indicate that it was William the Conqueror himself who was responsible for it. A timber tower was built on its summit, the building in which Robert, duke of Normandy, the eldest son of William the Conqueror, was held prisoner. (In the castle's Banqueting Hall, there is a carving of Robert gazing through the bars of his cell.) The tower was replaced *c.*1140 by a masonry shell keep. (Many decades must go by before a mound of soil can sustain a stone building.) According to Giraldus Cambrensis, the walls of the keep were scaled by Ifor Bach during the daring raid which led to the capture of William, earl of Gloucester, in 1158.

During the period 1199 to 1314 – the years of Cardiff's medieval apogee – the town and the lordship of Glamorgan were held by successive members of the Clare family. Gilbert de Clare (d. 1230) was probably responsible for the Black Tower, which stands in the middle of the southern wall of the old fort. (It now houses the museum of the Welch Regiment.) Cooper's Fields offers a view of the impressive octagonal tower abutting upon the western wall. It was commissioned by Richard Beauchamp, earl of Warwick (d. 1439), who was also responsible for the adjoining apartments with their vaulted undercroft, now the location of jolly medieval banquets.

In 1549, the castle came into the possession of William Herbert (d. 1570; earl of Pembroke from 1551), whose descendants held it until 1947, when John Crichton Stuart, the fifth marquess of Bute, presented to the city of Cardiff the castle from which it had sprung. The last addition to the castle before the late eighteenth century was commissioned by Henry, second earl of Pembroke (d. 1601) – the square tower located to the south of the Beauchamp Tower. Thereafter, nothing was done for two-hundred years. As the Herberts preferred Wilton, their mansion in Wiltshire, they virtually abandoned the castle. The situation worsened under their successors, the impoverished Windsor family (1683–1766).

Then, in 1766, the Windsor heiress married John Stuart, who in 1796 became the first marquess of Bute. Henry Holland was given the task of ensuring that Cardiff should have a residence worthy of their son, the heir of the Windsors and the Stuarts. Another square tower – the Bute Tower – was built abutting the west wall and the Beauchamp apartments were extensively revamped. Although the second marquess of Bute, owner of the castle from 1814 to 1848, left it virtually untouched, Holland's work attracted the contempt of the third marquess, a fervent champion of the Middle Ages who came of age in 1868. Hugely wealthy, he commissioned his fellow-enthusiast for things medieval, William Burges, to medievalize the castle. Burges died in 1881 at the age of fifty-four. It is difficult to imagine what further fantasies he would have created had he lived for another decade.

But the fantasies he did create are wonderful. They include the delightful clock tower, within which are the richly decorated summer and winter smoking-rooms. (The third marquess smoked heavily, partly in order to suppress hunger during his many fasts.) Equally ornate are the Banqueting Hall, the Library and the Arab and Chaucer rooms. The chief revelation is Burges's wealth of imagination. He abhorred the absence of ornamentation and drew upon themes from the classical world, the Bible, folk tales, nursery rhymes, Arab art, medieval literature and his own fertile inventiveness to create a wealth of serious, learned, playful and witty adornments.

The death of the third marquess in 1900 probably marked the passing of the only one of Burges's contemporaries who was totally devoted to his work. For most of the twentieth century, his accomplishments were held in low regard. When James Lees-Milne visited Cardiff Castle in 1942 on behalf of the National Trust, he suggested that the building should be demolished. Lees-Milne was a devotee of eighteenth-century neo-classicism, but his views were not dissimilar from those of Nikolaus Pevsner, that giant among architectural historians. Pevsner was enthusiastic about some of the more eccentric pioneers of modern design – Gaudí for example – but he declared that Burges's artistic work represented a cul-de-sac. Nowadays, we are more eclectic and we can delight in the knowledge that the heart of our capital city holds peerless marvels.

It was in the 1950s that I was first told that Cardiff has the finest civic centre in the world. At the time, I thought it was an example of an excessive desire to praise one's own patch. But after visiting Washington and New Delhi – the only credible competitors, it was argued – I realized that Cardiff does indeed have the finest civic centre in the world. My abiding memory of Washington is of a long strip of unkempt grass, and, in New Delhi, there is something peculiar in the way the presidential palace appears and disappears as one climbs the hill towards it.

Cathays Park exists because of the wealth of the Bute family. In 1766, John Stuart, son of the third earl of Bute (George III's prime minister), married Charlotte Windsor, granddaughter and

Armistice Day poppies on the grass near the Welsh National War Memorial

heiress of Charlotte Herbert, who inherited the Welsh estates given to her ancestor, William, earl of Pembroke, by Henry VIII and Edward VI. In 1766, Cardiff, with fewer than 1,500 inhabitants, was little more than a village. North-west of the castle lay a piece of scrubland, and it was the scrub (*[ge]haeg* in Middle English) which gave rise to the name Cathays. John Stuart became the first marquess of Bute in 1796. He avidly added to his land holdings in Glamorgan, and by his death in 1814 he owned almost all the land in the old borough of Cardiff and much in its immediate vicinity, acquisitions which later gave rise to accusations of chicanery. As the castle was half-ruined, he lived when at Cardiff in a house he acquired in Cathays, the grounds of which came to be known as Cathays Park.

The house was demolished soon after the first marquess's death. Little use was made of the land; as it was separated from the castle by North Road and by the Glamorganshire Canal, it did not become part of the extensive gardens which were being created for the third marquess of Bute (d. 1900). When the third marquess came of age in 1868, Cardiff was growing very rapidly, but, as he was so wealthy, there was no need for him to seek the income which would be forthcoming if Cathays Park were covered with houses.

For centuries, Cardiff's town hall had been located in the middle of St Mary's Street. The hall built on that site in 1747 was demolished in 1861. A new building was erected on the west side of the street, but, by the 1890s, it was inadequate for a town with almost 130,000 inhabitants. Cardiff also needed spacious law courts and a site for Wales's southern university college, which had been founded in 1883 in a small building in Newport Road. Furthermore, as the town's leaders were increasingly insistent that Cardiff was 'the metropolis of Wales', they considered that the town was the natural home for the buildings which would house the institutions that Welsh patriots were seeking to establish.

All the undeveloped land within easy reach of central Cardiff was part of the Bute estate. The estate would not part with the grounds linked to Cardiff Castle – Cooper's Fields, Sophia Gardens, Pontcanna Fields, Bute Park, Blackweir and Llandaff Fields – for the third marquess delighted in the extensive stretch of land visible from the windows of his castle. Cathays Park was not part of that extensive stretch; after a fruitless attempt in 1892, Cardiff Corporation succeeded in 1897 in purchasing the park – 23 hectares of land – for £159,323.

In laying out the civic centre, a simple plan was adopted – straight roads surrounding the rectangular Alexandra Gardens. (To Harold Carter, the fact that Wales's most ambitious piece of urban planning is centred upon a garden rather than a paved space – compare Paris, Rome or Florence – is proof that the Welsh lack a full sense of civic design.)

The first completed building was the Registry of the University of Wales (1903), but the ones that placed their stamp on the civic centre were the neo-baroque pair completed two

Television viewers outside the National Museum

years later – the City Hall and the Law Courts. (Intriguingly, the architect ensured that the clock tower of the City Hall was slightly higher than the clock tower of the castle.) They are clad in white Portland stone, and the decision to use the same stone to clad the other buildings erected in the park was the chief factor in imposing unity upon the entire scheme. Another such factor was the rule that the cornice line of the City Hall should determine the height of the main façades of all the other buildings, a rule sadly abandoned in the late twentieth century.

The main purpose in building Cathays Park was to acquire sites for buildings to serve Cardiff as a city (a status it was granted in 1905), as the county town of Glamorgan, and as the seat of Wales's southern university college. The wider ambitions of 'the metropolis of Wales' received recognition in the acquisition of the University Registry. They also find expression in the snarling dragon on top of the City Hall's cupola and in the building's massive statues symbolizing the unity and culture of Wales.

In subsequent years, the park increasingly became home to national rather than civic symbols. Work began in 1910 on the National Museum of Wales, a more compact and restrained building than the City Hall. It was not completed until 1993, and the final work was considerably less ambitious than was the original plan. The gallery of Welsh heroes (with one heroine: Boadicea) in the City Hall was opened in 1918, the Welsh National War Memorial in 1928, the Temple of Peace in 1938 and the Welsh Office in 1979. The Welsh Office – now the executive office of the Welsh Assembly Government – is a very odd building; it seems to close in upon itself, and has been described as conveying an impression of 'bureaucracy under siege'. It contrasts markedly with that transparent building, the Senedd in Cardiff Bay (2006). Perhaps the two buildings are symbolic of the difference between the Wales of 1979 and the Wales of 2006.

In Cardiff Bay, the explorer should begin at the place where once stood the lock-gate of the earliest of the Bute Docks, that opened on 8 October 1839. The opening of the dock was a major stimulant to the transformation of Wales and the transformation of the world. The dock's early months were not auspicious; in 1840, it handled 46,000 tons of goods, 43,000 tons of which were coal exports. However, by 1913, the Port of Cardiff, which included Penarth and Barry as well as Cardiff's Bute Docks, handled 29.8 million tons of goods, 26 million of which were coal exports. The worldwide price of coal was determined in Cardiff's Mount Stuart Square, at the Coal Exchange completed in 1888. By the early twentieth century, the Port of Cardiff was responsible for a quarter of the international trade in coal, and was therefore wholly central to the provision of the world's chief source of heat and energy. The industries and railways of France, Spain, Italy, Egypt, Argentina, Chile and Brazil depended on Cardiff for their fuel, and the oceans were traversed by ships powered by coal from Cardiff.

In revolutionizing the world, Cardiff was also revolutionizing itself and Wales. In 1801, when Cardiff had 1,870 inhabitants, there were in Wales twenty-four places which had larger populations. By 1901, the town had 164,000 inhabitants, 70,000 more than Swansea, its closest rival. Coalmining in the valleys of the rivers which flowed to Cardiff had caused even more revolutionary change in the central part of the south Wales coalfield. There, the population increased from less than ten thousand in 1801 to over half a million in 1901. Furthermore, the rest of Wales could not avoid the consequences of the massive growth in the south-east. Indeed, it was claimed in 1900 that fluctuations in the price of southern coal influenced marriage rates as far to the north as Merioneth.

The situation was not destined to endure. The fact that the

lock-gate of the first Bute Dock is no longer under water is proof of that. Most of the dock was filled in at the end of the 1970s, mainly with material from the Aberfan tip. Its southernmost part – the Oval Basin – was spared and the site of the lock-gate is now part of Roald Dahl Plass. The second of the Bute Docks (1859) has also lost its function. It is now a rectangular lake lacking access to the sea. The three other docks – Roath Basin (1874), Roath Dock (1887) and Queen Alexandra Dock (1907) – are still in use, but, as little has replaced the export of coal, Cardiff's dock system now far exceeds the needs of the city's maritime trade. The chief activity is the import of timber and sand, and trade in specialized forms of steel, although there are hopes that the three anchorages specially built for cruise ships will attract wealthy sea voyagers to the city.

In the third quarter of the twentieth century, there were many worried discussions about the future of Cardiff's docklands. The Coal Exchange closed in 1958 and coal exports ceased in 1964; by then, little took place in the mercantile palaces – Empire House, Baltic House, Cambrian Buildings and the rest – erected when the coal trade was at its height. Butetown was described as 'Cardiff's withered arm', and it was argued that cutting it away was the only option. Discussions were linked to equivocal attitudes towards the unique multicultural community that had developed there. Neil Sinclair, the chief chronicler of Butetown, described Tiger Bay as the only place in Britain 'where you can see the world in one square mile'. Members of the community were rehoused as blocks of flats were substituted for neighbourly terraced houses in places such as Loudon Square, causing Sinclair to ask: 'Who was the unknown architect whose dream created our nightmare?'

The 1970s saw the germination of the notion that Butetown could experience rebirth. The first seedling was the establishment of the Welsh Industrial and Maritime Museum (1975); it was followed by the South Glamorgan County Hall, which is handsomely mirrored in what remains of the 1859 dock. But rebirth proved to be sluggish. The 1979 plan to house Wales's National Assembly in the former Coal Exchange came to nothing, as did Zaha Hadid's innovative design for the home of the Welsh National Opera Company in Cardiff Bay. Even that harbinger of

The Norwegian Church at Cardiff Bay

the Bay's renaissance – the Welsh Industrial and Maritime Museum – was replaced by very nondescript buildings.

But dramatic innovation did eventually occur. The estuaries of the Taff and the Ely were turned into a freshwater lake, thus ensuring that Cardiff, which owes its existence to access to the sea, has now turned its back on salt water. On the lakeside are two of the capital's best-loved buildings – the delightful Norwegian Church and the Pierhead Building, aglow with warm terracotta. Alongside them are two of the capital's most significant buildings – the Millennium Centre (2004) and the Senedd (2005), the seat of the National Assembly for Wales. If anywhere in Wales has been reinvented, it is Butetown. What is particularly heart-warming is that an institution that represents all the people of Wales stands splendidly diaphanous at the very spot where Welsh industrial output began the transformation of the world.

There is hardly any other building in Wales that has suffered as many indignities as has Llandaff Cathedral. That complex manuscript, *Liber Landavensis*, compiled in the 1130s, claimed that Llandaff had, by then, been the centre of an extensive and well-endowed diocese for at least six centuries, but the place-name Llandaff does not belong to the era of Early Welsh. Indeed, the first reliable reference to Llandaff as a diocese dates from 1119.

No doubt there were bishops in Glywysing and Gwent from the time when the Christian religion first struck roots in those kingdoms. There may well have been bishops in hallowed places such as Llantwit Major, Llandough and Llancarfan, and Geoffrey

of Monmouth claimed that there was an archbishop at Caerleon in the age of King Arthur. The tenth-century inscribed stone in the south aisle of the cathedral suggests that there was a church at Llandaff before the coming of the Normans; elevating it to diocesan status was probably their work. They wanted a bishop who would be answerable to Cardiff Castle, their chief power centre in Glamorgan. (The same aspiration may be seen in the north-east, where St Asaph Cathedral was founded near the Norman stronghold at Rhuddlan.)

As bishops of St Davids, when seeking to expand the boundaries of their diocese, could cite the many dedications to St David, bishops of Llandaff felt that they too should look for dedications to 'saints' with Llandaff connections, among them Dyfrig, the earliest Welsh 'saint'. His associations were with Erging (Archenfield in south-west Herefordshire). His body was brought from Bardsey Island and ceremoniously reburied at Llandaff in 1120. Another was Teilo, a 'saint' whose dedications extended from Llandeilo Fawr to Gower, Brycheiniog, Elfael and northern Gwent. (Llandaff already had one of Teilo's three alleged bodies.) Yet another was Euddogwy, who was said to have been bishop of Llandaff in the sixth century, and who had dedications in eastern Gwent. *Liber Landavensis* was compiled in order to promote the dedications campaign, but, as the bishops of St Davids and Hereford were fiercely opposed to Llandaff's ambitions, all attempts to expand the diocese beyond the boundaries of the kingdom of Morgannwg were unsuccessful.

The earliest building work surviving at Llandaff was commissioned by Urban, bishop from 1107 to 1133. It includes the arch behind the high altar, one of the best examples of Romanesque architecture in Wales. In the thirteenth century, most of the cathedral was rebuilt; the work, which, unusually, included no transepts, culminated in the fine early Gothic of the western façade.

In the fourteenth century, the cathedral acquired traceried windows in the Decorated style, and, in the late fifteenth century, it benefited from links with the Tudor family. It is likely that it was Jasper Tudor, lord of Glamorgan from 1486 until his death in 1495, who financed the construction of the tower on the northern side of the western façade, a tower crowned with pinnacles similar to those on the tower of St John's Church in central Cardiff.

Llandaff's fortunate days came to an end with the death of Jasper. It had never been a wealthy diocese, and was further impoverished by the Protestant Reformation. The manor of Llandaff, source of a third of the diocese's income, was alienated. As a later bishop of Llandaff put it: 'I am the bishop of Aff, for all the land is gone.' The castle at Llandaff fell into ruin. The bishop's palace at Mathern, on the eastern edge of the diocese, was, by the early eighteenth century, also in ruin. Being bishop of Llandaff was not lucrative, so no one wanted to hold the position for long; indeed, it was claimed that the bishop of Llandaff was immortal, for no bishop ever died in office. The cathedral suffered severely. In 1576, it was believed to be beyond restoration, and, after a storm in 1723, the roof caved in and much of the stonework collapsed. In the 1730s, a temple was constructed within the ruins. It was quite a sophisticated building; designed by John Wood, its dimensions were based upon Solomon's temple ('the length thereof was three score cubits and the breadth thereof twenty cubits'). But, as it was so incongruous an addition to a medieval ruin, it was widely held in great contempt.

Nevertheless, it remained in existence for a century and a half. No attempt was made to restore the cathedral to its original glory until 1841, when the revival of Anglicanism was in full flood. The work continued until the 1860s under the supervision of John Prichard, the son of the cathedral's vicar choral and virtually the first Welshman to win fame as an architect. The climax of his work is the south-western tower, which gives the cathedral a distinction it had previously lacked, and adds a vertical emphasis to a building which might otherwise look as if it is squatting in its low-lying location.

The cathedral enjoyed almost eighty years of repose. Then, in 1941, a bomb exploded outside the south aisle. The roof caved in for the second time, the windows were destroyed and the entire cathedral was blackened by fire. This time, rebuilding was rapidly undertaken, partly in order to stabilize the structure, and partly in order to include in it elements of the modern world – a concept which would have been alien to medievalists like John Prichard. It was the bishop, Glyn Simon, who urged the architect, George Pace, to design a concrete arch between nave and chancel, and it was he too who commissioned Jacob Epstein to make the enormous aluminium Majestas placed above the arch, work which ensures that Llandaff is unique among the cathedrals of Europe. Llandaff's tribulations did not come to an end with the post-war rebuilding. In 2000, fire destroyed the organ. So far, however, that is the only ordeal that the cathedral has suffered in the twenty-first century.

Skansen in Stockholm, opened in 1891, is the oldest open-air museum in Europe. It was followed in 1893 by the Norsk Folkemuseum in Oslo, in 1901 by the Frilandsmuseet in Copenhagen and in 1909 by the Seurasaari Ulkomuseo in Helsinki. The first country to follow the example of the Scandinavians was Wales, with the opening of the Welsh Folk Museum at St Fagans in 1948.

The museum comes late in the history of the area. The roots of the place are very much older. There are prehistoric earthworks near the Ely, the remains of an eleventh-century ringwork south of the church, and the curtain wall of a thirteenth-century castle can be traced in the museum's gardens. In 1584, St Fagans was acquired by a member of the prolific Herbert family – perhaps the Nicholas Herbert who was elected MP for Glamorgan Boroughs in that year. By the end of the century, a splendid mansion had been built there. Although known as St Fagans Castle, it had virtually no defensive features, proof that the gentry of Glamorgan believed that, by then,

Inside St Teilo's Church at the National History Museum, St Fagans

ensuring the security of their residences was a matter that could safely be entrusted to the state. (The situation was different earlier in the century; St Fagans Castle should be compared with Llanmihangel Place and Llancaeach-fawr, where there are obvious defensive features.) The castle is remarkable for the perfect symmetry of its chief façade, evidence that the architectural ideas of the Renaissance were taking root in Glamorgan. (The belief that a building has a chief façade was alien to the thinking of the Middle Ages.)

In 1616, the castle was bought by Edward Lewis, the grandson of Edward Lewis of Van near Caerphilly, one of the most successful of Glamorgan's seventeenth-century estate builders. It remained in the possession of the Lewis family until 1736, and the fervid Parliamentarian, William Lewis (d. 1661), delighted in the Royalists' defeat on his land (the Battle of St Fagans, 8 May 1648). The Lewises died out in the male line in 1736, and the St Fagans estate passed to Other Windsor, third earl of Plymouth of the second creation, husband of Elizabeth, the heiress of the Lewises.

Elizabeth's dowry was worth having. By the 1880s, the Windsors owned 7,023 hectares in Glamorgan, including extensive properties in Grangetown and Penarth – lands rapidly rising in value in the wake of urbanization. (The family also owned 4,500 hectares around Oakley Park in Shropshire and 3,400 hectares around Hewell Grange in Worcestershire.) The family owned every hectare of the parish of St Fagans, a striking example of a 'closed community'. The Windsors spent lavishly at St Fagans and lived there for much of the year. The Stuarts of Bute, Glamorgan's leading aristocratic family, were generally absentee landlords, and thus the Windsors were at the apex of the hierarchy of Glamorgan. This was especially true during the inter-war years when Irene, countess of Plymouth, presided over county society.

The second earl of Plymouth of the third creation died in 1943, and in 1946 his son, the third earl, presented the castle and 40 hectares of land to the National Museum of Wales. The Welsh Folk Museum was opened in 1948, two years after the opening of Sturbridge, Massachusetts, a museum with not disimilar aims. The chief founder of the St Fagans museum was Iorwerth Cyfeiliog Peate, who was determined to follow the example of the Scandinavian open-air museums by re-erecting at St Fagans a wide range of Welsh dwellings and workplaces. Most traditional Scandinavian buildings were constructed of wood and most traditional Welsh buildings were constructed of stone, and thus the costs facing Peate were far greater than those facing Arthur Hazelius, the founder of Skansen.

The first building to be re-erected at St Fagans was the Esgair Moel woollen mill (1952). The choice was proof of Peate's interest in threatened rural crafts – perhaps an understandable concern in the 1950s, a decade when industrial Wales was experiencing something of a revival. The revival proved short-lived, but decades would go by before any structures from industrial Wales were re-erected at St Fagans.

The first fruit of the change of policy was the terrace from Rhyd-y-car, Merthyr Tydfil, now the favourite exhibit of those visiting the museum. (The gardens of the terraced houses are particularly interesting, including as they do objects such as rusty metal baths hanging on walls.) The most recent addition is

St Teilo's Church from the Llwchwr Valley. As it has been restored to look as churches did on the eve of the Protestant Reformation, its interior comes as a shock to those accustomed to the interiors of most of Wales's parish churches, almost all of which were transformed in the Victorian age.

Peate's intention was to add a building or a monument to the museum every year. Over forty have been re-erected there in the half century and more since the opening of the Esgair Moel woollen mill. Thus, his objective has not been fully realized. After all, there are over a hundred and fifty buildings in the Norsk Folkemuseum in Oslo.

Wales is rich in landmarks – Dolwyddelan Castle, for example, or Pentre Ifan cromlech, or the Foel Drygarn cairns and hillfort. Probably the best-loved of them is Castell Coch. When the Normans invaded the kingdom of Morgannwg in the late eleventh century, their central intention was the seizure of fertile lands. (Despite the fact that their origins lay in the fiords and mountains of Norway, they had become lowland arable farmers rather than upland pastoral ones.) The first region they seized west of the Rhymney was Cibwr, the southernmost commote of the cantref of Senghenydd. Cibwr, essentially the area now occupied by the city of Cardiff, was surrounded by a girdle of mottes – Rumney, y Twmpath (Rhiwbina), Whitchurch, Radyr and Caerau.

These strongholds were abandoned when an outer girdle was created – Cefn Mably, Morgraig, Castell Coch and St Fagans. Here, an intriguing question arises. Was the outer girdle under the unbroken control of the lords of Cardiff Castle? Between 1147 and 1183, the castle was in the feeble hands of William, earl of Gloucester, and when the Welsh lords of upland Glamorgan were receiving the patronage of the Lord Rhys, the powerful ruler of Deheubarth. One of those lords was Ifor Bach, Rhys's brother-in-law. According to the most reliable of the early historians of Glamorgan, Rice Merrick, Castell Coch was 'supposed to be builded by Ifor Petit, a gentleman… who… took William, lord of Glamorgan.' The statement dates from the late sixteenth century, but, if it is true, the earliest masonry work at Castell Coch was commissioned by a Welsh lord.

The same ambiguity arises at Morgraig on Caerphilly Mountain. In the second half of the thirteenth century, as in the second half of the eleventh century, the Welsh lords of upland Glamorgan had a powerful patron. Gruffudd ap Rhys, grandson of Ifor Bach, and a man eager to recognize the power of Llywelyn ap Gruffudd, may have commissioned the building of Castell Morgraig. However, in the late 1260s, when Llywelyn was seriously threatening the Lords of the March, Gilbert de Clare ensured that the whole of Glamorgan became subject to his power. Sutton stone, quarried at St Brides Major in the Vale, was being used at Castell Morgraig by 1270, proof that, by then, the castle was securely in Gilbert's possession.

The most obvious evidence for the success of 'the second conquest of Glamorgan' is Caerphilly Castle, where building began at 1268. There was also a perceived need to ensure control over the Taff Gorge. Castell Coch was therefore rebuilt. Three towers were constructed on top of the original motte; they were strengthened by spur buttresses which reach out like massive triangles. It is likely that, by the death of Gilbert de Clare in 1295, the castle had been completed. It was damaged during the revolt of Llywelyn Bren (probably Gruffudd ap Rhys's son), a revolt which followed the death of Gilbert de Clare's heir – another Gilbert – in 1314. The damage was not made good, and, for over five-hundred years, Castell Coch quietly fell into ruin.

With the coming of the Tudors, the castle and the rest of the lordship of Glamorgan became crown property. Henry VII's grandson, Edward VI, presented the lordship to William Herbert, earl of Pembroke. It was William's distant descendant, John Crichton Stuart, the third marquess of Bute (d. 1900), who opened a new chapter in the history of Castell Coch.

In 1865, when he was eighteen years old, the marquess met a man twenty years his senior – William Burges, an architect who delighted in the Gothic revival. Burges began working on Cardiff Castle in 1868. The marquess considered the castle to be the focus of the vast park he was seeking to establish on the banks of the Taff and was anxious that the vista from it should culminate in an attractive landmark. A report prepared by G. T. Clark in 1850, and another by Burges in 1872, affirmed that sufficient remained of the castle to enable its restorers to be fairly sure of its original shape. Rebuilding was therefore undertaken. When Burges died in 1881, the external work had been completed, and he had left so many sketches of his intentions for the interior that other architects – William Frame in particular – were able to complete the castle by 1891.

The most striking feature of what is visible today is loyalty to what survives from the thirteenth century, proof of Burges's profound knowledge of the architecture of that century and of his eagerness, when there was an element of doubt, to give priority to the picturesque. The three towers certainly rise from medieval foundations, but the differences in their heights and the acclivity of their roofs are the fruit of Burges's imagination. Much of the interior work was inspired by Chillon Castle in Switzerland and by the works of Viollet-le-Duc, the leading specialist on the

Gothic architecture of France – although the author of *The Penguin History of Art* declared that 'besides [the] integrity [of Castell Coch], the more famous restorations by Viollet-le-Duc at Pierrefonds and Carcassonne appear harsh and obviously modern'.

Burges recreated the essence of the building commissioned by Gilbert de Clare. In commissioning it, Gilbert wanted to ensure that Cardiff would not become part of the reinvigorated Wales which Llywelyn ap Gruffudd was seeking to create. As Cardiff is now the capital of a reinvigorated Wales, Castell Coch is not one of a girdle of strongholds defending Cardiff from the Welsh, but a sign to those travelling south along the A470 that the end of the journey is nigh.

Before the coming of industry, only two places within what became the south Wales coalfield were larger than tiny villages – Pontypool and Caerphilly. It was to the weekly market at Caerphilly that the farmers of the Rhondda, Taff and Rhymney valleys brought their cheese, butter and eggs (the Pontypridd bridge was built to facilitate their trade), and it was at the annual fairs at Caerphilly that the cattle, horses and sheep of the uplands were sold.

The key to the development of Caerphilly was the fairly level land west of the bend in the Rhymney. It was there *c.* AD 75 that the Romans built a fort which adjoined the road linking Cardiff with the Vale of Usk. The curve in the B4600 north of the castle is believed to follow the northern corner of the fort.

From the end of the Roman Empire until the late thirteenth century, Caerphilly, located as it was within the *cantref* of Senghenydd (the land between the Taff and the Rhymney), was under Welsh rule. Cibwr, the southernmost of the commotes of Senghenydd, was seized by the Norman, Robert fitz Hammo, in the 1080s. Cardiff Castle was built as Cibwr's chief stronghold and mottes were constructed along the borders of the commote.

If it were the Normans who constructed the twelfth-century Gwern-y-domen ringwork south of Bedwas, they did attempt, in that century, to advance north of Cefn Cibwr (Caerphilly Mountain). In general, however, the Norman lord at Cardiff was obliged to accept that the uplands of Glamorgan were under Welsh rule. That became a major issue as Llywelyn ap Gruffudd won increasing power. As they were leaders of Welsh communities, men such as Gruffudd ap Rhys, a descendant of Ifor Bach, were eager to accept the overlordship of Llywelyn ap Gruffudd rather than that of the lord of Glamorgan. Indeed, the Treaty of Montgomery (1267) contained a clause which transferred the allegiance of 'the Welsh barons of Wales' to Llywelyn, although it must be admitted that there is nothing in the treaty which suggests that anywhere in Glamorgan was to be part of Llywelyn's principality.

From 1262 until 1295, the lord of Glamorgan was Gilbert de Clare, the most masterful of the lords of the March. He exiled Gruffudd ap Rhys, and strengthened the borders of Cibwr by commissioning the rebuilding of Castell Coch and Castell Morgraig in stone. Unlike Caerphilly, which was built on level land, those castles had restricted sites. Building a new castle on an unrestricted site at Caerphilly was a clear indication that Gilbert intended to extend his authority beyond Cefn Cibwr and to affirm what is known as 'the second conquest of Glamorgan'.

Work on Caerphilly Castle began in April 1268, seven months after the sealing of the Treaty of Montgomery. Llywelyn's forces set fire to the unfinished building in October 1270, but Gilbert continued with the work. In 1271, Llywelyn besieged the castle with the assistance of two former enemies – his brother, Dafydd, and the lord of southern Powys, Gruffudd ap Gwenwynwyn. It has been claimed that Llywelyn was at the height of his power in 1271, although Beverley Smith, the chief authority on his career, has argued that the siege of Caerphilly was an example of the hubris which was so central to the history of the destruction of the Welsh principality.

Six years after the siege, Llywelyn's authority was confined to Gwynedd Uwch Conwy. He was therefore wholly incapable of challenging the power of Gilbert de Clare. As a stronghold on the Rhymney was no longer necessary, Gilbert could have abandoned Caerphilly Castle. But he carried on; indeed, the work did not come to an end until *c.*1326. The result is one of the most impressive castles in Europe. Among its most striking features is the fact that it was not a royal castle. Caernarfon, Conwy, Harlech and Beaumaris castles were built for a king who could draw upon all the resources of his realm, and those resources were also available to the monarchs responsible for Windsor Castle, the only

castle in Britain more extensive than Caerphilly. But it was a castle commissioned by an earl – a very wealthy earl, admittedly – that was built at Caerphilly.

That is only one of the peculiarities of Caerphilly Castle. It also combines two of the most sophisticated developments in thirteenth-century military architecture – concentric design and the use of water. A concentric castle consists of two wards, the inner wholly enclosed by the outer. Beaumaris offers the most perfect example of the design, but that castle was begun a quarter of a century after work was initiated at Caerphilly. The builders of Caerphilly Castle were therefore the pioneers. Even more impressive is the use of water. In 1266, Gilbert de Clare took part in the siege of Kenilworth Castle. That castle was surrounded by large-scale water defences and a siege of nine months was necessary before it fell to royal forces. Did Kenilworth's water defences inspire those at Caerphilly?

The lakes around the castle were refilled in 1950, the climax of restoration work which had been begun by the fourth marquess of Bute in the 1920s. Unlike his father, the third marquess, who commissioned fantasy castles at Cardiff and Castell Coch, the fourth marquess commissioned work at Caerphilly which was as similar as possible to what had been constructed in the Middle Ages. But, mercifully, he did not interfere with the most intriguing feature of the castle – the tower which is 10 per cent out of perpendicular, over 6 per cent more of a leaning tower than the one at Pisa. The restoration is at its best in the Great Hall, completed in the 1320s. The hall is licensed for weddings. Is there anywhere in Wales a more splendid place in which to begin married life?

Of all the local history museums in Wales, the most appealing is that at Pontypridd, partly because of the enthusiasm of its curator, Brian Davies. It is located in Capel Tabernacl, and adjoins Capel Eglwys Bach, which has the most lovable façade of all the chapels of Wales.

Greater importance belongs to another of the museum's neighbours – the bridge which, in a circuitous way, gives its name to Pontypridd. In the early eighteenth century, the track linking the farms of Llanwynno with Caerphilly market crossed the Taff slightly to the north of its confluence with the Rhondda. Because of the Taff's powerful current, the wooden bridges built across it were quickly destroyed.

In the mid-eighteenth century, a stone bridge across the Taff became an urgent priority. William Edwards (1719–89), who had already built a stone bridge across the Tawe, was asked to provide it. Edwards, the minister at Groesfaen near Caerphilly, was the most remarkable of Glamorgan's ministerial architects. His first bridge (1751), one with four arches, was washed away. Because of the strength of the current, Edwards decided that the only option was a single-arched bridge spanning nearly 43 metres, a wider span than had ever been bridged before. Two of his single-arched bridges were washed away, but he persisted, perhaps as a tribute to his father who had drowned in the waters of the Taff. His 1756 attempt was successful, partly because the weight of the structure was reduced by forming three round holes on each side.

The bridge, located in a verdant landscape, won fame for its beauty. It was portrayed on a plate produced by the Nantgarw Pottery for Thomas Williams (Gwilym Morganwg, 1778–1835) and on a Wedgewood plate painted for Catherine, empress of Russia. A segment of a perfect circle, the bridge stands 11 metres above the river's flow. But, although beautiful, it was not very practical. It was too steep for any traffic apart from a sledge or a packhorse, and when steps were added in the 1890s, it was only usable by pedestrians. The adjoining ferry was in use until 1857, when a three-arched bridge was built alongside the 1756 bridge, a structure which much undermined the appeal of Edwards's masterpiece. The 1756 bridge came to define Pontypridd. It gave the town its original name – Newbridge. Confusion arose between the Glamorgan Newbridge and the Monmouthshire Newbridge, so the Glamorgan Newbridge was given a new name. The Rhondda had once been crossed by a bridge which adjoined a mud cottage; that bridge was known as Pont-y-tŷ-pridd (the bridge of the earthen house) or Pont-tŷ-pridd or Pontypridd, the name adopted by the town which developed around the confluence of the Taff and the Rhondda. (As Ponty can be considered to be a contraction of Pont-tŷ-pridd, it is not – as is widely believed – an Anglicization.)

The memorial to Evan and James Jones in Ynysangharad Park, Pontypridd

The Pontypridd Rocking Stone and the boulders erected around it

The bridge is the place at which to start exploring Pontypridd. From the museum, Morgan Street leads to the Municipal Offices (1904). It is a building with considerable swagger and has no competitors among the municipal offices of the south Wales coalfield, apart perhaps from those at Maesteg. In the town centre stands the tower of St Catherine's Church (1870), which gives the profile of Pontypridd a fine verticality. It was designed by John Norton, whose tower at Neath (1869) gives that town a similar distinction. Nearby is Pontypridd's famous market, although it is only a shadow of its former self. (That, at least, is the impression given by contributors to Pontypridd's website, people who are constantly critical of their town.)

Pontypridd was first affected by the Industrial Revolution in the 1790s with the coming of the Glamorganshire Canal. It acquired its own industrial works in 1810, when the Brown Lennox Company began manufacturing chains there. The area

also acquired a romantic aura. In 1815, Iolo Morganwg announced that he would hold a *cadair ac eisteddfod* (a chair and eisteddfod) at the Rocking Stone, a huge boulder in a common above the Taff which was probably dumped there by an Ice Age glacier. Iolo believed that the boulder was the centre of the rituals of the ancient Britons. His 1815 ceremonies were the beginning of the most remarkable chapter in the history of Pontypridd – the druidical craze which lasted until the death of Morien (Owen Morgan, a *Western Mail* journalist) in 1921. Explorers should go to the Rocking Stone to see if they can make it rock, and to appreciate the marketing skills of Gwilym Morganwg in ensuring that his New Inn tavern would be the bibulous headquarters of the druids. Pontypridd's romanticism appealed to the strangest Welshman of the nineteenth century – Dr William Price, who was responsible for the construction of a pair of towers at Glyntaff in which he intended to house a druidical museum. As he was the

pioneer of cremation, it is fitting that it was at Glyntaff in 1924 that Wales's first crematorium was opened.

Pontypridd was also home to less eccentric Welsh patriots. In Ynysangharad Park stands a delightful memorial to Evan James and James James, the composer and author of *Hen Wlad fy Nhadau*, the anthem they created, as the memorial puts it, *trwy dynerwch eu cariad at Gymru* (because of the benignity of their love for Wales). When the cemetery of Carmel Chapel was cleared, Evan James's remains were reinterred in front of the memorial. Apart from Aberdare and Pontypool, Pontypridd has the most extensive stretch of urban greenery of any of the towns of the south Wales coalfield, but because of the discontent characteristic of its people, the park is the subject of constant grumbling.

The memorial to Dr William Price at Llantrisant

Of all the places that I have visited in Wales, the most intriguing is the Rhondda Heritage Park at Trehafod, five kilometres north of Pontypridd. Before going there, I had had my misgivings, for I had heard that what it offered was a tour which mimicked a visit to a real coalmine. I was pleasantly surprised, for what is on offer is simulation rather than mimicry. Simulation is rooted in respect; mimicry is rooted in contempt.

It must be immediately acknowledged that a visit to Trehafod does not provide the same experience as does a visit to Big Pit at Blaenavon. At Big Pit, the visitor can explore a complete colliery (a somewhat sanitized colliery, perhaps) which happens to be idle; Trehafod offers access to a very small part of a colliery that has been turned into something of a show-piece. To make a show of an occupation as dangerous as coalmining might be considered tawdry, but, as everything has been designed with sensitivity and with an earnest desire to inform, visitors get no sense of tawdriness. The visit is certainly entertaining, but it is also educative and sometimes heart-rending.

The road from Pontypridd reaches the point where the valley of Rhondda Fawr is at its narrowest. There, on the right of the road, pit-head gear comes into view – now a rare sight in the Rhondda. (In the inter-war years, there were over fifty pit-heads within the Rhondda borough.) The gear is part of what remains of the Hetty shaft of Tŷ Mawr colliery, and contains the south Wales's coalfield's sole surviving example of a winding-engine powered by steam. Trehafod is two kilometres further to the north, but, if resources permit, there are plans to ensure that the Hetty shaft will become part of the park.

The beginning of Cyfeillion Road marks the boundary between the coal deposits leased by the Great Western Colliery Company, owner of Tŷ Mawr colliery, and those leased by the Lewis Merthyr Consolidated Collieries Company. The latter was the creation of William Thomas Lewis (1837–1914; Baron Merthyr from 1911), a company which also owned the Great Universal colliery where 439 people were killed in the Senghenydd Disaster of 1913. The company had six pits exploiting the Rhondda's coal deposits – Trevor, Bertie, Lady Lewis, Hafod 1, Hafod 2 and Coedcae. The Lady Lewis pit was in the valley of the Rhondda Fach, the two Hafod pits were near Nyth-brân (home of the famous runner, Guto Nyth-brân) and Coedcae was located where the Heritage Park hotel now stands.

The Heritage Park is centred around the Trevor and Bertie pits, which were named after William Thomas Lewis's sons. The most striking feature at the entrance is the two-metre-high miners' lamp, unveiled in 2000 as a memorial to those who were killed or injured in the collieries of the south Wales coalfield – a long list bearing in mind that, when mining was at its height, a collier was killed every six hours and one was seriously injured every two minutes in Britain. (Proportionately, the statistics were far worse in the south Wales coalfield, which was much more dangerous than the other coalfields of Britain.)

In 1989, a Visitors' Centre was opened in the colliery's storehouses; it contains exhibitions, an art gallery, a café, and shop façades brought from other parts of the coalfield. The project was completed with the opening of the Heritage Centre in 1994. The main feature of the centre is a somewhat equivocal guided tour of the colliery. It begins at Trevor pit's winding-house, which contains ingenious machinery which permitted cages to stop at several places within the shaft. In the adjoining winding-house of the Bertie pit, the history of the Rhondda is interpreted through conversations (in Welsh among colliers and their families; in English among coalowners and agitators) conducted by full-size models. The models are disappointing, for, after almost two decades, they are rather dilapidated. It is more rewarding to talk to the guides, all of whom are hugely welcoming and informative former miners.

Then, the visit becomes rather surreal. On entering the cage in the Trevor pit, visitors experience what seems to be a very rapid journey to the bottom of the pit, 400 metres from the surface. But, on looking through the small window in the cage, it is apparent that the journey is very brief and very slow. This is a

matter of illusion rather than deception, for, at the end of the journey, everyone is aware that they are only some 20 metres lower than when they started. (It was the people who devised the journey at the Jorvik Centre in York who were responsible for the illusions at Trehafod.) The tram offers an even more surreal experience. Although it is stationary, those sitting in it have the impression that they are hurtling through tunnels full of life-threatening dangers. These are Disneyland tricks, but, as they offer at least some impression of the dangers faced by so many of our ancestors, they have a modicum of authenticity.

The tour finishes with a film providing a kaleidoscope of impressions of the Rhondda. Listening to the melodious, committed voice of the commentator is an emotional experience. It was only on leaving that I realized that I had been listening to the voice of Neil Kinnock. I had never imagined that I would be moved almost to tears by any pronouncements of his.

It is not everyone who realizes how central the Rhondda has been in the history of Wales. Its population reached its peak in 1924 when 167,900 people lived in the valleys of the Rhondda Fawr and the Rhondda Fach – more than the combined populations of the counties of Cardigan (58,290), Merioneth (43,710) and Montgomery (51,640). The figure 164,000 represented an 8303 per cent increase since 1851.

The most astounding development in the Rhondda between 1851 and 1924 was the building of over 30,000 dwellings. The inhabitants of those dwellings were fortunate that the Rhondda developed when it did. Extensive urbanization had occurred in places such as Blaenavon and Merthyr Tydfil in the late eighteenth and early nineteenth centuries, an era when little attention was given to issues such as clean water and sewerage. Some streets were constructed in that period in the Rhondda,

especially at Dinas, where Walter Coffin's employees began mining bituminous coal in 1809. But major urbanization did not occur until the 1870s, when the size of dwellings, the width of streets, and the provision of drains, pavements, lighting and clean water had become priorities.

Rhondda dwellings of the late nineteenth century may be seen at their best in Dumfries Street, Treorchy, where each house has a frontage of about five metres. The front room had a window facing the street and the middle room a window facing the back; the kitchen and the back kitchen lay between the house's middle-room window and that of the house next door. There were three bedrooms, and a lavatory was located at the bottom of the garden. Such houses attracted the envy of country dwellers, a visitor from Cardiganshire commentating in 1900 that 'we are fools to stay where we are when we could live in houses such as these'.

A further advantage was the fact that the houses were warm, for, in the Rhondda, coal was cheap; indeed, for many, it was free. Admittedly, the houses in Dumfries Street were superior to many of those built in the Rhondda. The Dumfries Street houses were erected on the fields of Glyncoli and Tyle-du, farms owned by the third marquess of Bute, whose officials favoured expansiveness in house building. A plaque in Treorchy's main street marks the boundary between the Bute estate and that of Crawshay Bailey, whose officials had more restrictive ideas.

Two-thirds of the land of Ystradyfodwg (the parish which eventually became the borough of Rhondda) was owned by four landowners – the marquess of Bute, Crawshay Bailey, the earl of Dunraven and Griffith Llewelyn. The four estates followed essentially the same policy – letting plots for house building on ninety-nine-year leases. Lessees paid ground rent, generally two shillings per foot frontage – usually £1.10 per house per year. The leasehold system had its merits. The estate had the responsibility for, and bore the costs of, marking the boundaries of the plots, laying out the streets and providing essential services. As the cost of a house did not include the cost of the land on which it stood, dwellings were more affordable. By the early twentieth century, nearly 60 per cent of the families of the Rhondda owned their houses – albeit as leaseholders – and the leasehold system is part of the explanation for that high percentage. Although serious problems arose when leases expired, it is difficult to imagine what would have happened had householders been allowed to build whatever they wanted, wherever they wanted – the system advocated by opponents of ground leases.

The great majority of the dwellings built in the Rhondda between 1851 and 1924 were similar to those in Dumfries Street, Treorchy. There were some exceptions. Strictly speaking, a street is a row of buildings facing another row of buildings; a terrace is a row of buildings facing the back of another row of buildings. Llwynypia offers the finest examples of Rhondda terraces. There, in the 1860s, terraces were constructed bearing names such as Inverleith, Argyle and Cameron; they were built to house the employees of the Scot, Archibald Hood, who had commissioned the sinking of a pit to the four-foot coal seam, the true source of the Rhondda's wealth. They represent Hood's attempt to attract key workers from Scotland to his 'Scotch Houses' at Llwynypia.

There is a dignity to the houses of the Rhondda, with their walls of Pennant sandstone and the brick surrounds of their windows and doorways; indeed, their architectural ancestors are the Georgian streets of places such as Dublin. Their original dignity has not always survived. There has been a vogue for false stone-cladding, Gwynedd slate has yielded to clay tiles and the skilled work of the Rhondda's carpenters has given way to the horrors of uPVC. As hardly any Rhondda families now have coal fires, thin pipes pushing out through roofs have replaced chimneys, the pots of which used to give such panache to the roofline.

But these are minor defects compared with the delights of gazing at the Rhondda's townscape. The shape of that townscape was determined by the nature of the landscape. South Wales has the sole mountainous coalfield in Britain, the key to its remarkable history. Although the standard of the Rhondda's

dwellings was comparatively high, the scarcity of fairly level land suitable for house building meant that congestion was rife in those places where such land was available. It is striking that it was the most congested areas – Tonypandy, for example, where population density could be as high as nine thousand people to the square kilometre – were the areas most prone to industrial discontent. (Housing which blurs the old distinction between built-up areas and the open mountain – the Penrhys estate on the high moorland, for example – has enjoyed little success.)

By 2001, when the population of the Rhondda had declined to 72,443, congestion was no longer a problem. What remains is the townscape. Similar streets may be seen in other parts of the southern coalfield – at New Tredegar, for example, and at Penrhiwceiber – but the abundance and compactness of the Rhondda's streets have given rise to a unique townscape. Those who have not seen a panorama of that townscape have not seen Wales.

Almost every area of industrial Wales experienced expansion in the 1850s. The most dynamic place was Aberdare, where the population rose from 14,999 in 1851 to 32,299 in 1861, an increase of 115 per cent. As Aberdare was home to the chief leaders of the denominational battle which raged in nineteenth-century Wales, and was a publishing centre of increasing importance, it was hardly surprising that there were those who declared: 'What Aberdare thinks today, Wales will think tomorrow'.

Industrial development had been afoot in Aberdare long before the 1850s. Ironworks were opened at Llwydcoed in 1799, at Abernant in 1800, at Gadlys in 1827 and at Aberaman in 1847, but, although they remained successful until the 1870s, they were minnows compared with the giants of Blaenau Gwent and Merthyr Tydfil. In 1840, when the Glamorganshire Canal conveyed 110,000 tons of Merthyr iron to Cardiff, it carried less than 13,000 tons of iron from the Cynon Valley. But as Merthyr has been so neglectful of its industrial heritage, Aberdare has richer evidence of the iron industry. At Gadlys, there are two intact blast-furnaces, together with calcinating furnaces, a blowing-engine house, and the earliest bridge in the world specifically built to carry a tramroad. Blaenavon is the best place to visit in order to understand the manufacture of iron in the early years of the Industrial Revolution; Aberdare is a worthy runner-up.

However, the particular significance of Aberdare belongs to another industry. If it is assumed (and who would contest the assumption?) that modern Wales was born a hundred and sixty years ago in the wake of the enormous growth of the numbers employed in the coal industry, then it is impossible to deny that modern Wales was born at Aberdare. In the late 1840s, the industrial world was excited by reports of the coal of the four-foot seam in the Cynon Valley. It ignited easily, produced intense heat rapidly, released very little smoke and left hardly any ash.

Consequently, the British Admiralty acknowledged that it was the best coal in the world for boiling water to produce steam power. As the British navy was then at the height of its prestige, that was an advertisement which created markets for Aberdare coal in all parts of the world.

The ascendancy of the Cynon Valley proved to be short-lived, for it soon became apparent that there was an even richer source of steam coal in the Rhondda Valley. The mining of steam coal continued in Aberdare long after the 1850s – it was the cradle of Powell Duffryn, recognized in the early twentieth century as the largest coal company in Europe – but the increase in its population was not dramatic. (Between 1861 and 1911, its population increased by 41 per cent; the increase in the Rhondda was 3860 per cent.)

Aberdare nevertheless remained the heartland of progressivism. It is frequently asserted that Merthyr was the cradle of Welsh

The Aberdare Constitutional Club

Ducks on the Aberdare Canal

radicalism, and the victory of Henry Richard in 1868 and of Keir Hardie in 1900 are cited as proof of that assertion. But it should be remembered that the two-seat constituency of Merthyr Tydfil included Aberdare, and that much, perhaps most, of the intellectual energy invested in the victories of 1868 and 1900 came from Aberdare.

As it was in the 1850s that the transformation of Wales was launched at Aberdare, it is fitting that the town centre – Victoria Square and the grids of streets north and south of the square – is a monument to that decade. (Glacial action must be thanked for creating the fairly level ground which made possible the creation at Aberdare of that rarity in the south Wales coalfield – a nucleated town.) The centre of the pre-industrial village was St John's Church, a building so modest that the patron of the parish, the second marquess of Bute, insisted that the growing town should have a more dignified Anglican place of worship. His campaign led to the construction of St Elvan's Church, completed in 1851. According to John Newton (*The Buildings of Wales: Glamorgan*, 1995), visiting it is like stepping 'into a seventeenth-century Dutch painting of a church interior'. The first vicar of St Elvan's was John Griffith, the most prominent

of the Welsh Anglican ministers of the day. Nearby is Calfaria, one of the handsomest Baptist chapels in Wales; it was built in 1852 for Dr Thomas Price, the most prominent of the Welsh Nonconformist ministers of his day.

As Aberdare was the most significant place in the Wales of the 1850s, it is hardly surprising that it was the location of the eisteddfod of 1861, widely considered to be the first National Eisteddfod. The urge to compete became ingrained in the town, as can be seen from the memorial in Victoria Square to Caradog (Griffith Rhys Jones), who led the South Wales Choral Union to success at the Crystal Palace in 1872 and 1873.

The town also has a memorial to the eisteddfod of 1861 – the *gorsedd* stones which stand in Aberdare Park. The Dare Valley Country Park is a much more extensive open space, and is a notable example of the restoration of land scarred by industry. Aberdare's most delightful piece of greenery is that surrounding a short stretch of waterway – virtually the sole surviving part of the Aberdare branch of the Glamorganshire Canal, the pioneering venture which did so much to promote the industrialization of this part of the world.

St John's Church, Aberdare

Aberfan is the most agonizingly poignant place in Wales. Suggesting it as a place to visit can imply distasteful curiosity. Yet, is it possible to comprehend the history of Wales – and especially the role of coalmining in that history – without reference to Aberfan? The story is harrowingly familiar – the flow of tip waste which on 21 October 1966 killed 144 people, 116 of them children under eleven years of age. The heartbreak is as real as ever, as the disaster website testifies.

Some details have not attracted attention. The village of Aberfan was built on the fields of the farms of Aber-fan Fawr and Aber-fan Fach, part of an estate whose roots can be traced to the lifetime of Richard ap Lewis of Llancaeach-fawr (*fl. c.*1520), a descendant of the Welsh lords of upland Glamorgan. When the area began to experience industrialization, the estate was owned by John Richards of Plasnewydd, Cardiff. In 1880, Arabella, Richards's granddaughter and heiress, married Donald Mackintosh of Moy Castle, Inverness-shire. He was the twenty-eighth Mackintosh of Mackintosh, and chief of Clan Chattan, among the most exalted of the grandees of the Scottish Highlands. It was this marriage which explains some of the names at Aberfan – Moy Road and Mackintosh Arms, for example – which came to be known around the world.

Although Aberfan was part of the parish of Merthyr Tydfil, the southernmost part of that parish was not industrialized until the last decades of the nineteenth century. The Glamorganshire Canal had been dug through the Aberfan farms in the 1790s, but the area was untouched by the original line of the Taff Vale Railway (1841), which ran through Merthyr Vale on the eastern side of the Taff. That was also the location of Pit 1 and Pit 2 of the Merthyr Vale colliery, the sinking of which began in 1869. The colliery was the venture of John Nixon, a mining engineer from County Durham, who was attracted to south Wales because of the second marquess of Bute's links with the Newcastle upon Tyne coalfield. The chief collieries of Nixon's Navigation Company – Cwmcynon, Deep Duffryn and Lower Duffryn – were in the neighbourhood of Mountain Ash, and the sinking of a pit at Merthyr Vale was considered to be a foolhardy act, for, in 1869, no one had reached steam-coal seams in the southernmost part of the parish of Merthyr Tydfil.

Although Nixon's Navigation became the third largest of south Wales's coal companies in terms of employees, the western bank of the Taff opposite Merthyr Vale underwent little development. Virtually nothing had been built on the fields of Aber-fan Fawr and Aber-fan Fach until 1890, but, between 1890 and 1910, the village of Aberfan came into existence; it included the Pantglas elementary school, built to accommodate 862 pupils.

By 1911, 8,551 people lived in the ward in which Aberfan and Merthyr Vale were situated; the great majority of the ward's families were dependent upon the Merthyr Vale colliery, where 2,500 men were employed. The colliery became part of the Powell Duffryn empire in 1936, and came under the authority of the National Coal Board in 1947. It was one of the Board's most successful collieries; £2 million was invested in it in the early

1960s. Although the colliery stood on the east side of the Taff, its waste was conveyed across the river and deposited on the slopes below Cnwc, a hill 378 metres above sea level. The dumping increased from 1958 onwards, and by the mid 1960s a substantial new tip – one of a cluster of seven in all – had come into existence above Aberfan.

Between the roundabout at Abercaniad and that at Quaker's Yard, the A470 crosses the place where the sodden Tip No.7 slipped down the slope. That part of the road was built in the 1970s. Had it been built a decade earlier, the engineers would doubtless have drawn attention to the instability of the tips, knowledge that had, in fact, been available since the late 1950s. The tribunal which studied the disaster came to the conclusion that it was the consequence of 'stupidity and lack of communication'. The behaviour of the National Coal Board attracted much criticism and, unbelievably, the government appropriated much of the money donated to the Memorial Fund, which was not fully compensated until the National Assembly for Wales took action in 2007.

But the intention here is not to examine the causes of the disaster, nor to discuss the years of insensitivity on the matter of the fund. The explorer should climb up to Cnwc. From there, the route taken by Tip No.7 is clear, and, at one point, a thin vein of coal pushes through the soil. Following the route of the tip is an emotional experience, and visiting the graveyard where the children's graves are linked by arches is overwhelmingly sad. But there is tranquillity in the Memorial Garden and a welcome in the Community Centre. Warmest thanks to both of them.

Pictures taken on 21 October 2006, the fortieth anniversary of the Aberfan Disaster

It is difficult not to lose patience with Merthyr. For much of the nineteenth century it was the world capital of iron manufacturing, but so great was the hatred of the ironmasters among later leaders of the town that, having apparently come to the conclusion that all evidence of Merthyr's iron industry had been personally constructed by men such as John Guest and William Crawshay, they sought to destroy as much as they could of that evidence. They had obviously not read the lines of the socialist dramatist, Bertolt Brecht: 'Who built Thebes of the seven gates? In the books you will find the names of kings. But did the kings haul up the lumps of rock?' (The rulers of East Germany accepted Brecht's message; almost the only virtue of that peculiar country was the fact that no guide informed visitors that Frederick the Great built Sanssouci at Potsdam, or that Augustus the Strong built the Zwinger in Dresden.)

Had it been more appreciative of its industrial heritage, it is Merthyr rather than Blaenavon that would have attained World Heritage Status. Yet, as ironmaking at Merthyr was on such an enormous scale, it has proved to be impossible to destroy everything. The largest surviving remains are at the Cyfarthfa ironworks – six of the seven masonry furnaces constructed when Cyfarthfa was the largest ironworks in the world (1800–20). They were built into the hillside so that the furnaces could be fed with iron ore, coke and limestone through gravitation. The molten iron would have flowed into shallow troughs to cool. As the cooled metal in the troughs looked like a sow feeding its piglets it was known as pig-iron. Sadly, the casting houses have been destroyed, and thus Cyfarthfa offers no clear idea of the process. (Blaenavon does.) From the ruins of Cyfarthfa ironworks, it is worth walking up to Heolgerrig in order to see the curious shapes of iron slag.

The most ingenious construction of Merthyr's golden age was the Iron Bridge which was built at Rhyd-y-car in the 1790s in accordance with the designs of the local engineer, Watkin George. It was the first bridge in Europe to be made of iron beams. (The Chinese had built such bridges centuries earlier.) The Merthyr authorities dismembered it in 1970, but the pieces were preserved, and, in a pang of repentance, it was rebuilt at Georgetown in the 1990s. Pontycafnau was equally innovative. It too was erected in the 1790s and was also the work of Watkin George. It had three levels; at the bottom was a trough that carried water to power the great wheel which produced blast-heating for Cyfarthfa's furnaces. The trough's covering carried a tramroad, and above that was another trough which fed the higher level of the great wheel. The structure proved innovative, for Pont Cysyllte can be seen as an offspring of Pontycafnau. Alas, the upper trough has long disappeared.

The former Town Hall, Merthyr Tydfil

The fountain in High St, Merthyr Tydfil

Merthyr does have one building which is an excellent example of the safeguarding and interpretation of the history of the iron industry – the Ynys-fach engine-house. Although iron production at Merthyr originally depended upon water-power, it had been realized by the 1830s that steam power was more reliable and efficient. The building at Ynys-fach (1836) is the most striking symbol of that realization, and the interpretive material it contains tells the story admirably. Plans are afoot to expand the exhibition and to compensate for the neglect of the past. There are also fascinating exhibits in the Merthyr Museum and the Cyfarthfa Castle Museum. (It is intriguing that by far the most impressive memorial to Merthyr's contribution to the world economy is a castle.)

Generally, however, searching for Merthyr's history is a matter of discovering remnants. It is now difficult to trace the course of the Glamorganshire Canal, the coming of which in 1794 hugely accelerated the growth of the town's iron industry. Some evidence survives of the Plymouth and Penydarren ironworks, but nothing remains of the Castle Hotel, the site of the bitterest episode in the 1831 Rising, of the Triangle, a remarkable example of nineteenth-century working-class housing, of the market, an elegant and well-built structure, nor of Garthnewydd, the cradle of a new wave in the history of Anglo-Welsh literature. The years have been kinder to the venture of Richard Trevithick, the pioneer of locomotion. There is a memorial to him at Pontmorlais Circus; much of the tramroad which carried his engine in 1804 can be traced, and some restoration work has been undertaken on the first bridge and the first tunnel in the world to be traversed by a locomotive. But the memorial to Trevithick is puny compared with the statue of the capitalist, Baron Buckland. So greedy was the baron as an asset-stripper that he was hated even by the members of the Cardiff Stock Exchange. When he died in 1928 after being thrown from his horse, they launched a fund to raise a memorial to the horse.

The engine-house at Ynys-fach

In the mid-nineteenth century, Dowlais was the home of the employer who had the largest labour force on Earth. The house in which he lived has disappeared. If Merthyr has been neglectful of its industrial heritage, Dowlais, its chief suburb (or perhaps its twin town) has been even more negligent. The only structure that survives of what was, in the mid-nineteenth century, the largest ironworks in the world is the Blast-engine House, a building which at one time was demoted to the status of a chocolate factory. Waste from the Great Tip which once dominated Dowlais's skyline was used to bury the ironworks' great amphitheatre of furnaces and to delete the evidence of Dowlais's rebirth as a centre of steel manufacture. (In 1856, Dowlais, was the earliest ironworks licensed to manufacture steel in

The Dowlais Reading Room, built in memory of J. J. Guest

accordance with the pioneering method invented by Henry Bessemer.) Pieces of masonry stick out of the soil in places – the sole memorial to the grandeur that was Dowlais.

The man with the largest number of employees in the world was John Josiah Guest (1785–1852). His home – Dowlais House – stood immediately opposite the Dowlais works. (As his brother-in-law put it: 'You have a very lucrative view'.) It was at Dowlais House that Lady Charlotte Guest translated the *Mabinogion* and planned the provision of schooling for Dowlais's children. Charles Barry, the architect of the Palace of Westminster, designed the school, one of several commissions he received from the Guest family. Impressively Gothic, it was opened in 1855 and was intended to provide education for 1,566 children. Needless to say, it has been demolished.

A few of the buildings financed by the Guest family do still stand. They include St John's Church, which is in a very dilapidated condition; J. J. Guest is buried in the churchyard. Dowlais's most dignified landmark is the building erected in his memory – the Library and Reading Room, opened in 1863. With its high podium and its Tuscan pillars, it dominates Dowlais's main street. (It has been converted into flats.) The most extensive surviving building linked to the Guests is the stable constructed in 1820 to accommodate the horses which worked in the ironworks. With two floors and twenty-one bays, it is better built than any of the dwellings constructed for the human employees of the works. It has been converted into sheltered housing.

Dowlais offers convenient access to the many attractions situated to the north of Merthyr Tydfil. Beyond Dowlais Top lies the new landscape created by refilling what was in the 1970s the largest hole in Europe – a vast opencast coalmine worked by what Harri Webb described as 'sunshine miners'. (The sun does occasionally shine at Dowlais Top.) To the north lies Blaen-y-garth whence the Brecon Mountain Railway runs to the north

The stables of the Dowlais Ironworks

The last ingot mould to be produced at the Dowlais Ironworks

Wales's finest viaduct – fifteen arches which rise 36 metres from the bed of the river. (There are close competitors at Porthkerry, Knucklas, Chirk and Pont-Gethin.) It carried the Merthyr to Brecon railway. The expense involved in its construction, and the construction of an almost equally imposing viaduct across the Taff Fechan at Pont-sarn, represented investments which offered very little hope of profit – proof of how venturesome, or foolhardy, were the railway entrepreneurs of the 1860s.

The journey should finish at Hen Dŷ Cwrdd, the Unitarian meeting-house at Cefn-coed-y-cymmer. The congregation first gathered in 1747 and became the source of much of Merthyr's radicalism. When Merthyr became a county borough in 1908, it had hundreds of chapels, almost all of them far more impressive than the modest meeting house at Cefn. Yet, of all the area's places of worship, this one was probably the most influential.

end of the Pontsticill Reservoir on rails laid on part of the track of the one-time Merthyr to Brecon railway, the line which, until its closure in 1962, offered one of the finest railway journeys in Wales.

West of Blaen-y-garth stands Morlais Castle, commissioned *c.*1290 by Gilbert de Clare, lord of Glamorgan, during a dispute between him and Humphrey de Bohun, lord of Brecon. It is sited at a location which offers wide views in all directions. In 1295, it was dismembered during a Welsh revolt, but, mercifully, the splendid vaulted undercroft survived. To the north, St Gwynno's Church, Vaynor, stands above the banks of the Taff Fechan. Described by John Newton as 'a crude performance', the church is notable for its burial ground where the tomb of Robert Thompson Crawshay (1817–79) bears the stark words: 'God Forgive Me'. His particular need for forgiveness is a matter of conjecture; it is known that, while conducting his photographic experiments, he behaved with impatience towards his wife and daughter, certainly behaviour which demands forgiveness.

It is worth following the Taff Fechan to Cefn-coed-y-cymmer, where it joins the Taff Fawr. That river is crossed by

The south Wales coalfield experienced frenzied urbanization from the late eighteenth century until the First World War, but instances of constructive attempts to plan the urbanization are rare. Morriston is an interesting example from the eighteenth century, and Oakdale from the twentieth century. In the nineteenth century, when the number of families living in the south Wales coalfield increased from less than ten thousand to more than a quarter of a million, Tredegar and Butetown offer virtually the coalfield's only examples of coherent town planning.

Butetown is the more appealing of the two. As its original name, Newtown, and its Welsh name (y Drenewydd), indicate, the intention was to build a new town on the west bank of the

Butetown church

upper Rhymney to house employees of the Union Ironworks established in 1800 on the river's eastern bank. The land belonged to the first marquess of Bute (1744–1814), but the statement displayed on the notice-board adjoining the entrance stating that Butetown came into existence because of the marquess's interest in 'health and harmony' is seriously misleading; indeed, it is difficult to imagine anyone with less interest in such matters.

A mere twenty-seven houses were built at Butetown, perhaps because the character of the iron company changed in 1803, when much of it was acquired by Richard Crawshay. The houses are a remarkable group. The most impressive section is the southern part, where Middle Row and Lower Row face each other. Had one of the rows stood in parkland with a drive leading to it, it could appear to be a grand country house. With their emphasis on symmetry, the rows were clearly designed in accordance with the principles of Andrea Palladio (1508–80). Both have a three-storey central block flanked by two-storey wings, the ends of which jut out slightly – a pattern which gives liveliness to a design which might otherwise look too static. To the north stands Collins Row, which, although its western end has been demolished, has the same wide eaves and the same layout as the other two. An intriguing feature of the design, and one which is at odds with the overall elegance, is the cellar dwellings underneath the back of Lower Row. Even odder is the fact that the three-storey central blocks – the most stylish part of the complex – were intended as barracks for unmarried men.

The Union Ironworks remained under the control of the Crawshay family until 1825, when it was amalgamated with a new venture – the Bute ironworks, which owed much to the resolve of the second marquess of Bute (1793-1848). (Unlike his grandfather, the first marquess, he did believe in 'health and harmony'.) During the amalgamation discussions, a wholly astonishing comment was made about the processes which were transforming the south Wales coalfield. David Stewart, the marquess's mineral agent, stated that he hoped that the Bute-Rhymney works would become 'the largest ironworks in Wales, and therefore, of course, in the world'. It was the association with the second marquess which led to the abandonment of the name of Newtown and its replacement (in English, at least) by Butetown.

William Forman, the chief investor in the Bute-Rhymney company, had ambitious ideas about the rebuilding of the works. By 1828, the banks of the Rhymney was graced with the second neo-Egyptian structure to be erected in Wales. (The first was a monument (1812) to George III built on the summit of Moel Fama in the Clwydian Range.) Nothing survives of Forman's temple but a picture of it can be seen on the notice-board. The Rhymney works continued to produce iron until 1890; remains of the furnaces of the successor to the temple works are visible on the eastern side of the river. Long before 1890, however, coalmining had become the main function of the Rhymney company, although in 1839 it did launch a brewery. The chief collieries of the company – Duffryn and Mardy – were located well south of the ironworks, and it was around them that

the town of Rhymney developed. Consequently, Butetown went into decline. Salvation came in 1972, when the place became a conservation area. It underwent restoration, and now the inventiveness of its design, the quality of its stonework and its blessed freedom from uPVC window-frames can be readily appreciated – although it is sad that the Butetown Museum had to be closed in 2007.

From Butetown, it is worth walking to the middle of Rhymney. St David's Church (1843), a severely solid building, was, until the 1970s, the only church in the diocese of Monmouth in which all the services were in Welsh. The churchyard abounds in Welsh epitaphs, although, as the stone is so friable, they are becoming less legible by the day. Nearby, the plaque on the childhood home of Thomas Jones (1870–1955) states that he was founder of Coleg Harlech, deputy secretary to the British cabinet, secretary of Gregynog Press, secretary of the Pilgrim Trust and president of the University College of Wales, Aberystwyth. The plaque on the home of the poet, Idris Davies, is more endearing. It describes him as '*un o'r anwylaf a'r enwocaf o feibion Rhymni*' (one of the best loved and best known of Rhymney's sons).

The Middle Row, Butetown

The most striking urban landmark in the south Wales coalfield is Tredegar's clock tower. As befits a town in which one of the coalfield's chief ironworks was located, it is made of iron. (In April 1910, a locally-produced film was screened within the tower, giving rise to the claim that it was the world's smallest cinema.) Erected in 1858, the clock commemorates the duke of Wellington, who died in 1852. It bears the words 'Wellington, England's Hero', but his victory at Waterloo was not the primary reason for the desire of the local ironmasters to honour him. They admired him above all because of his unyielding opposition to Chartism, an issue of importance to Tredegar employers, who had seen so many of their workers joining the march to Newport in 1839. (The Cambrian Inn, opposite the tower, was one of the Chartists' favourite meeting places.) A plaque on the tower states that it was financed by the money raised at a bazaar organized by Mrs R. P. Davis, the wife of the manager of the Tredegar Ironworks. A memorial to Mrs Davis in St George's Church stresses that she never drew attention to herself when undertaking good works.

Originally, the tower stood in a square located in front of the Tredegar market, which is now a Wetherspoon tavern. The circularity of the tower proved influential, for, within a few years of its construction, the square became a circle from which four roads radiate. In the nineteenth century, that to the north led to the ironworks that gave rise to the town. The earliest, Sirhowy, established in 1778, was the most significant of the ironworks of Blaenau Gwent, for it was the first to smelt iron using coke rather than charcoal, a process which released the industry from reliance upon the sparse timber of the area and allowed smelting to benefit from the abundance of coal. The company failed in 1797. Two years later, another ironworks was established on land which was part of the estate of the Morgan family of Tredegar House near Newport. It became known as the Tredegar works, a name

also given to the town which developed around it. It was not uncommon for a works to adopt the name of the estate on which it was sited – the Plymouth works at Merthyr, for example, or the Bute works at Rhymney or the Beaufort works near Ebbw Vale – although it may be relevant that the chief owner of the Tredegar works, Samuel Homfray, was related by marriage to the Morgans of Tredegar.

The Tredegar furnaces were the starting point of the Sirhowy tramroad, the most ambitious land transport venture created in Wales until Telford began constructing the road from London to Holyhead. A 40-kilometre pair of rails which linked Tredegar to Newport, it was completed in 1805 at a cost of £40,000; in the 1820s, the tramroad company paid a dividend of 30 per cent, making it one of the coalfield's most prosperous enterprises. The tramroad has long gone, but, near the roundabout which marks the beginning of the A4047, is a handsome bridge which once carried the tramroad across the Sirhowy.

Initially, the owners of the Tredegar Iron Company succeeded in ensuring that it benefited from the technological changes which the iron and steel industry underwent in the mid-nineteenth century. Eventually, however, the company became mainly concerned with the mining of coal, an industry which spurred

Aneurin Bevan and Jennie Lee portrayed on a floor plaque at The Circle, Tredegar

more population growth that had metal production. Tredegar's inhabitants increased from 9,383 in 1861 to 25,110 in 1921; in 2001, the town's population was 15,057.

The road going southwards from the clock tower leads to Bedwellty Park, which was originally the garden of the house in which the Morgans of Tredegar House stayed when they wanted to enjoy mountain air. The road passes the modest cottage in which Michael Foot stayed during his visits to his Ebbw Vale constituency. (Aneurin Bevan's home in Charles Street has been demolished; nowadays, the street's chief feature is the large number of stretch-limos parked in it.) In 1899, Godfrey Charles Morgan, the second Baron Tredegar (1831–1913) presented the house and garden to the people of Tredegar; plans are now afoot to turn it into a centre interpreting the rich history of the area. A 15-ton lump of coal, the largest single piece ever mined, is the chief feature of the park, apart from the beer cans which choke its pools and the vandalized mosaic commemorating the Chartists.

The road to the east provides access to the A4048, the main road which runs through the Sirhowy Valley. Between it and the Heads of the Valleys road (the A465) lies Waun y Pound, where what seems to be a version of Stonehenge comes into view. It is the memorial to Aneurin Bevan. One of the stones bears an inscription stating that it was at Waun y Pound that Bevan addressed the people of his constituency and the world; the others bear the names of the chief towns of the constituency: Tredegar, Ebbw Vale and Rhymney.

From the memorial, a road leads to the most remote of the settlements of the coalfield – Trefil, where much of the limestone used in the ironworks of Blaenau Gwent was quarried. The quarries have given rise to a remarkable landscape, but the most striking features of the village are its rubbish bins, which are crowned with iron work which would have delighted Charles Rennie Mackintosh. From Trefil, a track leads to the heart of the splendid countryside between Blaenau Gwent and the Vale of Usk. It would be delightful to follow it in the direction of Cwm Crawnon, but the road is closed to the public. Why, I know not.

There is substance to the often made comment that everyone in Wales lives in one valley or another. But that cannot be said of the inhabitants of Prestatyn, Beaumaris or Tenby. Admittedly, these are seaside towns. In inland Wales, almost everyone does inhabit a valley. The great exception is Brynmawr, which looks down upon the valleys of the Clydach, the Llwyd and the Ebwy Fach, but is not located in any of them. The loftiest part of Brynmawr rises to 410 metres above sea level, making it

Market Square, Brynmawr, today

MARKET HALL CINEMA

Wales's highest town. As Buxton, England's highest town, is only 307 metres above sea level, and as Scotland, oddly enough, has no lofty towns, it can confidently be claimed that Brynmawr (5,599 inhabitants) is the highest town in Britain.

That is just the first of the unique characteristics of Brynmawr. The second is more grievous. During the depression of the 1920s and 1930s, Brynmawr was the only town in Wales to be the subject of a thorough study of the causes and the effects of that cataclysm (Hilda Jennings, *Brynmawr, a study of a distressed area* [1934]). That is hardly surprising, for, in November 1932, unemployment among Brynmawr's insured males was 98.3 per cent, compared with 67.4 per cent at Ferndale in the Rhondda.

The third unique characteristic is especially appealing. In the inter-war years, Brynmawr was the only place in the south Wales coalfield that produced craftwork of the highest standard. The Quakers have to be thanked for that. In 1934, they established the Gwalia Works, and, until the venture was overwhelmed by the Second World War, the craftsmen of the works were responsible for furniture which is now sought by collectors all over the world. In accordance with Quaker tradition, the items of furniture were practical and unostentatious. Designed in the main by Paul Matt, a refugee from Poland, their style owed much to the Arts and Crafts movement and to the work of Charles Rennie Mackintosh. The earliest of the Brynmawr chairs were sold for a pound apiece, but a new mortgage would be needed in order to buy some of the pieces of Brynmawr furniture now on sale.

The fourth of Brynmawr's unique features is both a matter of celebration and of sadness. In the 1960 edition of Nikolaus Pevsner's *Pioneers of Modern Design* only three buildings in Wales are mentioned. The earliest is Kinmel Park near Abergele (1874), the second the Boiler House at Queensferry (1905) and the third was in Brynmawr. Sidney's Opera House, Cornwall's Eden Project and the Scottish Parliament in Edinburgh – three of the

The boiler-house of Brynmawr's rubber factory

most iconic constructions erected since the Second World War – have one thing in common; they all include work by the engineer, Ove Arup. So did the Brynmawr rubber factory.

The factory was completed in 1953; its purpose, according to its progenitor – the enlightened industrialist, Lord Forrester – was to create an innovative environment which could offer numerous jobs requiring high craftsmanship in what had been industrial Wales's worst-hit community. The most remarkable feature of the factory was the way in which Ove Orup succeeded

Market Square, Brynmawr, in the 1920s; a mural in the town

in roofing a space 155 metres by 155 metres with a minimal use of supporting columns. This was done through the construction of nine concrete domes which were cast *in situ* and were no more than eight-centimetres thick. The factory was acknowledged to be the most innovative building erected in Britain since the Second World War, and its interior space was hailed as 'one of the most impressive interiors built in Britain since St Paul's'. It was Britain's first post-war building to be listed, but sadly it was demolished in 2001, and now the sole surviving part is the Boiler House across the road from the factory itself.

Brynmawr is the gateway to the Clydach Gorge. The gorge, which links Brynmawr with Gilwern is a magical place. It lies in the shadow of Gellifelen, where in 1820 Carnhuanawc (Thomas Price) founded what was at the time Wales's sole Welsh-medium elementary school. Along the slope, land was flattened to carry the track of the Brynmawr-Abergavenny railway (1862). The line closed in 1958, and a walk along the track, with its numerous tunnels and its life-threatening precipices, is a memorable experience. The gorge is an open-air museum of industrial archaeology, offering evidence of centuries of iron smelting and tinplate-making.

Brynmawr is also the gateway to the valley of the Ebwy Fach which joins the Ebwy Fawr at Aberbeeg. The valley's fascinations include the two round houses at Nantyglo, built for Crawshay and Joseph Bailey, sometime in the 1810s or the 1820s. They are widely claimed to have been built to ensure the safety of the Bailey brothers, owners of the Nantyglo Ironworks, during periods of industrial unrest. A remarkable reminder of the stark conflict of the era, the houses may represent the last privately-built fortifications erected in Britain.

But the great glory of the Ebwy Fach Valley is the memorial at Six Bells. It is a 12.6 metre-high statue of a collier which stands on a 7.4-metre-high plinth. With a total height of 20 metres (65 feet), it is overwhelmingly imposing. The monument was designed by Sebastien Boysen, who was also responsible for the Chartist Man at Blackwood and for several of Newport's street sculptures. Unveiled on 28 June 2010, it commemorates all who have suffered as a result of the tragedies of the coal industry, among them 45 of the 48 men working at the Six Bells colliery on 28 June 1960 – the last major colliery disaster in Wales.

People can be ignorantly negative about Newport. Few realize that it was the centre of Wales's earliest post-Reformation Roman Catholic diocese. When the Anglican diocese of Monmouth was established in 1921, it was argued that Newport's St Woolos's Church was unworthy of being a cathedral. It received that status temporarily while diocesan officials examined the practicality of rebuilding Tintern Abbey; it did not become a full cathedral until 1949. When the archbishop of Wales left Newport to become the archbishop of Canterbury, London newspapers assumed that Rowan Williams's move to Lambeth Palace was from Cardiff. In 2002, when Newport became a city, many of its inhabitants thought that the place had been overpromoted.

This is all rather odd, for Newport has many virtues. It is Wales's sole example of a populous urban centre on the banks of a substantial river. As that river is the Usk, which has one of the world's largest differences between low and high tide, one of Newport's characteristics is a superabundance of mud. The mud preserved one of Newport's proudest possessions – the fifteenth-century ship buried in the river, a discovery of international importance.

The river Usk is also the key to Newport's greatest treasure – the transporter bridge opened in 1906. As the river was deep enough and wide enough to allow passage to large ships, traffic on the Usk survived far longer than it did on smaller rivers such as the Taff and the Tawe. At the end of the nineteenth century, Newport was developing rapidly south of the southernmost of the town's bridges, which was situated five kilometres north of Uskmouth. The inhabitants of southern Newport were greatly inconvenienced by their inability to cross the river other than by

The stairs to the deck of Newport's Transporter Bridge

ferry. A conventional bridge was not an option, for that would have interfered with shipping on the Usk. The answer to the problem was a transporter bridge, with a gondola pulled across the river by cables moving along a platform 54 metres above the water, and therefore high enough to allow the tallest ships to sail beneath it. The world has only eight surviving transporter bridges, and Newport has the most elegant of them. The earliest is that at Bilbao; it has received World Heritage Status, and moves are afoot to secure that status for the entire eight. The Newport bridge was closed for essential repairs in 2008; it is reopened in 2010, an aspiration which was aided by those who paid £5 to join the

Friends of Newport's Transporter Bridge (FONTB). For pedestrians, the journey is free, and now that the bridge has been reopened, the cheapest and most delightful diversion in Wales is a day toing and froing on the gondola watching Newport's mud appearing and disappearing.

But journeys on the gondola are only the beginning of Newport's delights. The southern end of the Monmouthshire Canal was situated a few metres above the western side of the bridge, as was the southern end of one of the most important ventures of the early Industrial Revolution – the Sirhowy tramroad. Nothing survives of either terminus, but the canal and

The gondola of Newport's Transporter Bridge

the tramroad were central to the remarkable growth of Newport in the first decades of the nineteenth century. By 1830, its coal exports – aided by the port's special tax status – were four times larger than those of Cardiff. Newport was the most populous town in south-east Wales, the main reason why it was in 1839 the chief target of the Chartists.

From the one-time terminus of the tramroad, Usk Way leads to George Street Bridge, which is as innovative as the transporter bridge – it was the precedent for the second Severn Crossing. North of the bridge lies Newport Castle, the ruins of which are cruelly squeezed between the highway and the river. It was the second castle to be built at Newport; the first was built in the early twelfth century, but its site has been destroyed. In the fourteenth century, a new castle was constructed as the principal stronghold of the lord of Wentlooge or Gwynllŵg; remains of well-appointed rooms survive on its eastern side. Casnewydd (new castle) is Newport's Welsh name, which suggests that, while the town's Welsh speakers (probably the majority until the middle of the nineteenth century) were impressed by the castle, its English speakers were impressed by the port. (Chepstow/Cas-gwent suggest a similar duality.)

From the castle, it is a short walk to the Westgate Hotel (now a block of flats) where the holes created by bullets shot at the building in 1839 by Chartists are still visible. The walk offers a view of the open-air sculptures which are such a feature of Newport. The walk up to Stow Hill passes the nightclub which contains Wales's largest metal dragon (the work of David Petersen), and Victoria Place, where television companies constantly film one of Britain's most attractive Victorian streets. St Woolos's Cathedral stands on the summit of Stow Hill; it is a fascinating building which belies the 1921 judgment that it was unworthy to be a cathedral. Its most attractive feature is the arch leading to the nave, one of Wales's finest Romanesque arches.

A visit to central Newport should end on the western side of the Brynglas tunnel, the only tunnel on the M4. That was the location of the Mole Molynx factory, the place which produced the Mole Wrench, the self-locking pliers, Newport's most splendid gift to the world.

Those wishing to see in close proximity two Welsh architectural marvels belonging to very different periods and built in very different styles have only one place to go. That place is the western fringe of Newport, the location of Tredegar House – Wales's finest late seventeenth-century building – and of the factory of International IOR Rectifier – Wales's most remarkable late twentieth-century building.

Tredegar House was built in the 1660s and 1670s when the Tredegar estate was the property of William Morgan (d. 1680). The family had been in the district long before the 1660s. In the early fourteenth century, Llywelyn ab Ifor, a man whose roots were in Dyfed, married Angharad, daughter and heiress of Morgan ap Maredudd of Tredegar. Their descendants proved adept at estate building, with the sons of Ieuan ap Llywelyn ap

The Tredegar House stables

Morgan profiting from their service to Henry VII. (By the late nineteenth century, the Morgans of Tredegar owned over 10,000 hectares of Monmouthshire, and had profited hugely from the industrialization of the county.) In the 1530s, John Leland praised the family's stone house, and part of that has survived within the present building. In 1664, the estate was inherited by William Morgan, who had become owner through marriage of Y Dderw estate in Breconshire. The Morgans referred to that estate as Thirrow – evidence of the family's Anglicization.

It was perhaps the additional income forthcoming from Breconshire which led William Morgan to commission the building of a new mansion. Little is known of its architect, but its similarity to other mansions has led to the surmise that it was designed by Roger and William Hurlbutt of Warwick. The path to the house takes visitors to its south-eastern façade, but they should ignore the signposts and seek to ensure that their initial view of the house is the north-western façade. That view, offering perfect symmetry and a wealth of warm brick, is truly delightful. A pavilion juts out at each end, both with two windows on the ground and on the first floor; between the pavilions is the central portion, with three windows on each side of the main portal on the ground floor, and seven windows on the first floor. Linking the main portal and the ten ground-floor windows is a stone garland; it forms a curved frieze and gives liveliness to a building which otherwise might look rather severe. The view from the portal is almost as appealing, for, between 1714 and 1718, screens and a wrought-iron gate were constructed in front of the house – work that can bear comparison with the masterpieces of the Davies brothers of Esclusham.

The north-eastern façade, with its portal flanked on either side by four windows, is almost as delightful. The stables (1684–8) are overwhelmingly impressive; they were commissioned by William's son, Thomas (1664–99), and suggest that the family's horses were far better housed than were the bulk of the estate's tenants. The park surrounding the house is less than a tenth of the size it once was, but it is extensive enough to have been the location of the National Eisteddfod on two occasions (1988 and 2004), occasions that are considered to have been among the most successful in the history of the festival.

The park is open daily, but the house itself can only be visited on designated days between Easter and September. The interior is worth seeing if only to view the richness of the Great Stair, to admire rooms which have survived intact from the seventeenth century (the Gilt Room in particular), and to investigate the Cedar Closet built as a safe room for the family's treasures. The house offers little evidence of the sanitary facilities of a late seventeenth-century mansion, although visitors delight in the vast bath installed on the first floor in 1905.

While necessary details are obscured at Tredegar House, they are wholly evident in the other masterpiece located on Newport's western fringe. Richard Rogers, architect of the factory built originally in 1982 for the Inmos Company, believes that the elements which make a building function should be visible on its outside – a notion that first found expression through his work on the Pompidou Centre in Paris (1977). This was wholly acceptable to Inmos, for, as the factory was built for micro-chip production, any non-wholly sterile activity needed to be rigorously segregated from manufacturing areas. Although the inquisitive explorer can only view the factory through a fence, a mere glimpse is memorable. With its blue, yellow and silver intestines displayed on its outside, Wales has no other building comparable with it.

A visit to what John Newman described in *The Buildings of Wales: Gwent* (2000) as 'the most remarkable concentration of late twentieth-century architecture in the whole of Wales' should end at Dyffryn, the westernmost of the suburbs of Newport. Dyffryn is an example of 'perimeter planning' – an attempt to squeeze in as many dwellings as possible in an environment that continues to appear to be rural. Built between 1976–9, it is the largest experiment in such planning ever attempted. It is worth wandering around Kestrel Way, Swallow Way, Cormorant Way and the rest, which meander in the shade of the trees of Dyffryn Woods. In comparison, even the streets of the Rhondda's remarkable townscape seem unimaginative.

The north-eastern façade of Tredegar House

The purpose of this book is to assess the most memorable contributions human beings have made to the way Wales looks today. It is not primarily concerned with the landscape, although there is hardly any place in Wales where human impact on the landscape is not discernable. That impact is at its most intense in the Gwent Levels, a landscape which looks more Dutch than Welsh, and, like many parts of the Netherlands, would be

very different if nature had had its untrammelled way. Without human intervention, the Levels would have been a salt-marsh frequently washed over by the sea, with salt water destroying all fertility. There is something awe-inspiring about a landscape that has been cherished so greatly. And the Gwent Levels – Wales's largest extent of land wholly dependent on human endeavour – has certainly been cherished.

The Levels have a western wing – the Wentlooge Levels which lie between the estuary of the Rhymney and that of the Usk – and an eastern wing – the Caldicot Levels which lie between the estuary of the Usk and that of the Wye. Constituting of 111 square kilometres, the Levels extend inland for up to six kilometres. Two-thousand years ago, they would have been covered by a thick layer of peat, but, after sea walls had been built, the peat disappeared under a covering of alluvial soil. The soil is believed to have covered a wealth of prehistoric evidence; indeed, the Usk estuary has yielded footprints from the Mesolithic Age – prints made by people crossing the estuary six and a half thousand years ago.

The Romans were probably the first to build sea walls. At the Caerleon Museum, there is a memorial noting that the first cohort of Legio Secunda Augusta (the legion at Caerleon) built part of a sea wall at Goldcliff. Thick grass grew on the land behind the wall, grass which was perhaps grazed by the legion's horses.

The defences against the sea may have crumbled in the post-Roman centuries, but they seem to have been restored in the era of population growth which began in the late eleventh century. As water flows unceasingly from Gwent's rainy uplands, drainage was necessary. For centuries, ditches were dug haphazardly, resulting in irregularly-shaped patches of land surrounded by gutters. More systematic drainage was undertaken from the mid nineteenth century onwards, a process which led to the formation of large regularly-shaped fields drained by wider water courses.

The extent of the drains is evidence of how labour-intensive was the work of creating the Gwent Levels. They contain 1,200 kilometres of narrow gutters, 137 kilometres of wide gutters and 64 kilometres of substantial water courses. The drains are called *reens*, which may come from the Welsh *rhewyn*, a word which possibly has the same origins as the river-name Rhine. Some ditches are known by Welsh names such as Gwter Fawr, Pwll

The plaque at the church of St Bride's Wentlooge commemorating the 'Great Flood'

Bargod and Rhosog Fawr, an indication that the inhabitants of the Levels were more Welsh in speech than is often supposed. When George Borrow visited Penhow in 1854, he found that a significant proportion of the village's inhabitants knew no English, and, until at least the late nineteenth century, Welsh-language inscriptions were carved on gravestones at Marshfield.

The greatest tragedy suffered by the inhabitants of the Gwent Levels was the great flood of 20 January 1607. (In the early seventeenth century, New Year's Day was the first of March, and, therefore, the flood was considered to have occurred in the eleventh month of 1606.) Shortly after the flood, a pamphlet was published bearing the title *Lamentable newes out of Monmouthshire in Wales*; it contains memorable pictures of drowning humans and animals, of people seeking safety in trees and of a church up to its roof in water. The flood was believed to have been caused by ferocious south-west winds, but, following the interest in under-sea earthquakes aroused by the tragic tsunami in south-east Asia on 26 December 2004, it was argued that the flood of 1606/7 was also the result of a tsunami – although experts are not unanimous on the matter.

It is believed that the coast of Monmouthshire was hit by a wall of water 5.5 metres high, moving at a speed of 100 kilometres an hour. If it is true that Jane Morgan drowned in her home, Gellibêr, north of Marshfield, the water penetrated at least three kilometres inland. Inscriptions recording the flood may be seen in the churches of Goldcliff, Nash, Peterstone Wentlooge, Redwick and St Bride's Wentlooge. At Goldcliff, the line denoting the highest point reached by the water is 68 centimetres above the floor of the chancel. Its dozen churches, the chief glory of the Levels, are proof of the wealth produced by the fertility of the drained land. The most intriguing is St Bride's Wentlooge with its twisted spire; the most interesting is St Mary's, Nash, with its elegant tower and its fine Georgian timber fittings; the finest are those at Redwick and Peterstone Wentlooge. They form a chain north of the sea wall. The wall extends for 35 kilometres from the neighbourhood of Chepstow to the most indispensable part of the Levels – Lamby Way, the end of the journey for the 300,000 tons of rubbish produced annually by the inhabitants of our capital.

St Bride's Wentlooge Church

Wanderers on the sea defences

The Romans must have gained a sound understanding of the geography of Britain; they realized that the Lowland Zone – the south and the east – is a unit, and that the Highland Zone – the west and the north – is divided. The lowlands around the Severn estuary separate the uplands of south-western England from those of Wales, which are separated from the uplands of northern England by the lowlands around the Dee estuary. The Romans planted wedges of power in the two lowland areas and a further wedge in the heart of northern England. The three wedges – the legionary fortresses of Caerleon, Chester and York – were the chief strongholds of Roman power in the province of Britannia. York and Chester grew to be substantial cities but Caerleon became little more than a village. Unlike the Roman sites at York and Chester, much of that at Caerleon was not built upon. Thus, excavation there was far less impeded, making Caerleon the most important Roman military site in Britain.

The fortress was founded *c*. AD 76 by Julius Frontinus, governor of Britannia (74–8). The advantages of the site included its position on the Usk, which made it accessible to sea-going ships, and its location within the territory of the Silures, a tribe that had vigorously resisted the Romans. Originally built of earth and timber, the fortress was rebuilt in stone *c*. AD 90. Its walls enclosed 20.25 hectares. (Compare the 3.7 hectares enclosed by the walls of the fourth auxiliary fort erected at Cardiff.)

Excavations at Caerleon have revealed little that is surprising. The internal organization of a Roman legionary fortress is predictable; at least sixty such fortresses were built along the borders of the Empire and they almost all follow the same pattern. Caerleon was no exception. A playing-card-shaped fortress was constructed there, with a gateway at the centre of each of the four walls; roads from the gateways met near the *principia*, where the legionary standard was housed. Around the *principia* were the residences of the leader and the officers of the legion, the baths,

the hospital, workshops and granaries. Most of the rest of the fortress's interior contained the barracks housing the sixty centuries of legionary soldiers and their centurions. By the time Caerleon was built, a century consisted of eighty soldiers; as each barrack-room housed eight soldiers, six-hundred rooms were needed to house the legion's infantrymen. Although Caerleon had the usual layout, there were a few anomalies. One was the length of the swimming pool – 41 metres, only nine metres shorter than a modern Olympic pool. Another was the location of the amphitheatre, which was sited almost within the fortress's moat.

The chief purpose of excavation at Caerleon was to ascertain the fortress's chronology. In its early years, it housed the entire Legio Secunda Augusta, but, as the Silures came to accept Roman rule, it became the legion's administrative headquarters and storehouse rather than a fully-manned garrison. The legion's soldiers contributed to the building and garrisoning of Hadrian's Wall, work on which began in AD 122. The fortress was maintained in a usable condition for at least two-hundred years after that, but, in the late third century, dismantling began, perhaps in order to carry off material to sites where there was a greater need for fortification – to Cardiff, for example, which was better placed to oppose the increasing threat from the sea. The military use of Caerleon seems to have come to an end *c*.320. A new chapter in Caerleon's story then began – the story of Caerleon in legend.

As the ability to erect ambitious constructions disappeared from Britain with the fall of the Roman Empire, the fortress came to be seen as an object of awe – as the work of supernatural beings. Such notions were undoubtedly widespread centuries before Geoffrey of Monmouth declared, *c*.1138, that Caerleon had been the site of the court of King Arthur. Giraldus Cambrensis (d. 1223) maintained that there had been an archbishop at Caerleon and that its archiepiscopal status had been transferred to St Davids. In 1405, the French soldiers who had been sent to assist Owain Glyn Dŵr made a detour to visit the amphitheatre at Caerleon. Legend held its sway for many centuries; in the mid nineteenth century, Tennyson felt that it was only by lodging at Caerleon that he could complete his *Idylls of the King*.

After centuries of desultory excavation, more systematic investigations were launched in the 1840s. The Caerleon Antiquarian Association was founded and a museum was opened in 1850, but sophisticated excavation was not undertaken until 1926. The work initiated in that year was of international importance, for it brought the advanced techniques pioneered by Mortimer Wheeler to world attention. Most of the remains uncovered were reburied, but Wheeler persuaded the *Daily Mail*

to ensure that the amphitheatre would become a public attraction. (The tradition that the amphitheatre was King Arthur's Round Table was Wheeler's main weapon in persuading the newspaper to finance the project.) In the late 1920s, V. E. Nash-Williams led the team which uncovered the foundations of the barracks in the western corner of the fortress, and he ensured that four of the barrack blocks were not reburied. Caerleon is the only place in northern Europe which has visible remains of Roman barracks. Half a century went by before more of the fortress became visible to the public. In 1985, the cover-building protecting part of the bath house was completed, and walkways were constructed to allow the public to understand the layout of the baths. In 1987, the museum was enlarged; it is worth a visit, if only to see what Mortimer Wheeler called 'King Arthur's small change'.

The Caerleon Amphitheatre under snow with Holy Trinity Church, Christchurch, on the horizon

Cwmbran is unique. It is the only town to be established in Wales under the New Towns Act of 1946. The act was inspired by the faith in social planning which was central to the vision of the Labour government elected to power in 1945. The concept of new towns had its roots in the garden-city movement which developed in the 1890s, a movement which argued that there was moral benefit in living in places which combined urban and rural virtues; they were places which did not have rural isolation, inner-city overcrowding or the drawbacks of outer suburbs. Wales has a long tradition of new towns – established by the Romans at Caerwent, by Edward I at Flint, Conwy, Caernarfon and Beaumaris, by landowners at Aberaeron and Tremadog, by the Admiralty at Pembroke Dock and by industrialists at Butetown and Oakdale. The 1946 Act led to the establishment of five new towns in Scotland, partly in order to solve Glasgow's gross congestion. It led to the establishment of

only one in Wales. (In 1967, it was decided that Newtown should be a new town, but that was a matter of enlarging an existing urban centre rather than starting *de novo*.)

Cwmbran was probably chosen as the site of Wales's sole new town because it adjoins populous areas and is located in an area unrestricted by steep hills, an inevitable restriction had Wales's sole new town been established within the southern coalfield. About 2,000 hectares were earmarked as the site of the new town. In the mid 1940s, the locality, which had a long tradition of iron and tinplate making, was home to some 13,000 people, a number which the Cwmbran Development Corporation intended should rise rapidly to 35,000, with 55,000 as the ultimate aim.

In 2001, Cwmbran had 41,275 inhabitants, causing it to be Wales's seventh largest urban centre. The town's most obvious feature is its multiplicity of roundabouts – at least thirty of them – on the roads which divide Cwmbran into twelve

undercover retail area. Its core is Gwent Square, with its Congress Theatre and its campanile – the tower which disguises the chimney of the boiler which heats the town centre.

Initially, the inhabitants of the rest of Monmouthshire were suspicious about Cwmbran, and there was much muttering about new-town blues – the unease of those who felt that they had been set down in an area where there was no community. However, doubts about Cwmbran had disappeared by 1963, when the headquarters of the Monmouthshire County Council were established there. The buildings became the headquarters of the Gwent County Council from 1964 to 1996, and those of the Torfaen County Borough Council in 1996. (Nothing came of the suggestion mooted in the mid 1960s that the University of Wales's Institute of Science and Technology should move to Cwmbran.)

Cwmbran is home to the Police Training Centre, attended by cadets from Wales and south-west England. Its main entrance, which stands beneath a roof shaped like a policeman's helmet, is particularly intriguing. Taliesin, a fine example of sheltered housing, is a smaller, but perhaps more cherished, building. The inhabitants of Cwmbran are particularly proud of their stadium, which for years contained Wales's only international-standard running track. Perhaps the town's most striking buildings are its schools, the Cwmbran Welsh School, opened in 1961, among them.

One of the most delightful features of the town is the six-kilometre stretch of the Monmouthshire Canal which runs through its western side. Between Newport to Pontymoile, the canal had 42 locks, almost half of them within what would become the boundaries of Cwmbran; the group of five locks surviving at Pontnewydd is particularly attractive. The path alongside Afon Llwyd on the eastern side of the town also has its charms; it leads to Llantarnam, the home in the early fifteenth century of Abbot John ap Hywel, the most zealous of Owain Glyn Dŵr's monastic supporters. A 180-metre-long barn erected in the thirteenth century survives on the site of the medieval abbey. The rest of the abbey's buildings have disappeared, as has the Welsh-language sign which boasted that Llantarnam's Green House Inn offered excellent beer and cider.

neighbourhoods, all of which are in close proximity to open countryside. Up until 1988, when it was abolished by Margaret Thatcher as part of her campaign to get rid of anything with socialist associations, the Cwmbran Development Corporation ensured that the town had sufficient dwellings for its burgeoning population. Its efforts resulted in the creation of several notable housing projects, although the spaciousness of those projects completed before the rise of car ownership has been compromised by the need to provide adequate car-parking space. The most radical attempt to deal with the challenge of the car can be seen off Windsor Road, Fairwater, where pedestrians and vehicles have been rigorously separated. The houses there are only accessible by pathways, in accordance with the principles developed at Radburn, New Jersey. (Wrexham, the only other town in Wales which has this type of town planning, was the first place in Britain to adopt Radburn principles.)

J. C. P. West, the Corporation's chief architect from 1950 to 1962, sought to create a shopping area in the town centre free of cars and wholly protected from the weather. This was an innovative aspiration at the time, particularly if the contemporaneous redevelopment of Swansea is borne in mind. Not all of West's hopes were realized, but, by the mid 1980s, the 170 shops in central Cwmbran represented Wales's largest

Pontypool was the launching pad for the industrialization of south Wales. As early as the first half of the eighteenth century, it was considered to be a town – the only place in what would be the valleys of the southern coalfield, apart perhaps for Caerphilly, which deserved the description at that time. However, until it gained urban status in 1894, Pontypool was part of the parish of Trevethin, whose St Cadog's Church is one of the few churches in the southern coalfield still containing medieval features.

Significant smelting of iron seems to have begun at Pontypool *c.*1425, using charcoal from the forests of Gwent and iron ore loosened through scouring the land with water. In the 1490s, the Weald, a wooded area in Sussex and Kent, became Britain's main centre for smelting iron in blast-furnaces – the process of pumping air into furnaces in order to raise the temperature within them. Pontypool was one of the earliest areas in Britain, outside the Weald, to acquire blast-furnaces. The pioneer was Capel Hanbury; he settled at Pontypool in 1565, establishing there the

The Monmouthshire Canal at Pontypool

longest-lived industrial dynasty in the history of Wales. In 1659, one of his descendants – another Capel – commissioned the building of Pontypool Park mansion, a century and a half before Crawshay thought of Cyfarthfa Castle, or Guest thought of Dowlais House. The son of the second Capel, John Hanbury (1664–1734), introduced to Pontypool a method of rolling iron into thin sheets which could be coated with tin to ensure that the iron would not be attacked by rust, a development which placed the town in the forefront of the rise of the tinplate industry. Some of the tinplate was used to make a variety of household goods – trays, candlesticks, teapots – and the goods were decorated with lacquer produced from coal. The result was Pontypool Japanware, a product associated with the Allgood family – Quakers who settled at Pontypool in the early eighteenth century. The Allgood products, which imitated the lacquered wood produced by the Japanese, were the only consciously artistic objects created in the wake of the establishment of heavy industry in the south Wales coalfield. (The north, where the wrought-iron masterpieces of the Davies family of Esclusham were produced, proved to be superior.)

Pontypool was not only an industrial centre. As it was on the edge of the fertile land of eastern Monmouthshire, its market proved popular. A covered market was opened in 1730, an occasion commemorated by a plaque in Welsh and English. In the first half of the eighteenth century, Pontypool was perhaps the most prosperous town in Wales. It was among the first to acquire a printing press; books in both English and Welsh were published

there from the 1740s onwards, half a century before there was a printing press in Cardiff. It was home to an early group of Congregationalists, Baptists and Quakers, winning fame as a religious centre. In the mid eighteenth century, it was home to two of Wales's best-known Nonconformist leaders – Miles Harry, minister of Penygarn Baptist chapel, and Edmund Jones, minister of Transh Congregational chapel. Edmund Jones invited Howel Harris to preach at Pontypool, and Miles Harry had the task of defending Harris at the Monmouthshire sessions after the authorities had accused him of inciting a riot. Nothing survives of the chapels of Jones and Harry, nor of the Nonconformist academy established at Pontypool in 1836, but the town still has some of the largest and most handsome chapels in Wales.

The arrival of the Monmouthshire Canal at Pontypool in 1799 boosted the town's prosperity. A walk along the waterway from Mamhilad to Croesyceiliog is delightful, but Pontypool's greatest attraction is the mansion and its park. The mansion houses St Alban's Secondary School, and its stable has become one of Wales's most attractive and informative local museums. The park contains a wide variety of attractions, among them the Pontypool rugby club's stadium, a leisure centre and an artificial ski-slope. It is worth going further into the park to appreciate the Italian garden, the American garden and, above all, the grotto, a building which is even more remarkable than that wonder – the shell house at Cilwendeg in Pembrokeshire. It was constructed in the 1830s, rather late for such a product of the Romantic Movement. Its walls are covered with shells, and the floor was made from the vertebrae of oxen.

From the grotto, paths lead through Pontypool's green heart to St Cadog's Church, Trevethin, where memorial plaques allow visitors to work out the Hanbury family tree. From the church, Folly Road passes Ysgol Gyfun Gwynllyw – the most easterly Welsh-medium secondary school in the world – and continues to the Tower, a folly commissioned by John Hanbury in 1762. As it seemed as if it were pointing to the weapons' store at Glascoed, it was demolished in 1940 to ensure it would not offer guidance to German bombers. So enamoured were Pontypool's inhabitants of the tower that they had it rebuilt in 1993. The views it offers of the Usk valley are superb.

A memorial to the 'Pontypool Front Row'

The grotto in Pontypool Park

Nowhere else in Wales has had such an impact on the world as has Blaenavon. That was acknowledged in 2000 when its industrial landscape was added to the list of World Heritage Sites. Of the 890 sites listed by 2010, nine are industrial landscapes: one apiece in Belgium, Chile and Wales, and two apiece in England, Sweden and Germany.

Although the other eight are impressive, there can be little doubt that Blaenavon is the most impressive, offering, as UNESCO put it, 'an outstanding and remarkably complete example of a nineteenth-century industrial landscape'. Everything is there: the gutters dug for the water which scoured iron ore from the rocks, the Pwll-du tunnel (the longest of its kind in the world when it opened in 1815), the Garnddyrys Forge with its remarkable slag heaps, the remains of the tramroad that slid down the Blorenge to the canal at Llanfoist, and Engine Row and Stack Square, built to house those employed at the ironworks constructed in a landscape that had previously been virtually uninhabited.

The building of the ironworks began in 1788, but its finest feature is the last structure to be built on the site – the hydraulic lift completed in 1839. Within the furnaces and cast houses, the entire process of pig-iron production becomes apparent: the cliff from which the raw materials were tipped into the furnaces; the blast pipes which delivered hot air into the molten mass they contained; the casting floors in which the cooling iron formed

Engine Row and Stack Square, Blaenavon

piglets which lay snugly alongside their sows. Tipping from the cliff was an essential convenience in the early days, but, with the coming of newer technologies, the enterprise was relocated at Forgeside – on flat land the other side of Afon Llwyd. The relocation explains the particular importance of Blaenavon. At most other iron-making centres – at Merthyr Tydfil, for example – redevelopment took place on the original site, with newer structures destroying evidence of the structures of the pioneering era of the Industrial Revolution. At Blaenavon, that destruction did not occur, and, therefore, the place offers the world's finest example of ironworks of that era.

The original works are only half of the story. It is the developments at the Forgeside works, established in the 1850s, which placed Blaenavon in the forefront of world history. Forgeside, in 1878, was the place where the solution was found to a problem which had been plaguing industrialists across the globe. In 1856, at Landore near Swansea, Henry Bessemer had invented a way of mass-producing steel, a more versatile product than wrought iron. However, it was soon discovered that the Bessemer method could not produce steel from iron ore containing

phosphorus. Phosphoric ore was the main ore mined in most of the world, especially in the United States and in much of mainland Europe. The problem was solved by Sidney Gilchrist Thomas and his cousin, Percy Carlyle Gilchrist, an industrial chemist at Blaenavon. It was Blaenavon which launched the vast industrial expansion of the United States, and facilitated the road to the First World War, for without the discovery made there, Germany's ability to manufacture weapons of war would have been slight. And, to mention a more benevolent consequence, one of the subsidiary products of Gilchrist's Basic Method of steel production was basic slag, a fertiliser which helped mankind to feed itself.

The prominence that Blaenavon has gained can give the impression that the upper Llwyd Valley was the south Wales's chief iron-producing centre. This would be unfair to Merthyr Tydfil, which in the 1830s produced ten times more iron than did Blaenavon. But, as Merthyr has been so unmindful of its industrial heritage, Blaenavon has come to be recognized as the place which offers the best interpretation of the history of the iron industry.

Nevertheless, it should be acknowledged that that reward was not the result of the farsightedness of the Blaenavon authorities. It would be more true to ascribe it to their indifference; the urban district came under frequent criticism from Monmouthshire's medical officer of health for its laggard attitude towards the town's housing problems.

Two of the casting-houses at the Blaenavon Ironworks

As with other iron-making towns of industrial south Wales, it was the post-iron era – the age of coal – which led to the most dramatic increase in population. Big Pit was established in 1860; its pit shaft was the first in south Wales wide enough to allow two trams of coal to be drawn up through it side by side. Mining in the colliery came to an end in 1973, but – typically of Blaenavon – the underground works were abandoned undisturbed and the surface buildings were left virtually untouched. Consequently, when the Big Pit Mining Museum was opened in 1983, its founders could boast that Blaenavon was the only place in the coalfield offering a full portrayal of the way coal was mined. The former colliery became Wales's National Coal Museum in 2005, the year in which it won the Gulbenkian Prize (£100,000), Britain's most substantial arts prize. Now, it is one of the most popular industrial museums in Europe.

There is much more to be said about Blaenavon. What of its splendid Workmen's Institute, the unique iron font in St Peter's Church, and the attempt to reinvent the town as a book-selling centre similar to Hay? But, surely, enough has been said to convince the reader that Blaenavon is the most significant place in Wales.

Pit-head gear at Big Pit, Blaenavon

With its busy market, its food festival and its wide range of activities for visitors, Abergavenny is a lively place. But the main reason for visiting it is not to celebrate life but to celebrate death, for Abergavenny's St Mary's Church has the finest group of tombs in Wales.

In the Middle Ages, the church was a Benedictine priory; founded in 1087, it was the third Benedictine house in Wales.

(Chepstow, 1071, was the first and Monmouth, 1086, was the second.) It was a daughter of St Vincent's monastery near Le Mans in France, and, as an 'alien priory', it suffered as a consequence of Anglo-French enmity. The townspeople came to cherish their church, organizing in the late fifteenth century a series of plays to finance the purchase of new bells for its tower. Following the Reformation, the parish church, St John's, became

Abergavenny's open-air market

home to the Henry VIII Grammar School (part of that building still stands in St John's Street) and the townspeople secured possession of St Mary's. Despite the strength of Nonconformity in the district – Catholic as well as Protestant – the church remained and remains the heart of Abergavenny.

Within the church are eleven major tombs spanning the years from 1257 to 1660. Four of them are those of members of the Hastings family, who held the lordship of Abergavenny from 1273 to 1389 – five, if Eva de Breos, grandmother of Henry, the first Baron Hastings, is included. Three are the tombs of members of the Herbert family of Raglan, one contains the body of David Lewis, the first master of Jesus College, Oxford, and two the bodies of members of the Powell and Baker families, who were prominent in seventeenth-century Abergavenny.

The north transept is the location of the finest of the tombs;

it is that of John Hastings (d. 1325) and is surmounted by a superb recumbent statue of him which was originally rich in colour. Eva de Breos (d. 1257), daughter of the William de Breos who was hanged on the order of Llywelyn ap Iorwerth in 1230, lies in the North Chapel. Generally, weapons of war are not portrayed on women's tombs, but a large armorial shield covers much of her body. There are seven tombs in the Herbert Chapel, which, until the early 1990s, were in a dilapidated condition, the result of years of neglect and of clumsy reconstruction. Following excellent restorative work between 1994 and 1998, they are now among the world's best funeral monuments. The location of the tombs is significant. The earliest are those of Lawrence Hastings and his half-brother William, both of whom died in 1348. The successors of the Hastings family as lords of Abergavenny – the Beauchamp and Nevill families – showed little interest in the lordship; consequently, the chapel ceased to glorify the Lords of the March. Its centre – the place of greatest honour – became the resting-place of William ap Thomas (d. 1446) and his wife Gwladus (d. 1444), proof that the age of the Welsh gentry had dawned. The tomb chest is richly sculptured, with effigies of the twelve apostles on one side, of twelve prophets on the other and a splendid carving of the Annunciation beneath the feet of the sculptures of the departed.

The tombs are not the only glories of St Mary's. Of Wales's one-time Benedictine churches, it is the only one which retains its medieval choir stalls. The fifteenth-century woodwork is superb, and it is delightful to examine the misericords – the carved shelves beneath the seats which allowed monks to give at least the impression that they were standing during their lengthy services. Another of the church's timber treasures is the carving of the sleeping Jesse. A tree trunk rises from Jesse's heart, and, originally, its branches would have borne effigies of the ancestors of Christ. As the Jesse carving is larger than life-size, it is difficult to visualize the massiveness of the sculpture when it was completed in the fifteenth century.

From the church, the explorer should wander past the Angel Hotel, where in the 1840s the gentry of Abergavenny would have stood at the windows to watch the processions of Cymreigyddion y Fenni. A little further up the High Street stands the Gunter

Carvings on the tomb of William ap Thomas and Gwladus, his wife

Mansion where, in the eighteenth century, the Gunter family had in the attic a secret Catholic church similar to the one beloved of visitors to Amsterdam. From there, it is worth going to the Town Hall; completed in 1874, it is a striking declaration of the civic pride which was such a feature of the towns of nineteenth-century Wales. Adjoining it is one of the largest covered markets in Wales. A road leads from the town centre to the fifteenth-century bridge across the Usk, and on to the site of the Roman fort of Gobannium, work on which began in AD 55. Of the adjoining castle, little remains, for it was largely demolished

following the seventeenth-century Civil Wars. The castle was the scene of the Abergavenny Massacre, when the men of William de Breos (d. 1211) murdered their lord's Welsh guests – the worst example of ethnic slaughter in medieval Wales. An old hunting cabin in the middle of the castle houses Abergavenny Museum; among its treasures is a painting of the Magi, made for the Gunter Mansion's church in the attic.

Wales is rich in remote valleys and the loveliest is the Vale of Ewyas which extends from Lord Hereford's Knob to Llanfihangel Crucorney. Giraldus Cambrensis was charmed by the valley – a mere arrowshot in width, he claimed – which lies snugly at the heart of the splendours of the Black Mountains. The journey up the valley offers many delights: the Llwyncelyn hall-house, memorials by members of the Brute family in the crooked church at Cwmyoy, and the Tŷ-Hwnt-y-Bwlch

longhouse. But the purpose of the journey is to visit Llanthony monastery, a religious house unique in the history of medieval Wales. Almost all the founders of Welsh monasteries were inspired by a desire for wealth and power. The one exception was Llanthony, the founding of which, argued J. E. Lloyd, was 'the outcome of unalloyed religious fervour'. (The name comes from Llanddewi Nant Hodni – the church of St David on the River Honddu.)

The founder was William, a member of the de Lacy family which seized Ewyas from the Welsh. William was hunting in the valley *c.*1100 when he came across a small chapel dedicated to St David. He decided to settle there as a hermit. News of his piety spread widely, and, in 1108, a new building, dedicated to John the Baptist, 'the pattern of all hermits', was completed. Demands arose for a more formal recognition of the holy place, and, by *c.*1118, there was in the Vale of Ewyas a priory belonging to the Order of St Augustine, housing as many as forty canons. So great was the enchantment of Llanthony that when its prior, Robert of Béthune, was chosen to be bishop of Hereford, he felt he was 'forced, like Adam, to leave paradise and become an exile'.

But the priory did not impress the native Welsh, who considered the monastery to be an alien importation. Llanthony received the patronage of Queen Matilda, but after her death (1118) and especially that of her husband, Henry I (1135), some of the monks came to the conclusion that there was no future for them in so remote a location. They retreated to Gloucester where they established Llanthony Secunda, a monastery which was in existence from 1136 until 1538.

The statue of the Virgin Mary at Capel-y-ffin

The de Lacys continued to be faithful to the original foundation. As members of the family had profited from their campaigns in Ireland, they could afford to finance extensive rebuilding at Llanthony Prima. Work undertaken there from *c.*1180 to *c.*1220 is the best example in Wales of the Transitional style between Romanesque and Gothic. Sufficient of the building survives – particularly the western façade, the nave and the southern transept of the abbey church – to offer a clear impression of Transitional at its best.

The monastery languished in the later Middle Ages and, in 1481, Llanthony Prima became the responsibility of Llanthony Secunda. As the priory is so remote, little of its stonework was carried away following its dissolution. Its slow decay was the result of neglect and the ravages of the weather. The collapse of the tracery of the great west window of the abbey church did not occur until 1803, when the antiquarian, Richard Colt Hoare, witnessed the stonework raining down. By then, part of the monastery had been turned into a shooting-cabin, a building which has been absorbed into the Abbey Hotel. (Llanthony is the only one-time monastery in Wales where it is possible to drink strong liquors similar to those which such institutions were once famous for producing.) In 1807, the Llanthony estate was bought by the English poet, Walter Savage Landor, who commissioned the building of Y Siarpal on the hillside above the monastery; work on the mansion ceased in 1813, when Landor was declared bankrupt.

But that was not the end of the story. Not only are there Llanthony Prima and Secunda, there is also Llanthony Tertia. In 1869, land at Capel-y-ffin at the northern end of the Vale of Ewyas was acquired by Joseph Lyne – Father Ignatius – a man determined to graft Benedictine monasticism upon the Church of England. He commissioned the construction of a cloister and part of an abbey church – the chancel – which was intended to be on the same scale and in the same style as Llanthony Prima. Following Lyne's death in 1908, the site came into the possession of the Anglican monks of Caldey Island. Although the Caldey monks were received into the Catholic Church in 1913, Llanthony Tertia retained the affection of Anglicans. Visions of the Virgin Mary were seen there in 1880, and Capel-y-ffin

became the only centre of Marian pilgrimage in these islands organized by Anglicans.

Llanthony Tertia's chancel collapsed in 1920; four years later, the cloister became home to a commune of artists led by Eric Gill, examples of whose calligraphic work may be seen in the neighbouring cemetery. The commune's members included the poet and artist, David Jones; as Jones spent most of his life in lodging-houses, Capel-y-ffin was probably the only real home he had during his adulthood. The commune came to an end in 1928, but, as the magic of the Vale of Ewyas is so powerful, who knows what other idealists will be attracted to this earthly paradise.

The most delectably rural landscape in Wales is that of northern Monmouthshire. Part of the magic of the district comes from its place-names, the most double-barrelled in Wales – Llantilio Crossenny, Llanddewi Rhydderch, Llangattock Lingoed. The best way to appreciate the area is to walk the 32-kilometre path which links White Castle, Skenfrith Castle and Grosmont Castle. The fit can do the journey in a day, but in order to explore the castles and to appreciate the attractions that lie along the path, it is worth devoting two or three days to the expedition.

The three castles differ in shape, and the transformation of the original earth-and-timber mottes into masonry castles had different motivations. Nevertheless, it is fitting to see them as a triad; they were in the same ownership for at least seven and a half centuries, and the original mottes were built as part of a single venture – the campaign of William of Breteuil, earl of Hereford, to destroy the Welsh kingdom of Gwent. By his death (1071), his castle at Monmouth had given him secure possession of the Monnow's confluence with the Wye. From there, a convenient route through the hills of northern Gwent was offered by the Monnow Valley. In that valley, he commissioned the construction of two mottes – Skenfrith and Grosmont; a further motte, the later White Castle, was built in the hills to the west of the valley.

The power of the house of Breteuil came to an end in 1075; over the following half century, the mottes came to have several

Skenfrith Castle keep

different owners. They probably fell into ruin during the 'Anarchy' associated with the reign of Stephen (1135–54). Proof of the instability of the area was the murder in 1136 of Richard fitz Gilbert of the Clare family in the thick forest on the border of Gwent and Brycheiniog. In 1138, ownership of the three castles was united under the crown, but, as Stephen's power was so limited, it would seem that no building work was undertaken at any of them until the 1180s. In that decade, curtain walls were built enclosing a pear-shaped area at White Castle, probably as a reaction to the attack of the Welsh of Gwent upon Abergavenny in 1182. The attack was revenge for the dreadful act of William de Breos (d. 1211) – the murder of his Welsh guests at Abergavenny Castle in 1175, a crime which still resonates locally.

No masonry structures were erected at Grosmont and Skenfrith until after 1201, when King John presented the three castles to Hubert de Burgh. By 1203, there was a rectangular hall block at Grosmont. De Burgh commissioned further structures in the 1220s, work inspired by the revolution in military architecture initiated in France in the early thirteenth century. He was motivated by his ambition to become as powerful in Wales as was Llywelyn ap Iorwerth. (As Saunders Lewis showed in his drama, *Siwan*, Llywelyn's desire to thwart de Burgh's ambitions was central to the prince's policy.) De Burgh gained possession of an arc of lordships from Montgomery to Cardigan, with the three castles at its centre. A rectangular hall range and a freestanding round tower were built at Skenfrith, and curtain walls and round towers came to adjoin the rectangular tower at Grosmont.

What is now visible at Skenfrith and Grosmont is essentially what remains of the structures built between 1201 and 1232. The three castles returned to royal ownership in 1243, and in 1267 they, along with the lordship of Monmouth, were given to Edmund, earl of Lancaster (d. 1296), whose elder brother became Edward I in 1272. With Llywelyn ap Gruffudd attracting the support of the Welsh of Gwent, there was an awareness of the need to add to the fortifications of White Castle, the most westerly, and therefore the most vulnerable, of the three strongholds. In the 1260s, building work there included towers to strengthen the curtain walls, a pair of round towers to defend a new formidable gatehouse and long walls to protect the outer ward.

The tower of St Bridget's Church, Skenfrith

The three castles passed in turn to Edmund's sons, to his grandson, Henry of Grosmont, the first duke of Lancaster (d. 1361), and to Henry's son-in-law, John of Gaunt (d. 1399). John's son became Henry IV in 1399; his grandson, the later Henry V, was born at Monmouth, which explains why Shakespeare considered him to be a Welshman. There was considerable excitement at Grosmont during the Revolt of Owain Glyn Dŵr. In March 1405, the failure of Gruffudd ab Owain's siege of the castle was an important factor in the collapse of his father's principality.

With Henry IV's accession to the throne, the lands of the duchy of Lancaster became the property of the crown, although they were administered separately from the crown lands, an arrangement which has lasted to this day. The income of the three lordships dwindled to nothing, and in the late eighteenth century they were sold. Bought by the duke of Beaufort, they remained Somerset property until the ninth duke decided to liquidate his entire Monmouthshire estate. The sale was one of the sensations of the early twentieth century. Raglan Castle, Tintern Abbey, twenty manors, twenty-six hotels and 11,000 hectares of land came under the hammer, and ownership of the three castles was

divided for the first time since 1138. White Castle and Grosmont Castle eventually returned to crown ownership and are now under Cadw's supervision; Skenfrith was acquired by the National Trust and also came to be under Cadw's supervision. Cadw's work at the three castles is an example of conservation at its best.

Grosmont Castle (left)
The chimneystack at Grosmont Castle (below)

The walls and moat of White Castle

Raglan Castle was the most voluminous structure erected *de novo* in fifteenth-century Britain. It does not have the elegance of a broadly contemporary building – King's College Chapel in Cambridge – but, as a statement of power, it has no competitor. When considering castles commissioned by Welshmen, Dolbadarn, Dolwyddelan, Dryslwyn and Ewloe should be forgotten. Raglan, commissioned by a man of full Welsh descent, is the most magnificent of the castles of the Welsh.

Its commissioner was William ap Thomas – *y marchog glas o Went* (the blue knight from Gwent) – whose rise owed much to his participation in the battle of Agincourt. He bought the manor of Raglan in 1432 for a thousand marks (£666.66), and married

Gwladus, described by the poet, Lewys Glyn Cothi, as '*y seren o Efenni*' (the star from Abergavenny). The building of the castle was proof of his self-confidence, as is his tomb and that of Gwladus at St Mary's Church, Abergavenny. *Tŵr Melyn Gwent* (The Yellow Tower of Gwent) – a massive keep separated by a moat from the rest of the castle – and the south gate to the later Fountain Court were William ap Thomas's main ventures at Raglan. The keep and the gate have gunloops, indicating that William ap Thomas did not believe that the coming of gunpowder meant the end of castle building. He was among the last to hold that opinion, and it could be claimed that Raglan was the last real castle to be built in the British domains of the English crown.

Carvings on the wall of one of the rooms in the Yellow Tower of Gwent

Following William ap Thomas's death in 1445, Raglan was inherited by his son, another William, who, in accordance with the increasing practice of the Welsh gentry, adopted a surname. Summoned to Parliament as Baron Herbert of Raglan in 1481, William Herbert was the first Welshman to join the ranks of the English peerage. It was his leadership which ensured the Yorkist victory at Mortimer's Cross (1461), the victory which enabled the Duke of York to ascend the throne as Edward IV. As he held many of the chief offices in Wales, and as he delighted in his Welsh roots, William Herbert was, to many of the Welsh poets, the long-awaited *mab darogan* (the son of prophecy). Guto'r Glyn urged him: *Dwg Forgannwg a Gwynedd / Gwna'n un o Gonwy i Nedd* (Bring together Glamorgan and Gwynedd / Unite [Wales] from Conwy to Neath).

Baron Herbert commissioned Raglan's greatest glories – the profile of the towers of the gatehouse range with their splendid machicolations, and the sweep of buildings adjoining the south gate. The construction of the Great Hall caused the interior space of the castle to be divided into the Fountain Court and the Pitched Stone Court, and it was probably in the living apartments on the south side of the Fountain Court that Henry Tudor spent the bulk of his childhood. William Herbert was beheaded following the battle of Banbury (1469). His son, another William (d. 1491), proved to be lethargic, and Raglan would not be in the hands of an energetic owner until 1492, when Elizabeth, the first William Herbert's granddaughter, married Charles Somerset,

a kinsman and ally of the Tudors. Charles's grandson, the third earl of Worcester (d. 1589), presided over the completion of Raglan Castle, commissioning in particular the splendid Long Gallery. The late sixteenth-century work, constructed of dark red sandstone, is easily distinguishable from the fifteenth-century work constructed in pale yellow sandstone.

It is now difficult to appreciate the luxury of aristocratic life at Raglan during the lifetime of the third earl and his two immediate successors, Edward (d. 1628) and Henry (d. 1646). Although loyal to the Roman Catholicism of their ancestors, they were among the most prominent figures in the kingdom, and the income from their extensive estates – in Breconshire, Gower, Chepstow and Raglan, in addition to their vast holdings around Badminton in Gloucestershire – financed their opulent lifestyle. By the 1640s, Raglan, surrounded as it was by one of the most splendid gardens of the age, was more a palace than a castle. But in that decade, everything came to an end. The fifth earl (the marquess of Worcester from 1642) was an ardent Royalist; indeed, it has been claimed that Charles I would not have considered fighting the Parliamentarians had he not been confident that he could rely on the wealth of the Somersets. The castle came under siege; its garrison accepted defeat in August 1646 and the marquess died in prison in December. The castle was damaged during the siege, but suffered much greater destruction following the decision to render it useless as a stronghold. The undermining of the great keep caused much of it to collapse; roofs were robbed of their lead and timber, and the walls became a source of building stone. Although the Somersets regained possession of the castle, no one would live there after 1646.

From the castle, it is worth going to St Cadog's Church, where the mutilation of the Somerset tombs is proof of the Parliamentarians' hatred of the family. It is necessary to go to St Michael's Church at Great Badminton to see what the Somersets can do when it comes to honouring dead ancestors. The funeral monuments there make royal tombs look modest.

There is something intriguing about Trellech. Why is there so large a church in so small a village? What is the significance of the standing stones? Why does the place have so many differently spelt names – twenty-six according to one commentator? Something dramatic must have happened here. The fertile land of eastern Gwent – a district where the number of inhabitants grew prodigiously in the High Middle Ages – abounds with villages that failed. For example, Runston, near Chepstow, was a considerable village in the late twelfth century, but, by the late eighteenth century, it was virtually uninhabited. But Trellech is not a failed village; it is a town which lost its function and shrank into a village.

Trellech's history was linked with the fate of the most prominent of the Marcher families. In 1115, Gwent Is-coed came into the possession of Walter fitz Richard of the Clare family. By the mid thirteenth century, the Clares owned large parts of Ireland (the county of Clare commemorates them), together with manors in almost every county in England. However, it was in Wales that they were at their most powerful. They held the lordships of Glamorgan, Gwynllŵg (Newport), Caerleon, Usk and Trellech, thus holding sway over territory stretching from the River Neath to the River Wye. The resources available to Gilbert de Clare, the Red Earl (d. 1295), exceeded those of his contemporary, Llywelyn ap Gruffudd, prince of Wales (d. 1282). So great was his power that when his father-in-law, Edward I, visited him at Cardiff Castle in 1284, the welcome the king received was that of a fellow sovereign rather than that of a subject.

Among Gilbert's chief resources were the forests and ores of the lordship of Trellech. In the early fourteenth century, sale of the charcoal produced in the forests added £100 a year to the Clare coffers. However, the bulk of the charcoal was used where it was produced, to smelt the iron ore mined in the lordship.

The charcoal and the ore were the keys which had enabled Trellech, by c.1300, to develop into a town. The place was the Clare powerhouse. It was the production centre for the iron necessary for the building of the Clare castles – Caerphilly Castle, the largest in Wales, among them. (The reward given to the amateur archaeologists who excavate at Trellech is a lump of medieval iron slag.) Trellech iron was the raw material of swords, spears, lances and hatchets – the weapons used by the forces which fought in the endless wars of the Clares. Trellech was the family's arsenal, and was therefore a factor of importance in the ending of Llywelyn's principality.

The Clares also came to an end, for Gilbert, the only son of the Red Earl, was killed at the battle of Bannockburn in 1314. The Clare empire was divided among his sisters' husbands –

Trellech's Virtuous Well with the tower of St Nicholas's Church in the distance

Glamorgan to Despenser, Newport to d'Audley and Caerleon, Usk and Trellech to de Burgh. A large arsenal was no longer needed and the planted borough of the Clares fell into decline.

At its apogee, Trellech was the largest town in Gwent, and, possibly, the largest in Wales. There were perhaps two-thousand people living in Cardiff *c*.1290, and two and a half thousand in Trellech. The most obvious evidence of Trellech's size in the High Middle Ages is the extensiveness of St Nicholas's Church, which was clearly built to serve burgesses rather than villagers. Excavation has proved fruitful, but, even without digging, the newest techniques allow archaeologists to obtain a good idea of what lies below the many banks of soil in the vicinity of the church, surveys which tend to confirm the notion that, in the late thirteenth century, Trellech was indeed the largest town in Wales.

Millennia before there were Clares or iron weapons, there was an urge to draw attention to this part of the world. That is evident from the three tall stones standing south of the village. It is believed that they were erected during the Bronze Age (2300–700 BC). Such standing stones are rare in the south-east and those at Trellech have been subject of much speculation. They are known – misleadingly – as Harold's Stones, for they have been linked with Giraldus Cambrensis's comment that Harold, earl of Wessex, recorded his victories in his campaign against Gruffudd ap Llywelyn in 1063 by ordering the erection of stones bearing the words *Hic Victor Fuit Haroldus*. Fairly similar words appear on another of the attractions of Trellech – the sundial carved in 1689 which stands inside St Nicholas's Church. To Fred Hando, celebrator of all things Gwentian, the sundial, which also portrays Trellech's remarkable Virtuous Well, is the oddest in Britain.

Several of the websites discussing Trellech note, rightly, that *llech* is the Welsh for slab, and insist that *tre* in Trellech comes from the Welsh *tri* (three); Trellech is therefore considered to mean Three Slabs. In his *The Buildings of Wales: Gwent/Monmouthshire*, John Newman is more circumspect, and offers the Town of Stones as the meaning of the place-name. However, Hywel Wyn Jones and Richard Morgan argue that emphasis on *tri* or on *tre* is misleading. The first syllable is the reinforcing prefix *try*; thus the probable meaning of the place-name is Very Highly Stoned.

The sundial in St Nicholas's Church, Trellech

Mentioning the church, the excavations, the menhirs, the sundial and the well merely touches upon the attractions of Trellech. Explorers should visit the valleys to the east, where charcoal production continued long after it had ceased at Trellech. A visit to Llandogo is a pleasure, if only to see what remains of the port on the Wye which gave its name to the Llandoger Trow at Bristol, the inn immortalized as the Admiral Benbow in *Treasure Island*. Days could be spent wandering around the communities of Trellech and Llandogo. The place to stay is the Lion in Trellech, recognized in 2003 as the best open-fire tavern in south Wales, and where visitors sleep in a bedroom adapted from a late sixteenth-century pigsty.

Although Strata Florida and Valle Crucis have their charms, Tintern is undoubtedly the most impressive monastic site in Wales. Along with Fountains and Rievaulx in Yorkshire, and Melrose in southern Scotland, it is one of Britain's quartet of magnificent abbey ruins. Not everyone is delighted with the place. I remember being at the Chepstow youth hostel in 1955, where I met a young traveller from Bristol who had cycled down the Wye Valley. 'There's a huge bombed building there', he said. 'It's appalling that it has not been cleared away.' (It is difficult for today's young to realize how threatening ruins can be to those who remember the war.)

Tintern Abbey was founded in 1131. By the 1130s, the wave of reform which had been gaining strength in Europe since the mid eleventh century was at its height. One of the chief centres of reform was Cîteaux in Burgundy, a monastery founded in 1098. Unlike the autonomy enjoyed by Benedictine monasteries, every Cistercian house was answerable to the abbot at Cîteaux. Again unlike the Benedictines, who tended to establish their monasteries in towns – in Wales at places such as Abergavenny, Brecon, Cardigan, Chepstow, Kidwelly, Monmouth and Pembroke – the Cistercians sought sites 'far from the concourse of men'. Although St Benedict had advocated simplicity, the wealth with which Benedictine abbeys had been endowed gave rise to pomp and luxury. (In the history of monasticism, nothing fails like success.) The Cistercians shunned pomp and sought to build austere abbeys, all broadly following the same design.

Such ideas won warm approval, and, by the mid twelfth century, Europe had 340 Cistercian monasteries. The first to be founded in Britain was Waverley in Surrey (1128) and the second was Tintern. By 1300, Britain had over eighty Cistercian houses, including fifteen (two nunneries among them) in Wales. Although they were all dissolved in the sixteenth century, there are in Wales today a Cistercian monastery on Caldey Island and a

Cistercian nunnery at Whitland. The majority of Wales's medieval Cistercian houses received the patronage of the Welsh princes, although Tintern, the wealthiest of them, was wholly dependent upon Marcher Lords.

Tintern's first patron was Walter fitz Richard, who gained possession of the lordship of Chepstow in 1115. It is likely that the abbey church, a modest Romanesque building consistent with the austere traditions of the early Cistercians, had been completed by Walter's death *c.*1138. The design did not wholly conform to the strict rules of the order. Cistercian cloisters were sited to the south of the abbey church, but those at Tintern were built north of the church, probably in order that the kitchen and latrine drains could flow into the Wye.

Details of the buildings financed by Walter fitz Richard are sparse, for they were demolished during the thirteenth-century rebuilding. The initial rebuilding was commissioned by the Marshal family who held the lordship of Chepstow from 1186 to 1245, but it was Roger Bigod (d. 1306), grandson of William Marshal's daughter, Maud, who financed the rebuilding of the abbey church. Indeed, he spent so much at Tintern that he was obliged to yield his lands to the crown in return for a pension. The abbey church, a building of great splendour, represented the abandonment of Cistercian austerity. Now, it is necessary to go to places such as Fontenoy in Burgundy to see an entire building which conforms to the original ideals of the Cistercians, although

The carving of King Tewdrig at the Old Station, Tintern

what remains at Margam does give some indication of the simplicity originally advocated by the order.

The grandeur of the hall built for the abbot in the fourteenth century further underlines the degree to which the Cistercians had embraced luxury and ostentation. The monastery was dissolved in 1536; the lead on the roof was sold and the noble complex fell into ruin. Little of the masonry was carried away. It has been claimed that the stonework survived because of the abbey's remote location – although that is not a convincing argument in view of the extensive traffic on the Wye. (All the stonework has disappeared at Strata Marcella, a monastery sited at a similar location on the banks of the Severn.) Mansions were built within the ruins of Llantarnam, Margam, Neath and Strata Florida; nothing similar was built at Tintern, although William Herbert (d. 1593) did consider founding a college for the Welsh on the site.

The Romantic Movement led to new interest in Tintern. The best-known Romantic to visit the ruins was William Wordsworth (1793, 1798), but the name of the abbey only appears in the title of his poem. Wordsworth's visit was undoubtedly inspired by William Gilpin's *Observations on the River Wye* (1782). Gilpin complained that the regularity of the ruins detracted from their picturesqueness, and argued that attractive fractures could be created by 'a mallet judiciously used'. The site lay undisturbed for centuries apart from some maintenance work financed by its owner, the duke of Beaufort, whose ancestor, Henry Somerset, received the abbey from Henry VIII in 1537. The ruins were acquired by the crown in 1901 and came under the care of Cadw in 1984.

The industrial remains at Tintern are almost as interesting as the abbey ruins. It is worth wandering around the Angidy Valley which contains remarkable evidence of metal production. The Mineral and Battery Company established a wire-making works there in 1566; by 1600, its workforce of six hundred made it by far the largest industrial venture in Wales. It was also the longest-lived such venture in Wales, for it continued in production until 1900.

There are signs on the approaches to Carmarthen welcoming people to the oldest town in Wales. The signs may be misleading. That Carmarthen was a town nearly two-thousand years ago is a supposition. That Caerwent was a town nearly two-thousand years ago is not a supposition. An inscribed stone discovered there makes that wholly clear. In 1903, a memorial to a former legate of Legio Secunda Augusta, the legion stationed at Caerleon, came to light at Caerwent; it was erected *ex decreto ordinis respublica civitas Silurum* (by order of the republic of the land of the Silures). A *civitas* was a territory based upon the tribal pattern which existed prior to the Roman invasion, a territory whose inhabitants could be granted autonomous institutions. Each *civitas* had its capital, and there can be no doubt that Caerwent – *Venta Silurum* (the market place of the Silures) – was the capital of the region which would later constitute the kingdoms of Gwent, Morgannwg and Brycheiniog. (Of course, the absence of a similar inscription at Carmarthen does not preclude the possibility that it was the capital of the Demetae – the inhabitants of the south-west – but Carmarthen has not yielded irrefutable evidence.)

The earliest Roman remains at Caerwent date from *c*. AD 75, although, as the Silures had offered long and bitter resistance to the Romans, it is unlikely that their territory had by then been granted *civitas* status. That recognition probably occurred during the reign of Hadrian (117–38), and may have resulted from the need for new arrangements in the south-east, where garrisons had been withdrawn for service on Hadrian's Wall. Excavation work conducted at Caerwent since 1988 seems to confirm that surmise, for the *forum-basilica* in the centre of town was built in the early second century AD. Unlike many of the other *civitas* capitals – Cambridge and Leicester, for example – which eventually became substantial built-up areas, Caerwent became little more than a village and therefore offers few obstacles to those seeking a

fuller understanding of the character of the Roman city.

It seems that the city took some time to get under way. Caerwent was at its most prosperous at the beginning of the fourth century. It is estimated that it was then home to some three-thousand inhabitants – far less than the ten thousand in Wroxeter or the forty thousand in London, but, after Caerwent's demise, Wales would have no town equal in size for at least a thousand years.

The most memorable remains at Caerwent are the masonry walls which enclose the 18 hectares of the fortified town. They were erected *c*.330 and are the most impressive Roman defences to survive in Britain, and probably in northern Europe. Admittedly, much of the masonry has disappeared. As the walls were built mainly of limestone, lumps were carried away and burnt to produce lime, a more important motive for stone robbing than the search for building material. The walls are at their best along the city's southern boundary. Originally, they were crowned by parapets and rose up to *c*.7.5 metres; there are stretches where only the upper quarter has disappeared, and where the walls are still five metres high. Along the south wall, there are six five-sided towers, which look like miniature versions of the towers of Caernarfon Castle. To have an idea of how Caerwent's walls originally appeared, it is worth going to see the reconstructed Roman wall on the north side of Cardiff Castle. It is likely that the same style – the style characteristic of the work of Caerwent's Legio Secunda Augusta – was employed at Caerwent *c*.330 as was employed at Cardiff *c*.280. The best way to obtain an impression of the size of Caerwent is to stand in the centre of Cardiff Castle and imagine an enclosed area five times as large.

Caerwent was divided into twenty *insulae* – rectangular plots – each the site of a variety of buildings. By now, parts of at least fifteen *insulae* have been excavated. During the extensive work

tone which refers to respublica civitas Silurum

undertaken at Caerwent between 1899 and 1913, excavation was followed by reburial; therefore, nothing was visible to the visitor apart from the walls. During the recent work there, it was decided that within the walls as much as possible should be visible to the public. As a result, visitors can now see the foundations of a Celto-Roman temple, a luxurious mansion, a row of shops and part of the *forum-basilica*. The decision to display these foundations and to erect admirable information panels has revolutionized the experience of visiting Caerwent. Those who have not been there since the 1980s, should go again. Sadly, Caerwent does not have a museum similar to the Legionary Museum at Caerleon. However, some of the finds from Caerwent can be seen at the Newport Museum – a further reason for visiting that attractive city.

The *decuriones* – the rulers of the *civitas* of the Silures – were no doubt recruited from among the elders of the Silurian tribe. After the fall of the Western Roman Empire, it was probably the descendants of the *decuriones* who established the kingdom of Gwent, which borrowed its name from Caerwent. (It may be significant that the earliest king of Gwent, whose name is known, was Caradog. Was he named after the Caradog [Caractacus] who led the Silures in their struggle against the Romans in the first century?) The kingdom of Gwent was destroyed by the Normans in the late eleventh century; that kingdom may well have represented a polity which had been in existence, in some form or another, for at least a millennia and a half.

Part of a mosaic floor discovered at Caerwent

It is difficult to think of as many as half a dozen architects who, over the past quarter of a millennium, have designed buildings of great distinction in Wales – Nesfield at Kinmel, Creswell at Queensferry, Rickards at Cardiff and Foster at Llanarthney certainly, but it would be difficult to add to the list. The masterpieces of engineers are far more numerous – Pont Cysyllte, Menai Bridge, Brunel's work on the South Wales Railway, Britannia Bridge, the Llanwddyn Dam, the Crumlin Viaduct, the Second Severn Crossing, the Millennium Stadium, and many more. The early engineers – Telford, Brunel and Stephenson – are commemorated; Telford's name is emblazoned on Menai Bridge, Stephenson's on Britannia Bridge, and, at the end of the South Wales Railway, there was a splendid statue of Brunel, now sadly stolen.

But where are the memorials to more recent engineers? Standing near that masterpiece, the Second Severn Crossing, I can see nothing informing the visitor that the bridge was designed by Sir William Halcrow and Partners and the French company SEEE. The Second Crossing offers a superb view of the Severn Bridge (1961–6), which was designed by Gilbert Roberts of Freeman, Fox and Partners in co-operation with Mott, Hay and Anderson. Neither the one bridge nor the other bears a confident assertion like that on the Menai Bridge: ENGINEER THOMAS TELFORD. (The names of the Second Crossing's engineers are noted at the interpretation centre on the English side of the bridge, but that does not compare with the splendour of the declaration on the Menai Bridge.)

One of the most popular publications of the second half of the nineteenth century was Samuel Smiles's *Lives of the Engineers* (three volumes, 1857), and, in Cardiff's Riverside, there are streets named after the engineers who played a role in the history of the Bute Docks – Rennie, Telford, Smeaton, Stephenson and Brunel. I have yet to see streets commemorating Halcrow, Roberts,

Freeman, Fox, Mott, Hay and Anderson – and certainly not SEEE. Perhaps the lack of recognition is the result of the fact that our masterpieces are now the work of a warren full of technicians working for big companies, and are therefore the product of a very different world from that of Telford, Brunel and Stephenson – although, surely, they too had their backroom boys.

This is merely an introduction to a paean of praise to the Second Severn Crossing. It is the last of the ninety-four bridges (thirty-six of them in Wales) which cross the Severn. There are about 380 kilometres between it and the most northerly Severn bridge – that in the Severn Forest less than a kilometre below the river's source. Until the 1960s, the river's lowest crossing was at Gloucester, which meant that anyone wishing to make the landward journey from Chepstow to the banks of the Severn immediately opposite – a journey of merely a kilometre and a half across the estuary – would have to travel 48 kilometres along the estuary's northern bank and a further 48 kilometres along its southern bank.

By sea, of course, the journey was much shorter, although crossing the strong current was dangerous, and, as the difference between low and high tide in the estuary is one of the highest in the world, reaching the water presented difficulties. Nevertheless, there was a ferry between Beachley near the estuary of the Wye and Aust in the Vale of Berkeley in Roman times, and it was probably at Aust in 601 that the bishops of Wales met Augustine, the archbishop of Canterbury.

By the sixteenth century, the Beachley-Aust ferry was central to travel between south-east Wales and south-west England. In the late seventeenth century, with travel between England and Wales increasing rapidly, a second ferry linking Portskewett in Monmouthshire with Pilning in Gloucestershire was established. This was the New Crossing, a keen competitor with the Old Crossing from Beachley to Aust. The New Crossing followed the

same course across the estuary as that chosen in 1873 for the Severn railway tunnel. The tunnel was completed in 1886, and so great were the construction problems that its completion was hailed as one of nineteenth-century Britain's greatest achievements. Until the opening of the Seikan Tunnel in Japan in 1988, it was the world's longest underwater railway tunnel. As it was dug through a vast well of sweet water, the pumping station at Sudbrook has to extract 50 million litres of water out of the tunnel every day. (Anyone who has drunk British-produced Stella Artois has drunk some of that water.)

The opening of the tunnel meant the end of the two ferries, but, in the 1920s, increasing car traffic led to the reopening of the Old Crossing. That ferry closed in 1966, a day before the opening of the Severn Bridge. (Harri Webb's verse claiming that all that bridge's tolls were collected 'on the English side' is misleading; both ends of the Severn Bridge are in England, although the Wye Viaduct, which is a continuation of it, does usher the M4 into, or out of, Wales.) So heavy was the traffic on the Severn Bridge that the need for a second crossing soon became apparent. The Second Crossing, which follows the course of the New Crossing, does indeed have its Welsh side.

Although the Severn Bridge is superb, the Second Crossing is even more beautiful. In both bridges, the central section is sustained by cables. The cables of the earlier bridge hang vertically from pairs of wires stretching from the summits of the pylons, but, in the later bridge, the cables of the southern section are at an angle from the southern pylon and those of the northern section at an angle from its northern pylon. This means that the earlier bridge is a structure in the tradition of the Menai Bridge, whereas the later one represents a far more innovative design. (The design owes much to the George Street Bridge in Newport [1962-4], the first such bridge in Britain.) It is the angles of the white cables which give the Second Crossing its magnificent profile. From the Severn Bridge, the Second Crossing looks like a vast sailing-ship in full glory.

It is difficult to overestimate the distinctiveness of Chepstow. The Great Keep of the castle is the oldest dateable masonry building in Britain. Before the establishment of St Mary's Priory in Chepstow, Wales was bereft of religious houses obedient to the rule of St Benedict, Latin Europe's most powerful unifying factor. St Mary's Church, Chepstow, is Wales's earliest example of Romanesque architecture. The two towers defending the southern wall of the castle's central court are the earliest examples of round medieval towers in Wales, and possibly in Britain. The walls built around the borough of Chepstow in the 1270s – 1,097 metres in length – were, until the construction of Conwy's 1,300 metre-walls in 1283–92, the most ambitious attempt in Wales to fortify a town.

The distinctiveness of Chepstow did not end with the Middle Ages. The town played an important role in the seventeenth-century Civil Wars. Cromwell himself was at Chepstow in 1648 initiating the siege of the castle, a castle of which he obtained personal possession following the victory of the Parliamentarians. The castle's Marten Tower commemorates the imprisonment there of Henry Marten, the only signatory of Charles I's death-warrant not to be executed following the Stuart Restoration.

Chepstow flourished as a port. In the 1790s, when the quay was the chief centre for the loading of goods destined for ports along the Wye and the Severn, it handled a greater tonnage than Cardiff and Swansea put together. In 1816, the town was linked to Tutshill in Gloucestershire by one of the most ingenious iron bridges ever built – the masterpiece of the engineer, John Rennie. When Isambard Kingdom Brunel began work on his masterpiece – the railway across south Wales to Neyland – his starting point was Chepstow, where he designed a tubular suspension bridge sustained by triple cast-iron Tuscan columns – an extraordinarily innovative concept. Chepstow is also the location of the Wye Viaduct, which leads to the splendid Severn Bridge (1961–6).

There was much activity in this part of the world long before the creation of these masterpieces. Chepstow has a Neolithic chambered tomb and an Iron Age hillfort, and the place was undoubtedly the chief port of the kingdom of Gwent. Maps still refer to the earthwork on the crest above the east bank of the Wye as Offa's Dyke, but, although Asser, the biographer of King Alfred, stressed that Offa ordered the construction of a dyke from sea to sea, it is unlikely that the earthwork was an integral part of Offa's project. Nevertheless, the earthwork, which continues across the Beachley Peninsula on the other side of the Wye from Chepstow, seems to stress that the Wye and its traffic belonged to the kingdom of Gwent.

The earliest recorded name for the area around the Wye

The central doorway in the western façade of St Mary's Church, Chepstow

The entrance to the Great Tower of Chepstow Castle

estuary is Striguil, which was long considered (wrongly) to come from the Welsh *ystrad cul* (narrow vale). Later, the names Chepstow (market-place) and Cas-gwent (the castle of Gwent) were adopted. Clearly, the area's English-speakers were primarily aware of the market and its Welsh-speakers were primarily aware of the castle. The Welsh-speakers were perhaps more perceptive, for the castle is undoubtedly Chepstow's greatest glory. Its most impressive feature, the Great Keep, was based upon the keep of Falaise Castle in Normandy, the birthplace of William the Conqueror. Indeed, it may have been built on the direct orders of the king himself.

Visitors to Chepstow should venture beyond the town's boundaries to explore Mathern or Merthyr Tewdrig. Mathern offers splendid views of the Severn Bridge and the Second Crossing and has a wealth of interesting houses, among them a one-time palace of the bishop of Llandaff. Its most intriguing feature is the inscription in St Tewdrig's Church which claims that it denotes the location of the grave of King Tewdrig. If it is true that, *c*.620, Tewdrig won a victory over the Saxons which ensured the continuance of Welsh rule over Gwent and Morgannwg, he should be hailed as the greatest figure in the history of Wales, for without Gwent and Glamorgan there would have been no Wales.

Also published by Y Lolfa:

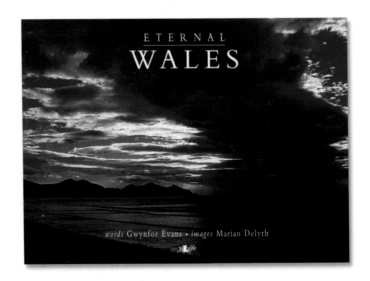

y Lolfa

www.ylolfa.com